EAST ANGLIAN LANDSCAPES: Past and Present

It's all theatre at the Windmill!
Alastair Liddell
Rubber Windmill

April 1990

Also by Jack Ravensdale

LIABLE TO FLOODS

HISTORY ON YOUR DOORSTEP

THE WEST FIELDS OF CAMBRIDGE (with C. P. Hall)

CORNWALL

THE DOMESDAY INHERITANCE

Also by Richard Muir

MODERN POLITICAL GEOGRAPHY

THE ENGLISH VILLAGE

RIDDLES IN THE LANDSCAPE

GEOGRAPHY, POLITICS & BEHAVIOUR (with R. Paddison)

SHELL GUIDE TO READING THE LANDSCAPE

THE LOST VILLAGES OF BRITAIN

TRAVELLER'S HISTORY OF BRITAIN AND IRELAND

HISTORY FROM THE AIR

NATIONAL TRUST GUIDE TO PREHISTORIC & ROMAN BRITAIN (with H. Welfare)

VISIONS OF THE PAST (with C. C. Taylor)

THE SHELL COUNTRYSIDE BOOK (with Eric Duffey)

NATIONAL TRUST GUIDE TO THE DARK AGES AND MEDIEVAL BRITAIN

SHELL GUIDE TO READING THE CELTIC LANDSCAPE

THE STONES OF BRITAIN

LANDSCAPE AND NATURE PHOTOGRAPHY

RIVERS OF BRITAIN (with Nina Muir)

HEDGEROWS: THEIR HISTORY AND WILDLIFE (with Nina Muir)

OLD YORKSHIRE

EAST ANGLIAN LANDSCAPES: Past and Present

by JACK RAVENSDALE
and RICHARD MUIR

'Topographic pursuits, my Doctor used to say, tend to preserve and promote the civilisation of which they are a consequence and a proof.'

Robert Southey, *The Doctor*, 1842

MICHAEL JOSEPH
LONDON

For Jill and Nina

MICHAEL JOSEPH LTD

Published by the Penguin Group, England, 27 Wrights Lane, London W8 5TZ,
Viking Penguin Inc., 40 West 23rd Street, New York, New York 10010, USA
Penguin Books Australia Ltd, Ringwood, Victoria, Australia
Penguin Books Canada Ltd, 2801 John Street, Markham, Ontario, Canada L3R 1B4
Penguin Books (NZ) Ltd, 182-190 Wairau Road, Auckland 10, New Zealand

Penguin Books Ltd, Registered Offices: Harmondsworth, Middlesex, England

First published by Michael Joseph 1984
This paperback edition 1988

Typeset by Photina

Printed and bound in Spain by Artes Gráficas Toledo, S.A.

British Library Cataloguing in Publication Data
Ravensdale, J. K.
East Anglian Landscapes, past and present.
1. East Anglia (England) – History
I. Title II. Muir, Richard, 1943-
942.6 DA670.E14

ISBN 0–7181–3064–2
D. L. TO:2261-1987

CONTENTS

LIST OF FIGURES

ACKNOWLEDGEMENTS

The authors and publishers would like to thank the following for permission to reproduce figures, which appear on the page numbers shown:

Vanessa Parker and Phillimore & Co Ltd, from *The Making of King's Lynn* (Chichester, 1971), 82; Royal Commission on Historical Monuments (England), from *City of Cambridge*, 93, and *West Cambridgeshire*, 117.

The following have given permission for figures to be based on their publications:

HMSO, from the guide leaflet to North Elmham Saxon Cathedral, 49; Hodder & Stoughton Ltd, from *The Suffolk Landscape* by Norman Scarfe, 64, 68; J. M. Dent & Sons Ltd, from *The Landscape of Towns* by Aston and Bond, 66; Norfolk Museums Service, from *Norwich: The Growth of a City*, 71.

The figures were prepared by Bernard Thomason.

LIST OF COLOUR PLATES

The Publishers regret that the captions to the colour illustrations facing page 160 have been transposed with those facing page 161.

INTRODUCTION

The identity of our region is strongly fixed in the popular imagination. Most minds will instantly respond to the mention of the name 'East Anglia' by conjuring visions of windmills, venerable houses of thatch and timber-framing, vast skies and low horizons. But ideas about the limits of East Anglia are much less finely tuned. To most people, we imagine, the area comprises the whole of that 'D'-shaped mass of land that bulges seawards between the Wash and the Thames estuary and which includes Essex as well as the core counties of the region. To some others, 'East Anglia proper' is a much more restricted area, embracing only Norfolk and Suffolk even though this definition of the region excludes the Isle of Ely and the Fens north of Cambridge. We have favoured a middle course, while recognising that geographical regions, unlike counties and countries, do not have sharp boundaries but gradually merge into their neighbours. Our East Anglia comprises Norfolk, Suffolk and Cambridgeshire; it drifts into the south-east Fenland margins of Lincolnshire, but fades away to the west of Cambridge before the formal county boundary is reached. This is *our* intuitive East Anglia although other minds will harbour different perceptions. Only with some reluctance have we surrendered the enticing fringes of Essex and the temptations of places like Hadstock, Thaxted and Saffron Walden.

Although the strong personality of East Anglia is not to be denied, the area embraces some very distinctive sub-regions, as different in their appearance and history as the Fens, Breckland and Broads. We have attempted to express both the history of this region – particularly as it is still expressed in the towns, villages, buildings and fieldscapes of the area – and the qualities of the distinctive rural landscapes. We are both pleased to be called 'landscape historians' and this book is mainly about the making of the East Anglian landscape. But our different disciplinary roots have influenced the way in which the contents have been divided.

Jack Ravensdale, a historian, has written chapters one to eight which explain the early settlement and the evolution of our churches, towns, villages, farming patterns and strongholds, while Richard Muir, a geographer, has described the distinctive sub-regions of East Anglia in the chapters which follow and has provided the illustrations. In a sense, the book is in two complementary portions, the first of which introduces the facets of the scene while the second concerns the coming-together of these facets to form unique landscapes. Inevitably, this approach has meant that some places mentioned earlier in the book are later revisited, but we have taken care to avoid unnecessary repetition.

Together, we have sought to provide the reader with a basis for *understanding* East Anglia and the forces which have moulded its scenery. This is certainly not a guide book in the traditional sense. It does not offer snippets of information about every village, mansion or church and it ignores the tradition in guide book writing which masks reality behind a cloying smokescreen of Olde Worlde charm, pretending that the world encompassed is a gutless and trouble-free place of amiable yokels and rose-hung cottages. In describing East Anglia, we have included some of the bad along with the good and so on the many occasions when we do enthuse about a building or landscape then the reader can be sure that the praise is properly earned.

But there is much in our region today that is bad and heart-breaking. East Anglia has borne the brunt of the assaults on the English countryside which have been launched by grossly subsidised modern farming and the selfish greed of the agri-business movement. If country-lovers from the, as yet, relatively unspoilt places like the Pennines, Clwyd or Grampian areas could be brought to see the scenic carnage which has been wrought around East Anglian villages like Thriplow, Great Shelford or Bourn amongst scores of others then they might realise the fearful price which submission to the masters of the countryside can exact. Many distantly held perceptions of the East Anglian scene are based on times long past when Suffolk could hold a place in the first rank of lovely counties. But the captivating world of hot, dusty lanes, smoke-free summer skies, rumbling harvest wagons and twining hedgerows is now only glimpsed in the collections of old photographs. Jewels in the East Anglian landscape, like Framlingham Castle, Oxburgh Hall and Long Melford Church have survived the devastation, but increasingly such places are standing like glittering islands above a pesticide and herbicide polluted mire of wheat and sugar beet. Yet amongst the carnage, embattled outposts of good countryside do still survive, although we will not be able to preserve them if we pretend that East Anglia is the scenic paradise of the pre-war years, rather than the conservational battlefield of the modern era.

While we can no longer entice the visitor with promises of uninterrupted vistas of captivating, hedge-patterned countryside, East Anglia still has much to offer that is, by any standard, superb. No other part of England, with the possible exception of Somerset, can offer such a splendid galaxy of medieval churches – and this claim is even more remarkable when one realises that the area is virtually devoid of good, weather-resistant building stone. The churches range from the unpretentious but enchanting flint round-towered buildings of the Saxon and Norman periods to the incomparable Perpendicular palaces of the later medieval centuries, with their sparkling panels of flint flushwork and wonderful timber roofs and fittings.

The wool-based wealth which spawned most of these great churches also supported many of the magnificent timber-framed houses of the region. No other province can surpass the quality of these dwellings and nowhere else do they still exist in such profusion. This glorious heritage of vernacular building extends down to the level of the smaller farmsteads and country cottages. Much that is fascinating endures even

The 40-ft or Vermuyden Drain: the Dutch engineer's schemes straightened, deepened and embanked the Fenland watercourses, restraining floodwater until it could be sent out with the tide

though this century has seen the replacement of many wheatstraw- or reed-thatched roofs with drab slates and incongruous synthetic tiles. But much thatch remains to face the dangerous curse of stubble burning which annually produces a host of little disasters, enrages the non-farming populace and dims the glory of our summer skies.

Our region also has a stranger claim to fame which derives from the staggering legacy of deserted medieval villages. In Norfolk, such relics are everywhere, and the tendency for most churches to be built of flint rather than of good, re-usable building stone has resulted in an array of towering ruins like those at Godwick and Pudding Norton. Norfolk was the most populous medieval county, but the ravages of the Black Death, the decline of its textile industry and the enclosure of its weakened villages which are well recorded still leave many questions unanswered about the vast scale of the depopulation.

East Anglia boasts a fine endowment of towns. Here the accidents of history have created just the right balance between the urban and rural components of the scene. There are no remote and town-less wildernesses but neither are there vast and sprawling conurbations. The spectrum ranges from the proud provincial capital of Norwich, through personable and historic centres of the middle rank like Cambridge, King's Lynn and Bury St Edmunds right down to the almost stillborn medieval townlets like New Buckenham and Castle Acre. Some towns have not escaped the worst follies of modern development: Cambridge has sacrificed the real old worldly charms of Petty Cury for a look-alike boutique bazaar, and Lowestoft and Wisbech have sad tales to tell. Peterborough, however, has an imaginative and expanding pedestrian area around its fine cathedral and the lusty civic ideals at Norwich have produced what may be the most civilised of all large British towns. A great town is incomplete without a great cathedral and East Anglia has three – Norwich, Peterborough and Ely – and the remains of several others. Ely is the best and is fit to be classed with Lincoln, York Minster, Salisbury and Wells in the highest division of magnificence. Though abbey ruins as breath-taking and comprehensive as those at Fountains and Furness have not survived in East Anglia, our region still has the stately grandeur of Castle Acre and a very rich endowment of smaller monastic houses.

Monuments and the countryside are the creations of people but it is not easy to distill the characters of East Anglian folk and the subtle patterns change from place to place. Cambridge has become such a cosmopolitan hotch-potch of visiting scholars, language school students and tourists that it can be hard to meet real Cambridge people, although in the Fenland the 'Tigers' still preserve some of their traditional insular, volatile and independent identity. This independence – bloody-mindedness, some might say – and a capacity for vivid and colourful conversation which is often masked by a veneer of reserve are perhaps the more easily identifiable facets of the subtle East Anglian character. East Anglia will not welcome the visitor with the extravagant bonhomie of western Ireland nor even the engaging warmth of the north or west country. Receptions vary from the cool and worldly indifference of Cambridge to the unassuming friendliness of many villagers.

In the matter of dialects, too, the region varies. Cambridge, being Cambridge, has its own élite version of the more celebrated Oxford accent, while the townsfolk speak in tones which the less discerning visitor may mistake for those of London. In the

The big fields give a very 'open' appearance on the thin soils over the chalk of the Cambridgeshire uplands, and could be mistaken for the product of modern 'prairie farming'. This farm has been almost hedgeless for centuries, but good husbandry with simple rotation and minimal spraying have kept the land in good heart and have left room for flora and fauna which are vanishing elsewhere. (Thanks to Mr J. Clarke for this information.)

rural backwaters of Norfolk, however, a strange and gloriously lilting dialect can still be heard and savoured, if not at first always fully understood. East Anglian dissenters and emigrants made up a substantial proportion of the early settlers in the United States and it is often said that the American drawl is a legacy of the migrations. This can be debated, but some of the thousands of US servicemen who came here during the last war are said to have mistaken East Anglian speakers for Americans and many of the words and phrases which sound like modern Americanisms have archaic East Anglian origins.

In fact, there is a schizophrenic quality to East Anglian culture. One side of this cultural coin is innovative, extrovert and represented by the historical role of the region as a reception area for settlers, refugees and all manner of new ideas from the Continent, and this capacity to absorb and revitalise change often placed East Anglia in the vanguard of British innovation. The other side is introspective and characterised by a deep conservatism; being insulated by the sea to the north and east and lying just far enough from London and the main north-south national routeways, East Anglia has been able to escape the full blast of the forces of centralised uniformity which have suffocated the provincial cultures of some southern and Midlands counties. Even in the nineteenth century, 'The Shires' beyond were often regarded with suspicion by the folk of Norfolk and Suffolk.

This conservatism and the apparent readiness to defer in most matters to the squire, his relations and the other masters of the countryside is evident in East Anglian politics. Only in darkest Cambridgeshire could a Tory parliamentary candidate be faced with the threat of deselection following discovery that his wife had joined an anti-bloodsports organisation. A stranger reading the correspondence columns of the local newspapers might come to believe that East Anglian sentiment favours compulsory floggings for the unemployed. But such superficial expressions of regional outlooks will fail to reveal another schizophrenic quality in the East Anglian make-up, for they give no inkling of the historic role of the region as a seedbed for radical dissent and revolution. This tradition runs back through the tithe wars of quite modern times, the writings of Thomas Paine and the trials of the Littleport Martyrs to the Kett's uprising and the rebellions of robber barons like de Mandeville and of patriots like Hereward the Wake. This facet of history is described in Chapter 8.

Having come to East Anglia from outside but having lived here for many years, both authors hope that we can merge the introspective and extrovert aspects of the region's character in an account which gives our personal views but which is not too insular. This is also a story of admiration and anguish: admiration for the remarkable legacy of buildings and monuments of all kinds but anguish that the rural setting of East Anglian life is being destroyed by the heedless, needless and selfish pursuit of agricultural profits. In past centuries, the quest for profit and status produced noble buildings and created fine countryside. Today, it is poisoning the land, polluting our water supplies and transforming lovely mature countrysides into sterile prairie. Only a massive public outcry can stem the devastation. Here we try to show that each facet of the old landscape has its own special story and that there is so much in East Anglia that should be handed down intact to our inheritors.

PART I

THE THEMES OF EAST ANGLIA

by Jack Ravensdale

1
ANCIENT EAST ANGLIA: THE SETTLER'S SHORE

I was on my last posting to RAF Beccles. The war in Europe was drawing to a close, but London was under rocket attack. We had had what seems in memory to have been an unusually generous ration of sunny days. From the airfield looking east into the dawn, we could now and again see an intense point of golden light climbing straight up from the horizon. It left behind a trail which widened out slowly in a zig-zag and paled against the sky, passing into the condensation trails from aircraft and streaks of cloud. This East Anglian airfield was the easternmost in England. We could not only see the enemy rockets rising over Holland, we could also pick up the radio messages from Beaufighters and Wellingtons flying low-down on shipping strikes over the North Sea, although curvature of the earth blanketed them from Group Headquarters. If the seas are narrower further south in the Straits of Dover, East Anglia is still near enough to the Continent for its coast to be attractive to an invader or settler.

There was a time when archaeologists too readily explained cultural change by treating every change and new style in pottery as the product of an invasion by new, warlike peoples from overseas. The long East Anglian coast sweeping round into the Wash, with the estuaries of the Fenland rivers announcing easy routes to the interior, must have invited settlers from the Continent. Even if we sensibly play-down the part of war and violence as a source of cultural change, the East Anglian coast has without doubt often been an invader's or settler's shore, whilst the sea has also favoured contacts for trade and cultural exchange. In the New Stone Age or Neolithic period, axes travelled both ways along the routes from several parts of Britain across to the Continent. We know from their survival that imperishable stone axes were exchanged, so there were surely more perishable trade goods as well.

In the misty mornings that so often came to this coast, the stillness and silence perhaps broken only by the yelp of an unseen dog or a curlew's call, curiosity must have tempted many an early boatman to probe further than he intended behind an apparently deserted shingle spit, and so to become an explorer.

Very little is known about the first East Anglians but they need not have been boatmen for the first human inhabitants arrived during the interglacial periods of the Ice Age or during 'interstadials' – the relatively warm episodes within the glaciations – and at these times southern England and much of East Anglia had a broad land link to what is now the Continent. People of the *Homo erectus* type might have reached this area 500,000 years ago or even earlier. There is conclusive evidence of the existence of human communities here during the interglacial period which lasted from

around 250,000 to 200,000 years ago, for although there are no human remains, their flint tools and even a well-preserved wooden spear have been found.

Although the richest discoveries of the flint 'choppers' made by these 'Clactonian' people have been in the beach deposits around Clacton in Essex, the sea was then far away. These hunting and fishing groups, whose culture probably extended into East Anglia, seem to have lived in riverside base-camps in an area which was then covered by pine and birch woodland which was gradually yielding to oak and alder forest. The Hoxnian culture, named after Hoxne and pronounced like 'oxen', in Suffolk seems to have developed in East Anglia a little later, perhaps existing at the end of the great interglacial period to which Hoxne also gave its name and which closed around 200,000 BC.

With its southerly position in Britain and its relative proximity to the Continent, East Anglia will have attracted new settlers whenever the glacial conditions ameliorated so that when the last deglaciation began around 12,000 BC, the last of the Old Stone Age and the first of the Middle Stone Age or 'Mesolithic' hunting and fishing peoples will have arrived here via the plains and mudflats of the continental land bridge which finally withered and perished in the course of the Mesolithic era. Thus the New Stone Age or 'Neolithic' peoples who introduced the revolutionary concept of agriculture to our area around 5000 BC must have arrived by boat.

In late Neolithic and Bronze Age times East Anglia was linked by the Icknield Way to the great cultural centre of Wessex, the region of Stonehenge and Avebury; this route has been in use in part ever since. Sections of it in Oxfordshire are still paved where the Romans surfaced the track and incorporated it in their road system. The Peddars Way, which links the Icknield Way to the Wash, is also in part Romanised, and seems to have run to a Roman ferry used to make a short cut across the Wash to the northward roads (*see also* page 210). Where these routes have been tidied up by the Roman surveyors, by later farmers fencing in as much land as they could claim as their own, or by the eighteenth- and nineteenth-century Commissioners of Enclosure, their appearance today may deceive us as to their prehistoric character, and as to their contribution to the prehistoric landscapes. The modern parallel-sided road of even width has very little resemblance to the ancient routeways. Air photographs can sometimes reveal their true nature: bundles of tracks, avoiding meres, puddles and rough-rutted areas, going generally in the desired direction, but with each traveller picking his own route, choosing his own diversions. Sometimes the air view can show a whole hillside marked and grooved in this manner, often where no living road exists today.

We know little of the Stone Age sailors or traders although chance finds of the routes by which they carried axes for exchange have given a few clues. Petrologists can identify the quarry of origin of most stone axes by the microscopic examination of a minute wafer of the stone. Peat has sometimes helped to preserve more perishable materials, and prehistoric dug-out canoes have been found in the Fens.

OPPOSITE: *The straightness of the Peddars Way betrays the fact that this prehistoric track, connecting the Icknield Way to the coast near the Wash, was once adopted by the Romans*

Much more can be learned from their manufactories and the most famous prehistoric flint-mines and axe-factories in England are Grimes Graves near Weeting in Norfolk. Even in the reign of Elizabeth I the earthworks were noticed by the antiquary Camden as being artificial, and already known to the locals by their present name, although even then no one knew what the name meant; memories of the Dark Age deity, Grim, had long since faded. The eighteenth-century Norfolk historian Blomefield thought the pits were a Danish camp where an army could hide invisibly but, by 1870, Canon Greenwell's excavations had established that they were prehistoric flint-mines. Between around 7000 years ago or even earlier and the final occupation of the site when the Bronze Age was giving way to that of Iron, various peoples occupied it intermittently for mining and working flint, although the main period of exploitation was in late Neolithic and early Bronze Age times from around 3100 to 2200 BC.

In a site of thirty-four acres, some 346 pits and their spoil heaps have left visible scars on the surface although the total area exploited may have been almost 100 acres. These pits take the form of shallow depressions, almost circular, with bare boulder clay and chalk crumbling in from the sides in any dry season. What slight traces the earliest and primitive pits left has been obliterated by later workings, or the number displayed would be higher. Other flint-mining areas are known, not only in East Anglia, but also in Belgium and in Sussex, where the top quality flint of the deeply buried 'floor-stone' revealed itself when erosion exposed it in the face of a chalk cliff or valleyside. Finds in pits from different periods, especially the mining tools, have enabled archaeologists to work out not only the methods of mining, but also to detect an increasing technical sophistication through the Neolithic period.

In the earliest pits, furnished with steps in the chalk for going down and coming out, the chief tools seem to have been the long bones of red deer and flint wedges. Later, pickaxes were used, made from antlers with all the branches or 'tines' removed save one. In the two pits now open, 244 antler picks were found. In pit number 15, open to the public, there were suggestions that it had become unworkable owing to a fault in the floor-stone. A heap of stone was left covered with antler picks beneath a shelf cut from the chalk wall. Here was set a figurine, female and pregnant. It is generally assumed that this was to defeat the barrenness of the floor at that level or to ensure the fecundity of future workings. Apart from the earliest pits – those which had steps cut in the chalk sides of the shaft – we do not know how access was gained to the working-floor often 30 or 40 ft below the surface or how the floor-stone and

---

OPPOSITE

ABOVE LEFT: *During the period of fullest activity at Grimes Graves, it seems that axes were 'roughed-out' on the site, but polished at their final destination*

ABOVE RIGHT: *The famous East Anglian flint mines, the so-called Grimes Graves, were developed to give prehistoric man access to a seam of flint modules that proved better for making axe-heads than flint found in shallower layers*

BELOW: *Except for the earliest shallow pits, where steps were cut in their chalk sides, we do not know precisely how the miners ascended and descended, or how the heavy blocks of flint were brought to the surface. Ladders and ropes of some sort were probably used*

other material were taken out. Ladders or ropes or both seem most likely.

Illumination in the tunnels or galleries radiating from the shaft floor was by lamps made from hollowing out blocks of chalk, and filling them with some sort of grease and a wick. Some of the soot marks on the chalk overhead may be from these lamps, but most are probably from the candles used by more recent generations of visitors. Ventilation may have been helped by the practice of connecting galleries to those radiating from adjacent pits, but many of these were blocked by back-filling as the excavation went ahead. With total excavation to date of only a very small proportion of the workings, and the greatest part of the web of tunnels left untouched, no skeletons of miners crushed by roof-falls have yet been discovered at Grimes Graves as in some continental flint-mines.

As well as the waste on the knapping-floors where the axes were roughed-out, some unpolished axe blanks have been found in the Grimes Graves area, but others found in distant regions show that this was an export industry. It seems to have been the practice to send away the axes as rough-outs, leaving the tedious polishing and sharpening, hours and hours of rubbing with wet sand, to the purchaser, if purchase was the nature of the transaction.

The flint lies in fairly level seams in the chalk and is not all of equal quality. Inside those shafts open to visitors, three seams can be detected. The upper two, known as top-stone and wall-stone, were not good enough for the stone-age implement maker and were treated simply as overburden – useless material overlaying the flint which had to be tediously removed. Floor-stone was what the miners were after. It comes in flat thick 'nodules' which split very straight and clean. Long, even, razor-keen blades can easily be struck from the dark, silky flint.

Very recent work, using the sophisticated techniques of atomic absorption spectrometry, suggests that most flint axes in this country, even in regions like Norfolk and Wessex where extensive flint-mines have been found, were made from Sussex flint. There is clearly much more to be said on the subject.

The most primitive pits were in the north of the site, where the floor-stone almost outcropped. Associated with these is the earliest phase of flint working at Grimes Graves which seems to be at the start of Neolithic technology or, even, perhaps before. There seems to have been a period of several centuries in a later stage of the early Neolithic period when mining was carried on in the intermediate pits, south of the more primitive ones. These early workings have left little sign on the surface but excavation has shown them, although still shallow, to be much wider than the first group and already to connect with one another. The latest pits, deeper and with dangerously low interconnecting galleries, are securely dated to late Neolithic times in the third millennium BC. This seems to have been the most intensive and productive phase of their use.

The Bronze Age and Iron Age people who lived at Grimes Graves may have worked and used the waste flakes of flint left about the site by the mining communities, but they did not themselves mine. No evidence of settlement later than the early Iron Age has yet appeared.

A Bronze Age barrow lies to the south-east of the site. There are clusters of such earthworks in north-west Norfolk (for example, at Bircham and Salthouse) possibly the remains of once more extensive 'barrowfields' – burial grounds which were perhaps used over long periods. Those barrows which survive visibly as mounds today are greatly out-numbered by those that like so many of East Anglia's other prehistoric monuments – such as 'causewayed camps', 'henges' and the earlier long barrows – have been ploughed flat, and can be detected only in air photographs. Not every mound that remains is a barrow; in some cases, only complete excavation can decide this. One mound that was examined some years ago in Norfolk proved to be a natural feature, but the archaeologist decided to finish the excavation and in so doing discovered a secondary interment. In other words, the mound had deceived the Bronze Age men who had taken it to be one of their own barrows, and had used it as they so often used theirs to insert later burials.

In East Anglia, there is little which is spectacular surviving from the ages of the early farmers, those of the Neolithic and Bronze Ages, but possibly their effects on our surroundings today are greater than those of any other era. A good deal of the forest clearance, which we used to think was the work of medieval man, may have been well begun in the days of the polished stone axe, and at Fengate near Peterborough, on the former margin of the Fens of north-west East Anglia, a Neolithic settlement and grave with associated field system has been excavated and is described on page 181. It now seems likely that some of the pattern of our early fields has survived continuously, once made, but in the lowland zone of England the chances of finding proof of such continuity are extremely slight. At Fengate the matter of dating was clinched by the unique discovery of the skeleton of a man buried with the Neolithic arrow head that killed him still in place.

One of the most valuable finds in the Fens was discovered by a peat digger in 1844 at Grunty Fen, Wilburton, in the Isle of Ely. It is a decorative collar or 'torc' of Middle Bronze Age pattern, twisted like a stick of barley sugar and curled up as an open coil. It is alleged that deposition of peat had compressed it and, in lifting his turf, the digger released the spring so that the torc shot up in the air.

The sites of finds of gold of that period suggest that Irish gold made its way to the Continent across the Irish Sea to the Anglesey region, and then overland to the North Sea around the Wash. Earlier and later, the principal route for their traffic was across Cornwall. This interpretation of the distribution, however, may be too simple. The Anglesey finds and the Grunty Fen torc may all be votive offerings thrown in watery places that had ritual significance, rather than travellers' losses by the roadside. It is beginning to seem that a water cult featured in the Bronze and Iron Age religions of Britain.

In contrast to the situation in Wessex, parts of the Midlands and most upland areas of Britain where scores of hillforts can be seen, the legacy of Iron Age monuments in East Anglia is relatively modest. It has often been suggested that East Anglia was relatively backward and sparsely populated in Iron Age times, but it is very hard to imagine that this could have been the case. Recent researches in the counties bordering our region, such as Christopher Taylor's surveys in Northamptonshire and Tom Williamson's work in Essex, have revealed the remarkable density of hamlets and farmsteads which existed in the centuries before the Roman conquest.

East Anglia contains some of the richest farmland in England and it would not have been neglected. A part of the misunderstanding must result from the relative lack of hillforts in the area, with Wandlebury near Cambridge being the best of a small number of examples. This paucity of hillforts cannot really be explained by the lack of East

Anglian hills which could be fortified, for lowland hillforts could also be built; the fine Warham Camp, close to the coast near Stiffkey in Norfolk, is a good example. Other perhaps similar hillforts may have been destroyed or lie unrecognised and the notion that the Norman 'motte' or castle mound at Thetford has re-used a double-ditched hillfort defence system has just come back into acceptance after a period of being rejected by most experts.

Even so, the shortage of Iron Age hillforts is quite real and so it seems that Iron Age East Anglia may have been less troubled by wars and skirmishing than other regions, organised its political affairs differently, or looked to other, less monumental forms of defenceworks. Some explanations of East Anglian backwardness during this period have concerned the nature of the dominant regional tribal federation, the Iceni. Whatever their other achievements may have been, the Iceni seem to have been a conservative people, less involved in the vigorous trading and in political contacts with the continental world than were the tribes to the south, which were more strongly influenced by the outlooks imported by the somewhat Romanised 'Belgic' immigrants. But there have been some extremely interesting and very recent discoveries at Iron Age sites in East Anglia, as are described in Chapters 9 and 10.

INTO HISTORY FROM PREHISTORY: THE ROMANS AND THEIR HEIRS

In AD 43, the Legions of the Emperor Claudius invaded and quickly conquered south-east Britain. They came, in this part of England at least, to a society which was already much influenced by contact with people who were under Rome's rule in Gaul. They already had substantial native 'proto-towns', tribal centres like Camulodunum (near modern Colchester). In East Anglia, in a period of inter-tribal rivalry and warfare, the Catuvellauni tribe living around Essex and Hertfordshire established their supremacy against the Trinovantes of Suffolk and Essex and the Iceni of Norfolk. The latter were centred on Venta Icenorum (Caistor St Edmund just south of Norwich).

It was at Camulodunum in AD 43 that the formal surrender to the Emperor Claudius took place. The Twentieth Legion was stationed at Roman Colchester and the Trinovantes came under direct Roman rule. On the other hand, Prasutagus of the Iceni was allowed to rule his tribe as a Roman client. The Ninth (Hispana) Legion moved north and in the museum at Cambridge there is a Roman brick from Tile House, Stretham, on the edge of the Fen south of Ely, bearing the Legion's stamp 'IX'.

In about AD 60 Prasutagus died. His widow, Boudicca, was not allowed to succeed; she and her daughter were ill-treated and abused by the Roman officials. She rebelled and the Trinovantes joined the Iceni in a terrifying uprising, as a result of which Camulodunum was sacked. In the museum at Chelmsford is a bronze head of the Emperor Claudius found in a river where it appears to have been thrown after the sacking. The Roman Governor, Suetonius, meanwhile was in Anglesey trying to pacify the island, and was unable to get his forces back in time. London and Verulamium (St Albans) were overrun. The Ninth Legion's infantry was wiped out, and it could only be re-formed around its cavalry wing. Suetonius, when he did get back, dealt with the rebellion so severely that he was recalled. It used to be thought that the

Iceni prisoners were forced to dig the Car Dyke, but it is now realised that the date of this great Roman canal is too late.

All the archaeological evidence suggests that the second century was a period of prosperity, but a foreboding of things to come became apparent in AD 198. Clodius Albinus withdrew the legions from the area for the first time in order to try to support his claim to the Imperial throne. Some years ago, workmen digging a trench at Barway in north Cambridgeshire came across a pot full of coins. The collection started off with pre-Conquest coins of Mark Antony and finished about AD 190. At the inquest, it was shown that hoards with almost identical distribution of dates had been found all over the country. The furtive burial of capital is hardly a sign of confidence and economic prosperity. The unknown owners had intended to return in less troubled times. They never made it.

During the third century, the Roman Imperial Government lost control. Swelling military expenditure for an empire that had overreached itself and was now hopelessly over-extended led to runaway inflation. Law and order broke down.

There was superficial recovery for a time, especially under the series of emperors known as the Antonines. Signs both of chaos and of reorganisation are to be found in decaying and shrinking towns. Verulamium appeared to archaeologists as if it had been blitzed and, when the town was restored, the theatre was no longer used as a centre for culture but used as a rubbish tip for the greengrocers from the local market. As in most Roman towns, Cambridge (where the Roman settlement lay north of the River Cam around Castle Hill) acquired new walls, possibly stone-faced this time, but the new walls were set back on a shorter perimeter, guarding a reduced town.

Pottery from the little farms of the southern Fen Edge often showed a long gap in the sequence of dates in the third century. Sometimes the pottery sequence finished by AD 230; sometimes this resumed after about 270; sometimes a site showed nothing previous to this. John Bromwich worked out the significance of this after seeing what happened in the great Fen flood of 1947. The Romans had committed the folly of linking the River Cam and the River Ouse, in spite of the difficulties of drainage in the area. Their canal, the Car Dyke, was fed from a natural source, and its levels had to be controlled by some kind of sluice. When a period of neglect was followed by a period of strain, perhaps heavy rain and exceptional tides in the Wash, as in 1947, the gates blew, banks burst, and the water went the wrong way for the next forty years, pouring out and drowning the low land bridge south of what now became the Isle of Ely.

When the Car Dyke was in operation again, after 270, it was possible to re-occupy some, but only some, of the old sites below the 20-ft contour, but on occasion completely new sites had to be used. Most of the farms placed above that contour were then able to continue functioning into the fifth century, possibly under new management. The government was more and more attempting self-financing defence by settling barbarians as *federati* who, it was hoped, would defend the empire against their Saxon kinsmen. Possibly management changed yet again in some of these places if the numbers of broken slave chains discovered mean what they appear to tell us. The latest pottery on many of the sites that survive right through tell the same story: different people were living there.

Late Roman defence of Britain was split between commanders on sea and on land,

the Count of the Saxon Shore, and the Duke of the Britons. The Saxon Shore was so-called because of pirate raids launched across the North Sea on to the East Anglian coast, and further south against Kent, Sussex and Hampshire. A chain of coastal forts was built from Brancaster in Norfolk at Burgh Castle and Bradwell, also in East Anglia; then beyond the Thames estuary at Reculver, in Kent; at Richborough, the centre of this scheme, and others on round the southern coast to Portchester. Another East Anglian fortress was at Walton Castle near Felixstowe, but the remains were destroyed by coastal erosion in the eighteenth century. These forts were manned by auxiliaries rather than regular legions, under the direction of the Count of the Saxon Shore. At Richborough, there were some regulars, a detachment from the Second Augusta Legion. The Roman fleet, based on Boulogne, met with success against the North Sea pirates, but its Admiral, Carausius, who was in trouble with Rome for corruption, came to Britain and seized power as Emperor. Thanks to treachery from his second-in-command, he was assassinated and afterwards his successor too was murdered. Imperial rule from Rome was re-established, and the sea defence reorganised to avoid repetition of Carausius's bid for power: the fleet was split between the forts, and naval defence became more localised.

In the fourth century, the threats of Saxon coastal raiding were coupled with the pressures from the northern barbarians while within the Roman province economic and organisational problems taxed the system. In 367, the Picts broke through the northern wall, and for two years were found raiding as far south as London and Kent. Both the Count and the Duke were killed. In 369, Count Theodosius arrived and restored Imperial power again. It was from his reorganisation of the defences that the province gained the coastal signal towers between the shore forts. It has even been suggested that the Devil's Dyke in Cambridgeshire (*see* page 30) was dug to protect his bridgehead during the re-conquest. This is not very likely, but what is certain is that he settled a continental people, the Alamanni, in Britain as *federati*, and began the large-scale establishment of Germanic tribes in Britain as defence against the barbarians from across Hadrian's Wall, preparing what perhaps became a gigantic Trojan Horse. Some such settlement had taken place before but on a much smaller scale.

Dr J. A. L. Myres discovered what he termed Romano-Saxon and Anglo-Friesian pottery in settlements outside walled towns all down the eastern side of England. Characteristic sword-belt buckles, standard items of auxiliary equipment, help to identify these barbaric defenders of Britain against the barbarians. A large village or camp has been excavated at Mucking in Essex, overlooking the vulnerable approaches up the Thames Estuary. Much of the coarse pottery that appears in the latest strata on Romano-British sites has now been shown to be of a pagan Saxon type. Romano-Saxon pottery was found in quantity on the site of the Roman town, Caister-on-Sea (Caister by Yarmouth), although much less was inside Burgh Castle shore fort, close by across the estuary.

OPPOSITE: *The Roman Car Dyke, which connected the rivers Cam and Ouse and had extensions to Lincoln and the north, is still clear for much of its length through Cambridgeshire although, in most places, its profile has been distorted by drag-lining and other modern techniques for cleaning ditches. This photograph shows it near the crossing with the old Roman road*

The Devil's Dyke, running over seven miles from the old forest to the old Fen, has so far kept its origins and purposes secret

---

A great concentration of pottery of this date has been found in the Anglo-Saxon cemetery outside Caister-by-Norwich called by the Romans Venta Icenorum, the old tribal capital of the Iceni (and today known as Caistor St Edmund).

The immigrants to East Anglia in the late Imperial era seem to have been mostly Angles from Schleswig, in the south of Denmark, more or less as Bede tells us they were, and the place-names of Norfolk and Suffolk have a coherence which suggests common language. T. C. Lethbridge, a generation ago, suggested that this language, spoken well before the withdrawal of the Legions from Britain in 410, was a form of Low German.

In one East Anglian pagan Saxon village, West Stow near Bury St Edmunds, which was deserted in the seventh century and covered in sand-dunes, the archaeological record shows a small Saxon community, rearing sheep and weaving cloth, trading with its Romano-British neighbours in a state of peaceful co-existence. Hundreds of other villages have wandered to new sites, buried their earliest remains with later building, or lost all traces of dwellings. But West Stow, fortuitously covered by wind-blown sand, was not only preserved and excavated, but is now partially reconstructed.

The East Anglian Roman roads seem to converge on Caister-by-Norwich, and this suggests that the Roman provincial centre was the native tribal capital as well, both before the Romans came, and after they had gone. When the Legions withdrew, according to the picture drawn by the late Charles Green, Anglian settlement seems to have been planned by a sub-Roman Governor based at Caister-by-Norwich. By the sixth century this organisation had gone.

Before then, a new authority had appeared, the East Anglian kingdom based on Rendlesham in the Suffolk Sandlings (a region known for its sandy soil between Ipswich and the sea), and early in the seventh century one of their kings, Redwald, followed Ethelbert of Kent as 'Bretwalda', the 'High King', with nominal precedence over the other kings.

THE DARK AGES

The Dark Ages are still very dark. We blunder blindly when we try to generalise about the end of Roman rule and the rise of successor kingdoms in England, but the discoveries of 1939 in the ship-burial at Sutton Hoo threw blazing light on part of the story in East Anglia. It was not only the century's richest find in Europe north of the Alps in terms of the quality of the ship and the grave goods, but the written sources and the archaeological investigation have slowly and with patience come together. Over the years, guesses have been transformed into history.

Four miles north of the barrow cluster which contained the ship-burial is Rendlesham, traditionally associated with royalty, and recorded by Camden as a royal site under Redwald. Here, in about 1690, it was reported that a silver crown weighing 60 ounces was found, although crown-wearing was not yet a royal custom in Redwald's time. Bede has more evidence to give which makes it clear that Rendlesham was a royal centre, suitable for receiving other royalty and also suitable for royal baptism, probably with one of the earliest East Anglian churches. Sutton Hoo appears now to have been the royal burial ground for the dynasty of East Anglian kings, the 'Wuffings', who lived at Rendlesham.

At first there was a major difficulty of interpretation in that no human remains were found beneath the burial mound, but chemical tests after the Second World War showed that a body may originally have been placed in the chamber on the ship, and subsequently have disappeared as the bones dissolved. The probability that this was after all a tomb and not a cenotaph is generally now accepted. The iron standard and the whetstone sceptre identify it as the tomb of a king. The shield was Swedish, and old at the time of the burial, for which it had been repaired; the helmet was also Swedish. The sword had a blade from the Rhineland, a pommel from Sweden, and was finished in England. Some of the jewellery probably came from the same workshop as the so-called Jutish finds in Kent, and Swedish themes appear to have been worked by an English jeweller. The coins, except for three blanks which made up the total to match the number of rowers including the helmsman at the steering oar, were each from a different mint. They seem to represent the rowers' fees, as in ancient times Charon was paid for the trip across the river Styx.

The finds make it clear that these people, living in the Sandlings in the seventh century, were involved in a network of coastal trade from Kent to their ancestral home in Sweden. At this time, and in view of the structure of the ship, it is not likely that sail was used very much, if at all. Yet it appears that an East Anglian kingdom based on sea-power lasted until it was vanquished by Mercia in the middle of the eighth century.

Sea-power made Rendlesham ideal as a base, with the Deben estuary as refuge or escape route, whereas Norwich would have been a trap for mariners. A site so far south as Rendlesham would have had much to commend it if contacts with Kent were to be maintained. It would help as well in taking advantage of the shorter passage across the open sea. The trade routes of the Sandlings folk are shown by the trail of their characteristic pottery (the hand-made Middle Saxon 'Ipswich ware') along the coast, up the rivers, and not along the main roads. Apparently, unlike other Germanic settlers, these people kept and maintained their boats after landing (the Sutton Hoo boat was patched) and continued their trading ventures as a source of wealth. In the seventh century, the pagan rite of ship-burial was practised only at either end of the trade routes in Sweden and Suffolk.

Among the grave goods placed closely beside where the body would have been, were two silver spoons, inscribed Paul and Saul, ten silver cruciform bowls, and a scabbard mount with cross decoration. Saul as well as Paul must seem unique in a Christian context except in a context of conversion. Redwald was the first of his line to accept baptism, although later, under his wife's influence, he installed a pagan altar for sacrifice alongside the Christian one in the church.

Re-examination of the coinage makes AD 625 (the date of Redwald's death) quite acceptable for the date of the ship burial. Redwald's religious history makes him the perfect candidate for the mysterious inhumation, as does the magnificence of the tomb; he was the only Bretwalda of his line.

If there is now less mystery about the early story of the Wuffings dynasty of East Anglian kings, we are faced with an unyielding mystery about its end: the Cambridgeshire Dykes. There is a series of four great linear earthworks of ditch and bank which run across the Icknield Way, between forest and the Fen, and all face south-west, as if people in East Anglia are defending themselves against attackers from inland. There are other linear earthworks in north-west Norfolk, mostly across Roman roads, and facing west. The greatest of all the Cambridgeshire dykes, the Devil's Dyke, has had archaeological attention for a long time, but it is not even possible to identify any original gate or entrance through it: probably there was none. The top has often gone, mainly from chalk robbing, and one cannot tell if it ever had a palisade. At the excavation by Professor Hope-Taylor a few years ago, a late Roman coin was found sealed in the original ground surface. One interment in the bank, which looked like an execution, dated from the thirteenth century, and after a small but very expert excavation which revealed much of the detailed method of construction, it still cannot be dated more closely than between late Roman and late Saxon times.

In spite of the attractions of other candidates as builders, notably the British 'king' Arthur's Saxon opponents fleeing eastwards (evidence from the Friesian islands suggests returning emigrants in the first half of the sixth century), the widely suggested period for the erection of these massive barriers is the wars between East Anglia and

Mercia. They are usually thought of as the retreating, defended frontiers of the East Anglian kingdom in the eighth century. Even so, during his previous incarnation as a political geographer, one of the authors (Richard Muir) studied the Dykes from the standpoint of military geography and they seemed most credible as defences against cavalry attack from the west, so that the 'British resurgence' theory cannot be ruled out.

Mercian overlordship was eventually accepted by the East Anglians. Probably the rise to importance of Thetford came then: the late Saxon pottery known as Thetford ware, which replaced Ipswich ware, was certainly being manufactured there.

The next great change came with the Norman Conquest, when the new rulers characteristically brought together church and state and commerce, symbolised by the castle, cathedral and new French borough in Norwich: the latter was the new part of the town built for the French and other Normans.

THE CHURCH AND THE STATE

Closely entwined with dynastic politics is the religious history of the region. The power and condition of kingship at the time meant that a faith which captured the ruler would probably win the people as a bonus. The most successful missionaries worked on the 'old boy network'. Redwald himself was converted during a visit to Ethelbert's court in Canterbury. He was succeeded by his heathen son Eorpwald. In 632, Eorpwald, persuaded by Edwin of Northumbria (who had himself been converted by Paulinus five years before), was converted. Almost immediately he was killed by the heathen Richbert. By 635, Sigebert, Eorpwald's brother who had been baptised in France, became king of East Anglia. Sigebert had a key role in the effective introduction of Christianity. During his reign, Felix, who was sent to East Anglia by the Pope, was installed as Bishop at Dunwich. Fursey, an Irish monk (the part played by the Celtic church in the conversion, even that of remote East Anglia, has been much underrated) set up a monastery, as good Irish missionary monks should. For this holy purpose he was given the old Saxon Shore fort at Burgh Castle. Sigebert himself founded a monastery at the future town of Bury St Edmunds, and took up the life of devotion there, handing over his duties to his co-ruler Ecgric. He was later compelled to emerge to lead the defence of the East Anglians against the aggressive pagan King Penda of Mercia. Both Sigebert and Ecgric were killed.

The junior line of the Wuffings, which was descended from the sons of Ecgric, Redwald's brother, ascended to the throne. Anna, who for a time was considered likely to have been the king to whom the Sutton Hoo burial had been raised as a cenotaph, became king. He was Christian, founded a monastery at Blythburgh, and enriched the Burgh Castle monastery of Fursey. His second daughter, Etheldreda, founded the abbey at Ely following the failure of her marriage, and his eldest daughter married the king of Kent, Erconberht. On being widowed she, too, went to Ely and succeeded her sister as Abbess. Anna's third daughter became an abbess in France. It was in Anna's reign that Penda of Mercia established himself as overlord of the East Anglian kingdom, and it was in a dispute with Penda that war was renewed and Anna killed. His brother Aethelhere marched north with Penda against Oswy of Northumbria only to be routed, and both Penda and Aethelhere lost their lives.

The next king, Aethelwald, was sponsor for Swithhelm of Essex at his baptism at Rendlesham. The dynasty seems to have died out in about 740, although there were later East Anglian kings until the line ended when Edmund was murdered by Danes in 870.

For all the branches of the Christian Church involved in the conversion of England – Celtic, Gaulish and Roman – monasteries played an important part. By 640, these had all made their contribution in East Anglia, and at least five monasteries had been set up. Dunwich was probably the site of the bishopric and convent of Felix, who had come from Burgundy. A rival interpretation places them at Walton Castle near Felixstowe. Fursey had been installed in the old Roman Saxon Shore Fort, Burgh Castle. Sigebert had set up the first foundation in what was to become Bury St Edmunds. Anna had started the house at Blythburgh and St Botolph's community has been identified with Iken on the Alde.

In the late seventh century, the East Anglian see was split. Norfolk acquired its own bishop at Elmham. The Mercian and Danish wars destroyed the East Anglian bishoprics until a united see was restored at Elmham in about 955. We are still not sure that this was North, and not South Elmham, or that the older stone church of which so much remains was the cathedral. This will be discussed later (page 48) but one should note the suggestion by Norman Scarfe that the earlier see was based at South Elmham and that it was after its restoration that it went to North Elmham. In 1071, it moved to Thetford and was taken by the Normans to Norwich in 1095 – a typical Norman action, emphasising the unity of Church and State.

OPPOSITE: *The Saxon church at Beechamwell*

ABOVE: *The interior of Ely cathedral from beneath the octagon*

OPPOSITE: *Ely cathedral silhouetted against the sunset*

ABOVE: *Medieval glass at Long Melford church*

BELOW: *An interior view of Norwich cathedral*

BELOW: *The impressive remains of Binham Priory*

2
RELIGION IN THE LANDSCAPE

The conversion and the subsequent growth of Christianity, and then the slow filling up of the countryside with churches, probably suffered as much interruption from the pagan barbaric Danes in East Anglia as anywhere in the country.

PAGANS AND CHRISTIANS

Practically nothing remains visible in the landscape to mark the Danish invasions, and yet East Anglia is littered with Scandinavian place-names, such as -thwaite, -thorpe and -toft, and Norfolk dialect is rich in words loaned by Danish settlers. In the Domesday Book of 1086 we can see some of the social effects of that settlement, a much higher proportion of freemen and 'sokemen', their Danish equivalent, a lower proportion of villeins who were unfree peasants, and a number of manors in the hands of a group of freemen with no lord between them and the king. The fewer feudal bonds here seem to be the result of settlement by groups of free Danish soldiers.

At Horningtoft, south of Fakenham, is an early Danish camp, easy to pass unnoticed, but very impressive when time is found to stop and look. The modern farm gate is still across the original entrance. What is not immediately apparent is that the ditch and bank running alongside the road in both directions continue right around this very large polygonal field of old permanent pasture. Inturned banks run back some thirty or forty yards alongside the entrance from the gate, and on the south side there is a platform in an ideal place for a guardhouse. Considerable gravel digging has taken place in the middle, confusing the earthworks which suggest a central headquarters, but it was these destructive gravel diggings which produced the chance finds of Danish weapons which identified the camp. Not far from here, the pagan Great Host over-wintered in East Anglia for the first time in 865.

Danish leaders, like Guthrum, began to be converted to Christianity either when defeated or, later, when settling in England. Any churches that survive from this period are almost invariably described as 'Saxon'. The complication of the period is illustrated by one church at Hadstock in Essex, where the 'Saxon' church door was covered with the skin of a 'Dane'. Fragments of the skin are still in the museum at Saffron Walden. If such an outrage were true, what right have we to call the church Christian? Even so, one can understand the fear and loathing which the poorly defended villagers directed towards the terrifying Danish raiders.

PARISH CHURCHES AND CHAPELS

Churches, strangely enough, are the most likely places to find survivals of pre-Christian pagan beliefs. At Whittlesford in Cambridgeshire, in what seems to be Norman work in the tower, there is a *sheila-na-gig*, a Celtic image of a naked woman anxiously awaiting possession by a human-headed bull or goat. The carving seems to have been reset and perhaps come from some pagan shrine. There is another *sheila-na-gig* in the church at Moulton in Suffolk. Green men, human heads with leafy vine-shoots growing out of their mouths and sometimes obscuring their faces, are relatively common. There are splendid examples in the Lady Chapel at Ely Cathedral from the first half of the fourteenth century. The authors of this book found three in the fifteenth-century woodwork at the parish church of Landbeach, a few miles north of Cambridge.

Ancient beliefs cast long shadows. One of the commonest features of East Anglian fonts is four wild men with clubs between four lions as supporters of the bowl. St Mary's at Happisburgh, on the Norfolk coast, has a good example of the type.

ABOVE: *One of the finest examples of the Decorated style of architecture is the Lady Chapel in Ely Cathedral. This very delicate carving was made in clunch (hard chalk) and the carvers showed a sense of form in three dimensions*

OPPOSITE: *These photographs show flint being used for the round towers in the absence of better building stone. Kilverstone, Belton and Burgh Castle churches show the persistence of this East Anglian feature over the centuries*

Much of the early work in East Anglian churches must date from the years of uncertainty as to who would rule in the long run, Saxon or Dane, and the question was in doubt politically right up to the Norman Conquest. Harold's defeat of the Norse Vikings at Stamford Bridge may have cost him his own defeat soon after at the hands of transplanted Norsemen from Normandy in 1066. The Norwegian fleet which appeared in the Wash during Hereward's revolt against the Normans was the last dying flicker of what had seemed a possible North Atlantic Scandinavian Empire, based on sea power.

One of the most frequent characteristics of early East Anglian parish churches, both before and after the Conquest, is the round tower. The reason for such large numbers of these has a structural explanation: the absence of good free-stone. The local builders used the best of the flint pebbles that were to hand but whatever its other qualities, it is not practicable to form 'quoins' or corner stones from flint pebbles. With flint

as the only available stone, a round tower is much stronger than a square one. Where a Saxon builder managed to obtain enough free-stone for his quoins, using flint for the rest, as at Newton near Castle Acre, the tower is square, even in this area with round towers nearby.

Another suggestion, deriving from the fact that so many of the towers have no original door at ground level, is that they were defensive retreats used during Danish raids. But used so, they would have been traps for the local people faced by barbarian enemies who would have been only too pleased to fire them from below.

Rather more sense lies in the suggestion that many of the round towers were erected by late tenth-century 'thanes' or nobles as look-out and bell towers to watch for Vikings sailing up the estuaries and rivers. The king had placed such an obligation on thanes, and many of the towers give magnificent views towards the coast. Although many would hardly be apt for this chore of coast watching, bells ringing from tower to tower could spread the warning inland, just as centuries later the siren spread its urgent message.

The first-floor entrance giving access only from inside the church has encouraged many to consider the defensive argument seriously, but a considerable number of years ago the Taylors, who made the most exhaustive study of Anglo-Saxon churches, showed how such doorways had been used in conjunction with western galleries in an elaborate ritual brought back from St James of Compostella in Spain.

One of the most attractive of these round-towered early churches is the little thatched church of St Mary's at Beechamwell, not far from Swaffham in Norfolk. Much Saxon work is visible here. Neat Saxon 'long-and-short' work on the south side of the nave indicates the original aisleless building. In the tower, in the original bell stage, are the two kinds of typical Saxon belfry openings, two lights on the north and west with triangular heads, and on the south and east there are round ones. There is now a very plain door into the tower at ground floor level, and a smaller, and probably earlier one on the first floor. These doors are not properly aligned with each other or with the church. This might indicate different periods of construction: it might also indicate unsolved problems in properly aligning a church.

In the unpretentious simplicity of this church and its setting, East Anglia is epitomised. Of the 180 round towers in England, 119 are in Norfolk, 41 in Suffolk and 8 in Essex. Possibly a tenth of those in Norfolk are Saxon. Most of them are very difficult to date, and none can be placed earlier than mid-ninth century. Some are indeed primitive. At West Lexham near Castle Acre, where the rendering had broken away at one point, construction seemed to be of flints set in clay, held together by sand and lime rendering which was in turn held together against the rain by coats of lime-wash. It had nevertheless lasted well. St Nicholas at Little Saxham, near Bury St Edmunds, is the opposite end of the scale of sophistication of a round tower, with elaborate pure Norman blind arcading on its top stage.

At Weybourne on the north Norfolk coast a different example of Saxon work survives in the ruined tower of the old parish church, a church to which a house of Augustinian Canons was attached in the thirteenth century. Still clearly visible on a large square central tower are 'pilaster strips', raised bands apparently imitating timberwork in stone, very typical of late Saxon external decoration. It also has very characteristic Saxon windows, circular, triangular-headed, and keyhole-shaped. We owe its survival

This ambitious late-Saxon arch in the tower of St Benet's church in Cambridge shows that a wealthy church and settlement must have existed on the east side of the river Cam long before the Norman Conquest. The piers at the side show typical Saxon 'long-and-short work' and the carved capitals are slightly elaborate versions of typical late-Saxon 'through-stones'

---

to its usefulness as an aid to navigation, and this saved it at the Reformation. Some authorities suspect that it belongs to a continuity of Saxon style during the years just after the Norman Conquest. In the Middle Ages, this one church was used by parish and priory, and one man was both prior and vicar.

Cambridgeshire is probably the poorest of the three counties in Saxon work. Apart from the shaft of the memorial cross to Ovin, St Etheldreda's steward, which was brought from Haddenham to the Cathedral at Ely, there seems to be nothing of architectural substance from the early Saxon period in Cambridgeshire, in spite of a rich endowment of pagan Saxon cemeteries and settlement sites. Even later, the region has little that is complete. Tomb slabs, in whole or in part, mostly with tenth-century interlacing decoration, are built into later walls as at Balsham, Little Shelford, Rampton and Stapleford. There is rather more at St Giles in Cambridge, if it is really late Saxon rather than early Norman in date and most of all in St Benet's on the edge of the market area, where the church is grand enough to show that the market town which developed on the opposite side of the river from the old Roman town and the Norman castle, was a place of some importance before the Norman Conquest.

The tower at the west end of St Benet's is a particularly fine example of late Saxon

THIS PAGE AND OPPOSITE: *East Anglian parish churches show an amazing variety. Here Kirtling church shows rich Norman ornamentation with a 'Christ in Majesty' over the doorway. Greensand afforded a moderately useful building stone in some parts of the region, and here it is shown used particularly freely at Denver. South Lupham church shows Norman blind arcading on a very typical Norman central tower still surviving, a pattern that was once common. The buttresses on West Stow tower show an effective if simple use of flint to help out what little good building stone was available*

construction. Built of rubble, it has light long-and-short work at its quoins. The openings at the bell stage are unmistakably Saxon, a lathe-turned stone baluster supporting a slab corbel with round heads cut into it. It also has a pilaster strip of stone present or traceable from the bell-windows to the summit. Inside there is a round-headed doorway into the tower at first floor level, and below it a round-headed tower arch with moulded 'through-stones' which approach the form of capitals surmounted by weird beasts – either a dimly perceived memory of continental styles of the time or a precursor of things to come once the Normans were thoroughly settled in. The jambs of the arch show the mason caught in two minds, continuing the half-roll moulding of the arch as half-round and half-pillar over the long-and-short work, rather like pilasters. What impresses the visitor about St Benet's is that the tower has survived so well in an urban core where anything less splendid would have been re-built.

The surviving Norman work in East Anglian parish churches, in contrast to that in former monasteries, is fragmentary and insignificant. The glory of East Anglian parish churches came later. Most of them relied on flint for the bulk of their fabric as other building stone had to be brought from a great distance, notably from Barnack in the far north of modern Cambridgeshire. The earlier builders used intractable flint and rubble, the walls being faced with large flint pebbles which were plastered over.

Then came the use of dressed flint in which the region was to excel. In the earlier forms of such work, flint stones were split and both halves set in the wall with the new faces exposed. Because of the irregular spaces between the stones, flint chips were sometimes set in mortar as 'galletting'. This practice continued and was later used in brick walls. The perfection of the use of flint in church building bifurcated into two distinct styles. In the less common style, as represented by the fourteenth-century wall of the present Bridewell Museum in Norwich, the flints were knapped into cubes, sorted into size and matched and laid so that not even the slimmest knife could be pushed between the stones. The other style – the pride of our late fifteenth- and early sixteenth-century church-building, and dominating the churches still left today – was 'flush-work', the use of dressed flint and dressed stone in patterns. The designs at Woodbridge are particularly fine examples of what could be achieved with the intractable flint.

Churches built shortly before the Reformation in East Anglia tend to be the biggest and finest, and the ones which used flushwork to best advantage. Salle, almost deserted today, Cawston and Worstead are on a scale which underlines the industrial wealth of Norfolk of the fifteenth century, and in later medieval times there was a shift in the direction of the pious endowments from the religious houses of friars and monks, back to parish churches. There is a marked tendency for the churches in areas of the greatest economic prosperity to be particularly lavish – St Peter Mancroft looking down across the market in Norwich must have been a wonderful setting for showy competitive displays by the great merchants' wives, and perhaps something of the same spirit entered into the fabric of the building itself. Bury St Edmunds similarly had the two largest parish churches of Suffolk standing close to the Abbey.

It is significant that the popular title, 'Cathedral of the Fens', is disputed by more than one parish church. Sutton in the Isle of Ely is not the meanest claimant, and

Lavenham church was built, to the greater glory of the Spring family, over three generations. This family of clothiers has left its merchant mark as a recurrent theme in the stonework

other marshland churches can be on the same scale, such as Walpole St Peter and Terrington St Clement, both lying a few miles west of King's Lynn. The coastal villages of both Norfolk (as at Blakeney, Salthouse, Cromer and Winterton) and Suffolk (as seen in the belt of Lowestoft – Kessingland – Covehithe – Southwold – Walberswick – Blythburgh – Aldeburgh) exhibit the same grandeur. Above, all the cloth villages around Sudbury and Lavenham not only have unsurpassable churches, they often have them in an unsurpassable surviving townscape of the same period. Size is far from everything in a parish church, but this may not have been the opinion of the Spring family of merchants at Lavenham who built the soaring tower over three generations. Still not finished, it looks too tall for the church – or for almost any church.

Its neighbour and rival, Long Melford, managed to stop growing in time; partly this is due to improvements in the years around 1900 which, Pevsner says, enhanced the purity of the style. The Clopton Chantry records the principal clothier family amongst those responsible for the re-building in the fifteenth century. It repays close examination as does the whole church. Dated inscriptions recording all those who gave money run around the whole interior, including the very unusual Lady Chapel which is approached through a narrow passage from the east end. A rectangular chapel under a three-ridged roof, it takes the form of an ambulatory around a canopied shrine. Much medieval glass survives at Long Melford. Perhaps the most exquisite is

Also built from the profits of cloth-making, the church at Long Melford attained an even higher quality in its flush-work of knapped flints and stone

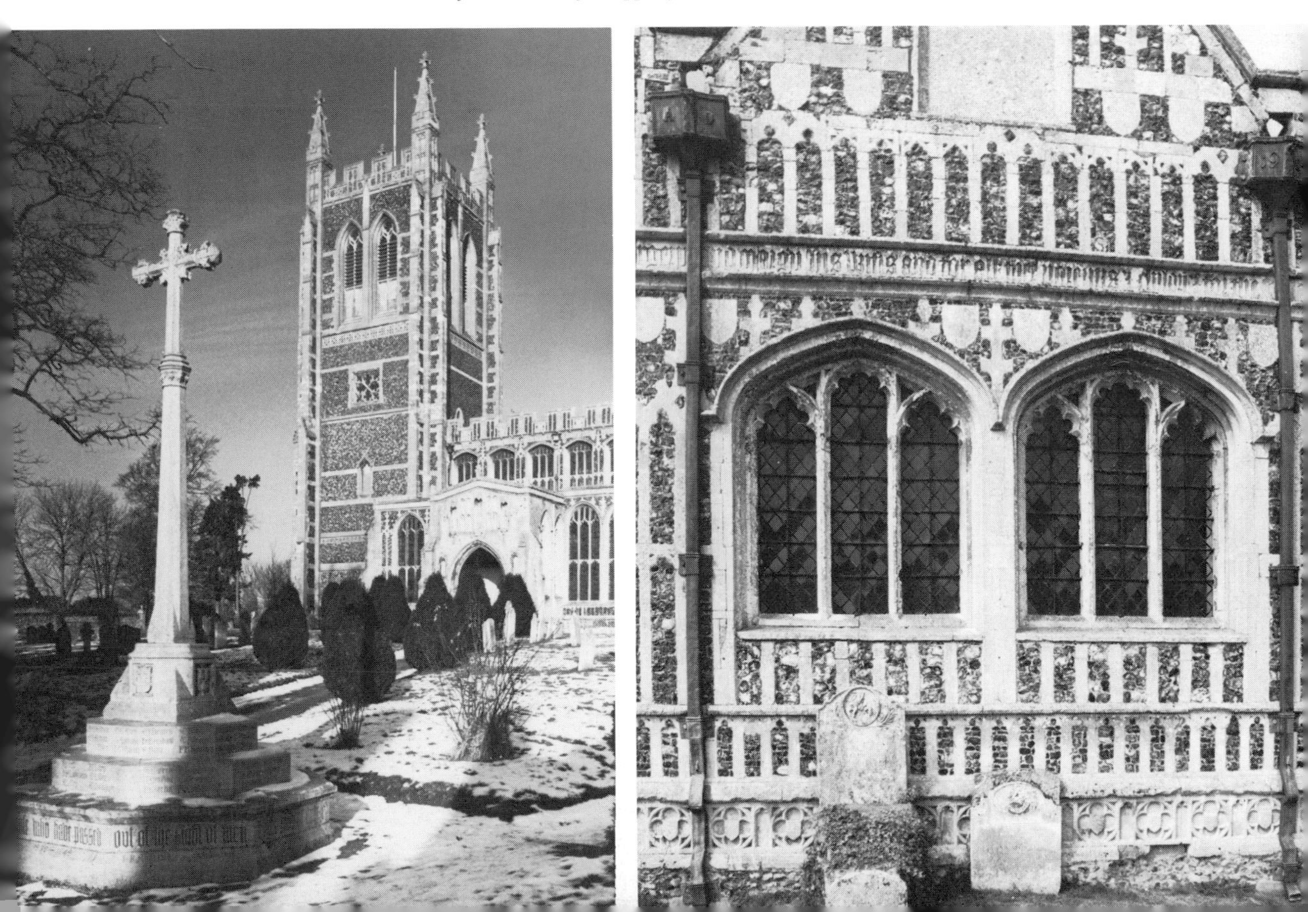

On the edge of the Fens, wealth from farming produced another magnificent parish church at Mildenhall. The upper storey of the porch is a Lady Chapel which opens out into the nave, and has elaborately carved spandrels on its tie-beams

---

the Lily Crucifixus in the Clopton Chantry. All in all, this church is one of the richest treasures in the region.

Less obviously placed, but still in Suffolk, and still telling of prosperity, is Mildenhall, situated between the Fen and the Breckland. The church of St Mary and St Andrew is again very large, and very original. The seven-light east window is exquisite enough to stop passing traffic. It shares a feature with nearby Fordham, a Lady Chapel in the upper room over the porch. This opens into the body of the church from a lofty position up among the delightfully carved spandrels of the arched braces of the principal trusses. Again, this church will repay a long stay.

East Anglia exhibits special regional preferences in its churches which differentiate it from other regions. For instance, it has few spires but a number of spirelets, as in St Peter Mancroft in Norwich. It has a number of priest's doors entering through or under a buttress on the chancel. Most of its towers are at the west end, as normal, but a few are over a south porch. As well as its western tower, Blakeney has a slender beacon-tower for the benefit of ships. At Beccles, the tower is detached, being built alongside the main building at the west end. The special glory of East Anglian churches, however, is in the roofs, and in the interior furnishings: fonts, font-covers, screens, pulpits, benches and stalls. Most of the woodwork was once painted, and a good deal of medieval painting remains, although for most of the early work and much of the later, the glazes have gone, leaving only the under-painting.

Whether splashed on by Puritans destroying 'superstitious images', by Victorians bringing defective walls back to standard, or applied to cover the anatomically frank (if not always accurate) depiction of vices in action, covering coats of white-wash have preserved as well as destroyed. Sometimes the best and worst intentions, however, have combined to produce maximum damage. At Sutton in the Isle of Ely, the splendid statue of the Madonna in the Lady Chapel has not only been defaced, but most of the blue of her robe seems to have disappeared under the ministrations of generations of cleansing hands.

From the fragments that remain of medieval wall-painting, it would seem that some churches had all their walls painted in this manner. Neighbouring Rampton and Willingham in Cambridgeshire are in this category, and some of what little remains in nearby Over is fine. Both Rampton and Willingham have had paintings of St Christopher in the traditional place opposite the main entrance. Other paintings are of scenes from the Life of Christ or of the saints and scenes from biblical events, like the Last Judgement.

The Judgement often appears in the form of the 'Doom pictures' over the chancel arch, depicting the rising from the dead and submission to the judgements of St Michael the Archangel who is shown with sword drawn and scales to weigh the souls. The saved then go up to Heaven to be crowned, and the damned (amongst whom even mitred bishops may be seen) are bound in red-hot chains and prodded by little devils into the jaws of hell. These have fangs like sea-monsters and are full of fire. Quite a lot of the Doom survives in Willingham, just mentioned. One of the clearest, if not exactly the most finely executed, is in the little Suffolk church of Wenhaston near Halesworth. A panel that had filled the top of the chancel arch above the screen was recognised and brought back to the church where it is protected from the weather and can now be seen in the north aisle. It is easy to see where the crucifix, or the 'Rood', was fastened on the panel. A surprising amount of the surrounding 'Doom' survives in full colour.

Elsewhere, wall areas were covered with painted imitations of squared and dressed masonry, not unlike the Norman decoration found and restored on the eastern side of the chancel arch at Norwich Cathedral. Other motifs were stylised vine rods with bunches of grapes and leaves, or roses on curving stems. Favourite themes for special places are the Apostles in the panels of the dado of the rood-screen, or the Early Fathers in the panels of the pulpit. St James, Castle Acre, has very good examples. Binham Priory, in north Norfolk was reduced in size and preserved as a parish church at the Reformation. The rest of the screen has gone but the dado remains. It was painted over with white as a background for texts painted in black gothic lettering. The texts have a familiar ring, but seem not quite as remembered. They were painted in the early years of the Reformation and use the earlier Tyndale and Coverdale translations of the Bible. Where the paint has begun to flake, well-preserved saints peep out.

The richness of the carving in the Lady Chapel at Ely is matched, or perhaps surpassed, by the roof-bosses of about the same date in the cloisters of Norwich Cathedral

The whole region abounds in good roofs. In Suffolk, Woolpit's double hammerbeam roof is as near perfection as any that could be imagined; the wall-posts themselves rest on angel brackets, both hammers have angels and there are more fluttering in two tiers on the wall-plate. The richness of the decoration of the rest is hardly noticed among all the angels with outstretched wings. March in Cambridgeshire and Knapton in Norfolk have roofs of similar quality and pattern.

One of the most essential pieces of furniture in a Christian church is the font. They have exceptional powers of survival. Far more churches have Norman fonts than substantial Norman masonry. Where they use figurative decoration, the result has a primitive rustic charm. There are two very good Norfolk examples, with figures in little Romanesque blind arcades running round the bowls, at Fincham and Burnham Deepdale; the latter's figures are engaged in the 'labours of the months'. At St Peter's, Ipswich, there is an excellent font of imported Tournai marble, with most delightful animals.

In the later Middle Ages, East Anglia developed its own characteristic types of font. The commonest type, as previously mentioned, has four seated lions, usually with four wild men – all hairy and armed with clubs – between the animals. On the bowl are the signs of the Four Evangelists with four more lions or instruments of the Passion, or decorative flowers, or even the symbol of the Trinity. From this developed the Seven Sacrament Font, with an octagonal bowl on which are depicted the sacraments of Baptism, Confirmation, Ordination, Penance, Matrimony, Holy Communion and Extreme Unction. The eighth panel usually had a scene from the life of Christ. At Blofield, east of Norwich, all eight panels have such scenes instead. Such seven-sacrament fonts are almost exclusive to East Anglia; Suffolk has thirteen and there are twenty-five in Norfolk.

In the panel depicting the Last Rites on the font at Badingham in Suffolk, the priest is showing the dying man the Gospel Book, the widow to be is at the foot of the bed, veiled and weeping. Underneath are depicted not only the patient's slippers but also a used chamber pot! In this earthy setting, we can see the agony, and the sunken eyes of the man in bed tell us that he is not long for this world. A country carver

ABOVE LEFT: *The font at Burgh Castle church is supported by four lions, a feature with many East Anglian parallels*

ABOVE RIGHT: *This simple font with shallow blind arcading at Oakington in Cambridgeshire is thought to be very early, possibly dating from before the Norman Conquest*

RIGHT: *The grand font at Binham Priory displays a picture of each of the seven sacraments around the basin, and is a fine example of a type of font common only in East Anglia*

immortalised the real people of the Middle Ages in stone.

Fonts are, with scarcely an exception, made of stone, but the covers are always of wood. Here East Anglia has no rival and, within the region, Suffolk is supreme, and in Suffolk, Ufford leads the field. The perfection of an East Anglian art in this village, north of Woodbridge, is most appropriate since it probably takes its name from Uffa, the founder of the dynasty of Wuffings in the Sandlings. Delicate pinnacles of woodwork, built up to an enormous height, sit on the bowl until it is needed for a christening. Most such covers are now counter-weighted and can be raised and lowered at the touch of a hand, or are telescopic. That in SS. Peter and Paul at Salle is operated from the ringing chamber by a crane and pulley over the balcony.

If Norfolk cannot rival the best of the Suffolk font covers (in spite of those like the one at Castle Acre), it has two font-canopies at St Peter Mancroft in Norwich, and Trunch near Mundesley. The canopy at St Peter Mancroft is in dark wood and appears very heavy, particularly if compared with the finer covers which have usually been painted in medieval colours, and maintained in some measure.

The parclose screen in the Spring Chapel at Lavenham is an exceptionally fine example of this kind of ornamental painted woodwork. St Edmund's church in Southwold has some very good examples of the kind of medieval woodwork that went into church furniture before the Reformation. The rood screen runs across the whole very wide building, nave and two aisles. Thirty-six painted figures can be detected in the dado. The medieval pulpit is mounted on a 'trumpet stem'. The stalls here are special: the misericords would be remarkable anywhere but East Anglia.

The figures or scenes that tell a story on misericords and bench-ends exist in profusion in East Anglia and record with amazing rustic vigour the people of the time: the well-dressed lady taking her dog for a walk, and the well-equipped thatcher (both in Ixworth Thorpe near Bury St Edmunds); ideas of piety, and the revelation of vices such as Pride at Blythburgh, with nightmares and spotted devils, and the 'skiapod' at Dennington, the monster whose one foot grew so large that he could lie down and shelter beneath it.

Material of this kind occurs probably as freely as anywhere (with or without post-Reformation woodwork such as Jacobean three-decker pulpits) throughout East Anglia. Unlike the later woodwork with its elegant panelling, bench ends and misericords, it forms an eloquent folk art. This sort of decoration is of course absent from the post-Renaissance churches and chapels with their restrained Classical designs. Very few Anglican churches belong to this period compared with those of the Middle Ages. St George's, Great Yarmouth, is an exception: it is a Queen Anne church by John Price who got his inspiration from Wren's work. The result is unexpected and eye-catching.

But the best of the later woodwork is to be found in some of the Nonconformist chapels, of which rather more were built than churches since most of the country needed to start from scratch when Toleration arrived. Probably the best is the Unitarian Meeting House at Ipswich, built by a carpenter using plaster applied over a timber frame. It has panelled box pews around three sides. Above there is a gallery with two elegant columns to support the ceiling. On the fourth side, there is a carved three-decker pulpit reached by curved stairs with turned balusters. It is a remarkable building.

Norwich has two very fine meeting houses in Colegate, north of the river, which almost touch each other. In both, the red brick of the period is particularly attractive, and in the Old Meeting House built in 1693 it has been very well exploited in shallow, generous pilasters with stone bases and well carved Corinthian capitals. Rubbed brick is used well for the window and door opening, and the cornice is elegantly dentellated. The windows are claimed as the earliest sash windows in Norwich, and the date seems right for this. As in Ipswich, the interior has box pews on three sides, with a gallery carrying more pews above, and the open side is again devoted to the pulpit. The good early organ is still *in situ*, and a possible use for the chapel – very secluded, it has drawn on a wide area for support for many years but is now more than the congregation can manage – is as a schools' music centre.

Hard by, but built fifty years later, is the Octagon Chapel which Thomas Ivory built for the Presbyterians but which became Unitarian in 1820. It is a simple brick octagon with an octagonal pyramid roof. Small dormers with round windows are in the roof, and the taller windows of the upper storey break the heaviness of the rather plain structure. The entrance is a well-moulded, pedimented portico on four slender Ionic columns. Inside, round Renaissance arches are carried on slim Corinthian columns, and one bay only is occupied by the pulpit, desk and organ.

The former Presbyterian chapel, now a Pentecostal church, in Churchgate Street, Bury St Edmunds, must rank as one of the finest buildings of its very good period. Built in 1711–12, again of attractive red brick, it is enhanced by rubbed brick decoration. Its brick pilasters are surmounted by a large segmented pediment above the entrance. Even the lead guttering and rain water disposal system adds elegant detail. Again, the interior has panelled box pews and galleries on three sides, and a pulpit opposed to the main door. The building is not merely saved but being used by the Pentecostal church.

Only a few of the finest of the Nonconfirmist chapels have been described here; there are enough to fill several volumes. The purpose and function was clear: Classical taste had evolved a very satisfactory use of red brick in domestic patterns so that provincial towns acquired self-confident public buildings sometimes of exceptional and lasting beauty, both for the emancipated Nonconformist congregations, and also for civic and cultural purposes. Churches were in many respects the civic buildings of the Middle Ages and several of the purpose-built civic buildings of the post-medieval period matched churches in their splendour (*see* page 76).

Both Nonconformist self-confidence and civic pride, often closely allied, enabled the best architectural tastes of the age to find permanent expression. And what a good age it was for architecture! The best was Classical, deriving its elements ultimately from the temples and other public buildings of an alien, ancient religion. So town halls are strangely at home as part of the contribution of religion to the landscape. The same service was performed in the next generation by motifs from medieval Christian churches when Gothic Revival architecture supplanted the infatuation with Classical styles.

THE GREAT CHURCHES: MONASTERIES AND CATHEDRALS

East Anglia boasts three splendid cathedrals and, until the Dissolution, it had many abbeys and priories, great and small. The English custom of serving cathedral churches

The east end of the Saxon cathedral or parish church at North Elmham finishes in a shallow apse. The main body of the nave was much altered to make a country house for Bishop Despenser in the fourteenth century

with Benedictine monks from attached monasteries was well illustrated in medieval East Anglia, but the region is uniquely endowed if the ruined church at North Elmham really is the *Saxon* cathedral. It was mentioned earlier that doubt has been cast on this and the suggestion is that, instead, it represents the first parish church, built when the cathedral was moved to Thetford in 1075. The excavators who started work in 1948 found remains of a wooden building underneath, possibly the real cathedral. South Elmham has its own old ruin of what appears to have been a minster church. Minsters predated most 'field' or parish churches and were religious centres which despatched clergy to preach to the surrounding churchless communities.

The North Elmham ruins have remarkable features, however. The plan is different from those of all other East Anglian churches. A long aisleless nave with a square western tower is usual enough. But the transept changes the plan into a Greek 'Tau' cross, a very early Christian symbol. The apse is only a shallow sector, not a semi-circle as was early Norman practice. The square cells with differently disposed doors, and situated in the angles between nave and transepts – labelled 'Tower' on the official plan – are remarkably like the Saxon porticus as it developed from a burial chamber

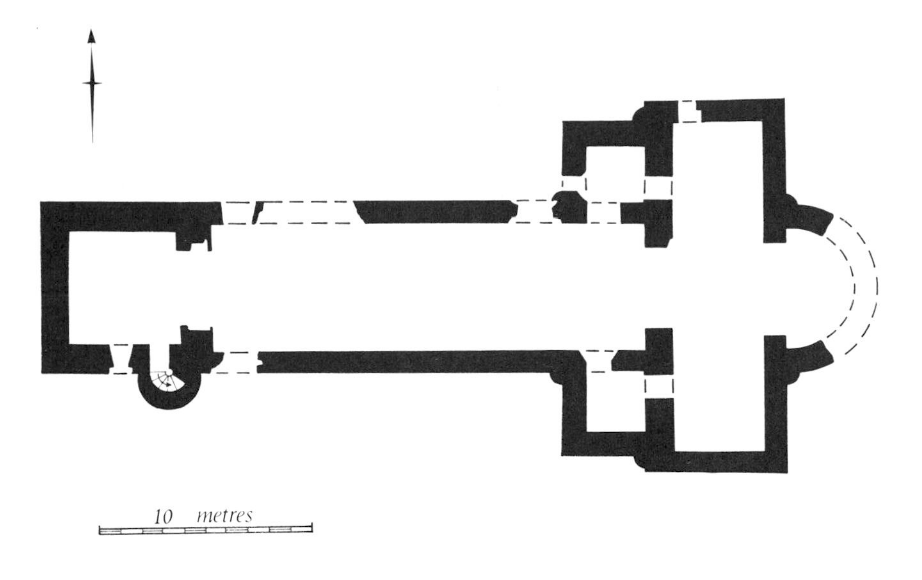

FIG. 1 NORTH ELMHAM
The remains of the Saxon Church, usually claimed as a cathedral

to a place with a function in the church service. This again would be Saxon and not Norman practice. The controversy continues, but the church remains are well worth inspection, and the issues are still there to be pondered.

On flint foundations at the east end, the rest of the early building is faced with carefully coursed blocks of lumpy red ironstone conglomerate. This is well preserved all along the south side, with quarter round 'fillets' carrying this finish around the angles. The result is very handsome. The western tower has the remains of a circular stair in a half-round tower. Opposite, another half-round tower was added in the fourteenth century, including a lodge for the porter of what had then become a fortified house. The difference in material and treatment between the eleventh- and the fourteenth-century work at this point enables one to make out the detailed changes such as blocked doors, garderobe or lavatory pits cut through old floors of the church, and later wall divisions.

After the see moved to Thetford, the Bishop retained the manor of North Elmham and the former cathedral probably served as a chapel and burial place. In 1370, Henry Despenser became Bishop, having gained promotion for his military rather than his spiritual services to the Pope. He was to gain notoriety for the vicious savagery with which he suppressed the Peasants' Revolt in Norfolk. Down the centre-line of the nave runs a row of foundations for the piers of the undercroft of the fortified house which he converted from the old church or cathedral. It was apparently used as a hunting-lodge, a place for carousals, even a house of ill-fame. Later generations avoided it.

Leaving aside Celtic monasteries and some Gaulish influence, most of the work of the conversion in East Anglia seems to have been done by Benedictine monks. In the centuries before the Norman Conquest they began to become powerful and privileged but many communities, possibly all those in East Anglia, were destroyed by Danish raiders, and re-founded in the tenth century.

Thorney is typical. The Abbot of what we now know as Peterborough Abbey founded a house for female hermits on an island a few miles from the abbey and remote in its fenland fastness. In 870, it was sacked and destroyed by Danes, and left desolate in an almost inpenetrable thicket of thorn bushes. From this, the island acquired its name. It was re-founded, or perhaps more realistically, founded, in 932 by Aethelwold (one of the great founders of monasteries under King Edgar and St Dunstan) as a retreat house for Lent. Some lucky acquisitions arrived in the form of attractive relics, and so it was set for six centuries of life.

The story of neighbouring Crowland in Lincolnshire is similar. The hermit Guthlac came to his 'island of pigs' in the deep fen in 699 and, we are told, heroically withstood the torments inflicted upon him by Welsh-speaking demons. This is usually taken to mean the hostile British, who had survived in the Fens where no Anglicised stranger could go. Dr Margaret Spufford points out that this might perhaps neatly describe a Welsh-speaking contingent in a Mercian war-band. Tradition says Ethelbald of Mercia, a Christian, founded a Benedictine abbey there. In the tenth century, it was ravaged by the Danes, but re-founded and endowed by Turketul, a courtier of King Edgar, in about 946. Turketul himself entered the religious life there and died as Abbot. Such a practice, virtually buying an insurance for the next world, seems quite in keeping with the feelings of the time.

Ramsey began similarly as a fenland cell with a wooden chapel for three monks, and was soon converted into a monastery with a big stone church, dedicated by St Dunstan and Oswald.

In these early monasteries, close personal interest from courtiers and royalty often created monastic houses which were, in wealth and power, to become of major national and international importance. The winds of reform were already blowing through the monasteries on the Continent by the time of the tenth-century re-foundations in England. Oswald who, with Ethelwold, was the great founder of monasteries, had been in a reformed house, and Cluny, which takes pride of place among the reforming houses, was greatly admired by William the Conqueror. William wished to buy a dozen monks to become abbots in his new foundations, and not surprisingly earned the rebuke from Abbot Hugh that his monks were not for sale! William de Warenne, one of William's more tactful courtiers, acquired four monks for his monasteries.

Cluniac houses were not common in England, but East Anglia could boast two fine examples: Thetford and Castle Acre priories. Much is visible of the excavated house at Thetford, but few sites in southern England can rival Castle Acre. The Cluniac houses were all priories, dependent on the mother-church at Cluny where the Abbot was based. They devoted themselves to worship with elaborate ceremonial, and paid full heed to the words of the psalmist, 'Worship the Lord in the beauty of holiness.' Something of this can be detected in the use of iron-stained stone in the remains of the piers in the aisles and crossing at Castle Acre. The surface was broken up by parallel bands or a chequer board of brown and white stone. The magnificent west façade

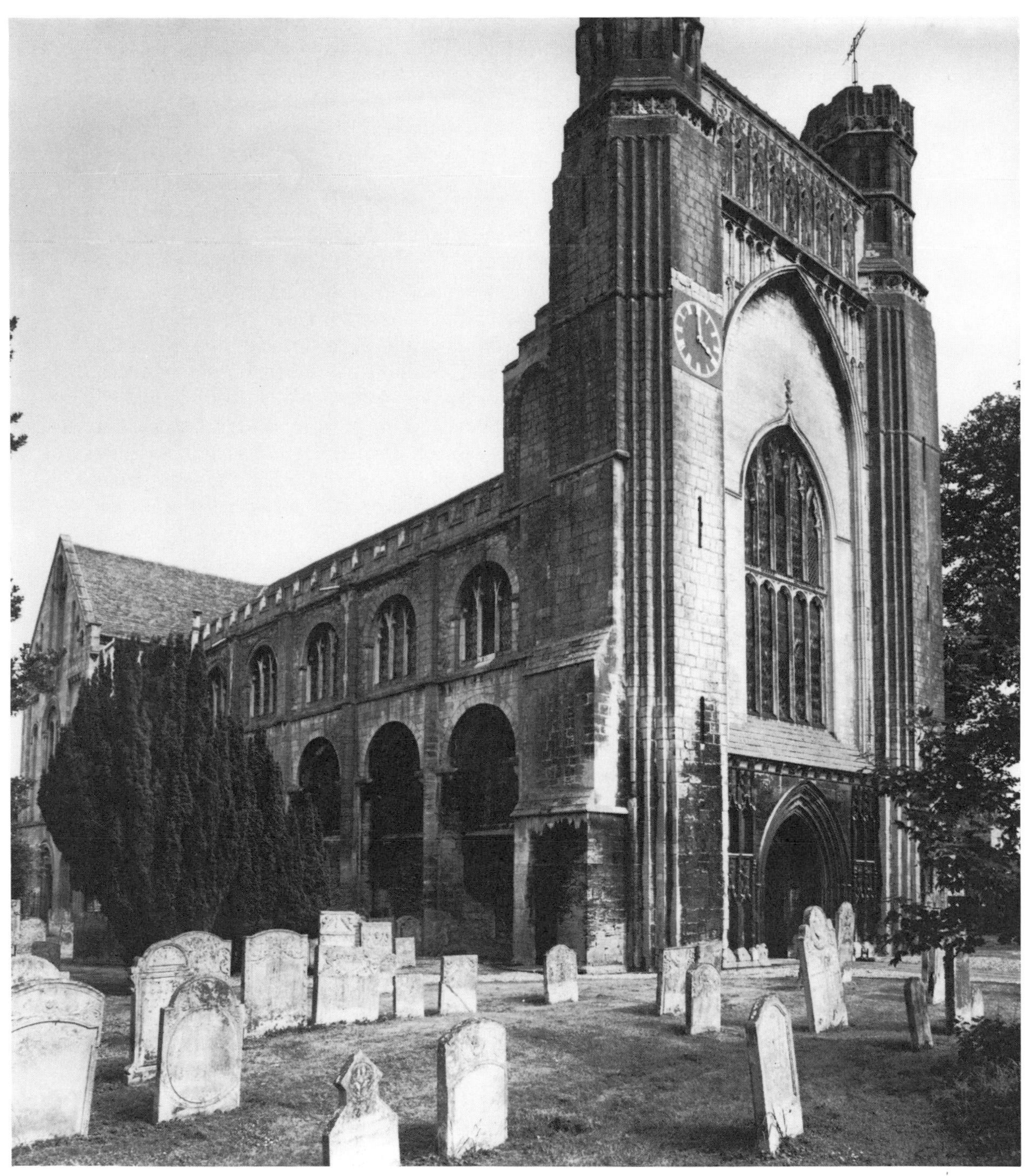

The former large Norman church of the Benedictines at Thorney was converted into a parish church at the Dissolution of the Monasteries by removing the aisles, the clerestory and the east end

of the church shows late Norman work at its best, varying and contrasting the patterns of decoration on symmetrical structures. Early Norman masonry was massive, as at St Albans in Hertfordshire, relying, often unsuccessfully, on its sheer weight to keep the structure standing. As time passed so the Norman builders somewhat increased the repertoire of decoration, and built lighter, more advanced structures, but they never quite learned how to unify structure and decoration.

But Castle Acre in any of its moods – and these shift with the slightest change of light – is one of the triumphs of English medieval architecture. At the top stage, just where they can be most effective, the first pointed windows appear, stretching Heavenwards: they are Early English in shape but made entirely of Norman shafts and mouldings, which were just about to become obsolete. Something of the same happy change of style at the top of the west façade can be seen in Ely Cathedral.

The amount of Norman work that survives in the big monastic churches of East Anglia is astonishing. The wealth and resources that arrived later when technically and aesthetically superior styles became available might easily have caused the removal of much more Norman work. Chances of survival for Norman work were best when the church had another purpose to complement its monastic uses. Where it had doubled as a parish church, something substantial was usually left to maintain this communal function, as at Wymondham, which is spectacular outside but an over-gilded lily within. Binham Priory in Norfolk also had its nave converted for parochial use and, looking east, beyond the superb façade of the thirteenth century, much of the older work survives. At Thorney, the Norman church was reduced in size at the Dissolution of the Monasteries; at Crowland, the nave was burned down after it became a mere parish church, leaving just the Norman north aisle to take over its role. At Ramsey, a magnificent late-Norman hospital was converted for parish use in the early seventeenth century, re-using much Gothic material from the rest of the buildings. Where a church did not acquire this parochial function, as at Bury St Edmunds, the crossing, the crypt of the Lady Chapel, and the decorated 'ashlar' or facing stone that still remain on some of the massive flint rubble cores of the piers, give us the faintest hints of what splendour we have lost.

Where Norman work survives in all its glory is in the monastic cathedrals: Peterborough, Ely and Norwich. In England, many cathedral churches had monasteries to serve them, and it is to this custom that we owe the preservation of the big Norman churches.

At Norwich, a great deal survives of the Norman east end. The Bishop's throne, re-used from an older church, faces westward across the High Altar towards the congregation. Sitting centrally, between assistant clergy seated on either side of him, with a semi-circular processional way around them, the Bishop presided according to an ancient rite. This pattern has been widely revived in this century by the Liturgical

---

OPPOSITE: *The nave of Peterborough Cathedral, and the central tower and nave at Norwich show finely developed Norman work. The west tower of Ely Cathedral shows Norman shafts and round arches giving way to pointed Early English arches as building fashion changed during the later stages of the work*

Movement. Perhaps the most famous feature of Norwich Cathedral is its cloisters, with the superb display of decorated stone tracery and the stone vaulting enlivened by carved scenes of Biblical narratives on the bosses. Viewed from outside, it becomes immediately obvious that the decoration hides a two-storey Norman structure.

MONASTIC TRADE AND TRANSPORT

Criticism by their 'Puritan' rivals, the Cistercians or white monks, did not prevent the old large Benedictine houses from flourishing in East Anglia nor, for that matter, did it prevent the Cistercians, after their phenomenal success in recruiting members, from becoming men of the world in their turn, raising sheep, buying and selling wool, and giving credit.

Endowments in the Middle Ages were normally in the form of land, or rents charged on it. As their estates grew by pious donations, the Benedictine 'Black Monks' of the twelfth century let most of them out for rent. When prices began to move upwards from the 1190s, more and more manors were taken back into the hands of their lords and exploited by direct cultivation, with the peasant bailiff and reeve on the spot, supervised in turn by an itinerant steward with a staff of scribes and auditors. Estate management was taken very seriously and nearby manors belonging to the same monastic house were organised on the basis of specialisation and division of labour, producing particular goods for particular markets. On Crowland's three adjacent manors in Cambridgeshire – Dry Drayton, Oakington and Cottenham – all the substantial demesne flocks of sheep were sheared at Oakington, while Cottenham bred cattle, providing necessary replacements for the plough-teams of all three manors. Cottenham also provided the depot for the Abbot's narrow barges which took the produce to Crowland itself before the fen water subsided each spring. Cottenham may also have been the malting centre.

Fenland waterways may often at first have been cleared or dug to enable building stone to be taken to the sites of churches. It is common in the Fenlands to find a stone-built church at the end of a lode (a ditch for barge traffic) on the first solid high ground above the sodden peat. Later they formed a network of commercial routes, for collecting and taking the produce of the outlying manors to the home barns at the abbey, and from the abbey to and from the great international fairs. Here European buyers came to purchase English wool and other agricultural products. At Crowland, there is a three-way bridge once spanning the junction of two tributaries of the River Nene, though now with only tarmac below it where once the barges were poled through. Around it are unexpectedly wide roads where the old medieval docks have been filled in.

Perhaps the greatest piece of medieval dockland is the Great Whyte and the Little Whyte at Ramsey. These enabled the boats to come up to the Abbey and the Fair Green in front of its gates. About a century ago, a brick culvert was built over the watercourse which ran down the middle of the Whyte, joining the two banks to form the present wide thoroughfare. The name 'Whyte' appears to be a deep fenland vernacular version of the name 'waits' which was used for quays where barges tied up. There is a pen and ink sketch of the Great Whyte before it was covered in, with the vessels lined along its side. All this area was supposed to have been burned down in the eighteenth century, but medieval crown-post roofs have been found in houses on both sides, so the fire must have been very selective.

If, when looking at such sites, a little imagination can recreate the busy waterside at fair time, we can attempt to do a little of the same on the tiny canal network which links so many villages in and on the edge of the Fens. Some of the best examples are Reach (*see* page 198) and nearby villages. The pattern there is of one main public wharf with other lesser ones running up as basins for small craft into the gardens behind the principal houses which back on to the main lode. It is difficult to imagine even the slenderest of vessels coping with such narrow ditches, but cope they did. At Cottenham, what appears to be a sunken path is really the 'cut' or canal leading to a place for barges to turn where the stone for building the church was unloaded. Legend has it that the Devil insisted on this site by moving the stones each night – such silly tales are common and the Devil provided excuses for hosts of lazy workers. Both Waterbeach and Landbeach seem to have had a similar arrangement with a subsidiary deep-water dock for unloading stone near their churches.

In an area, low-lying and flat, with watercourses both natural and artificial, Roman and later canal schemes all mixed together in one highly specialised transport system, it is possible to detect differences between Roman and medieval hydraulic engineering. The Roman Car Dyke (*see also* page 25), designed for moving supplies produced on the southern edge of the Fens to the Legionary fortresses, first at Lincoln, then at York, cut through the low watershed in Cottenham Fens right across the lines of the natural drainage. Water to fill it was provided near this point by a now vanished water-course. There must have been sluices or weirs of some sort to control the water level in this section which still has high banks. The Saxon and medieval ditches ran along the lines of natural drainage; they coped with the problem of traversing the gravel ridge between the Cam and the Ouse by using the section of the Roman canal at that point. It was still being so used in the seventeenth century. The old names for this canal, the Twilade or the Old Tillage, meaning a place where one barge is unloaded and the cargo transferred to another, may indicate the medieval use of the Car Dyke without the benefit of locks.

The rural trade that this network of Fenland waterways served was probably at its peak in the thirteenth century, when population locally was as high as it would be again until well into the nineteenth century. Village markets, with or without benefit of a formal charter to authorise them, sprang up, flourished and served local needs. Fairs serviced a wider clientele, and enabled the cash-hungry landlords to take advantage of rising prices, and dispose of the produce squeezed out of their demesnes. The Fenmen and the dwellers on the Fen Edge were able to profit from these institutions, small and large, from tiny fairs near village wharves to great international gatherings held on the waterways at Boston, St Ives and Stourbridge near Cambridge.

It is hard for us to picture these centres in their great days. A thirteenth-century villein on the Cheney Manor in Longstanton in Cambridgeshire had to carry his lord's corn to market either at Swavesey or Cambridge (Swavesey was a new town without a charter). Trade had to find a way to escape feudal bonds: kings and lords depended on it too much.

In the early fourteenth century some of the Landbeach villeins had to carry members

The prior's quarters at Castle Acre: the left-hand block in the photograph is the result of heavy expenditure in the decades before the Dissolution. The rest of the wing, including the grand entrance, became the heart of a farmhouse afterwards; other parts seem to have been relatively neglected in the last years of the priory

of the lord's family by water to Cambridge when required, and to carry food parcels to his sons at university there.

In such circumstances, the great estates, especially those of the old big Black Monk houses of the Fens like Ramsey, Thorney, Peterborough, Crowland and Ely, turned into what Professor Postan long ago described as 'federated grain factories, producing largely for cash'. The Black Monks came to dominate the economy of the medieval Fenland, and their manors and waterways shaped the landscape. The economic power and political power deriving from great possessions, made medieval abbots increasingly feudal lords and less men of God. This is a tale told by some of the ruins.

The splendour of the western façade of Castle Acre Priory has already been mentioned. Apart from the insertion of the great Perpendicular windows in the fifteenth century, the west end is unchanged Norman work, and enough of the ashlar facing of the piers remains to indicate little subsequent change. The east end of the quire saw the replacement of the Norman apse by a square-ended Lady Chapel of the fifteenth century. Most of the rest of the buildings show Norman style with little alteration but the west range, where the cellarer had his guest hall over the storage in the undercroft, and where the Prior had his private parlour and chapel, not only has some fine

Norman work, but also the latest and most comfortable additions before the Dissolution. The splendid gatehouse, in rubbed red brick, with its heated upstairs hall where the steward and the outside world of the tenantry met as men of business, is from early Tudor times. The west range appears to have been luxuriating as English monasticism drifted on towards disaster. Already vocations were too few to fill all the rooms. Dilapidation and decay caused abandonment of some of the buildings, and the few monks that remained spent more of their time in the west wing.

It was this wing, later converted in part into a farmhouse, that was the most attractive. The quality of the available rooms, the Prior's parlours and his chapel where a fireplace was inserted, show some of the best work amongst all of the house's building periods. The domestic standards provided for the Prior had raced ahead of their time: steps and stairs to a private lavatory with a built-in wash-basin – a secular and generous version of the piscina – far surpassed current lay standards of hygiene. A large fireplace was inserted into the old entrance porch, and the uncomfortably large Great Hall was abandoned. From all the choice buildings available, the elements of a splendid family farmhouse were selected. Even before the Dissolution, the centre of the house's life had been farming. Excavations near the bottom of the slope, west of the kitchens, are beginning to reveal specialised farm buildings on a suitably generous scale to match the contemporary religious buildings. The lay farmer who moved in after the Dissolution had a well-equipped start.

3
TOWNS, MARKETS AND PORTS

The religious houses of the Middle Ages, which preserved western culture through the trials of the barbarian invasions and the Dark Ages, have left an enormous legacy to the English landscape, both in countryside and town. As well as romantic ruins in lovely sites, much of the forest that had grown in the Dark Ages was cleared and many of England's fields were created and tended at the direction of monastic landlords. Their pioneers went into the wilderness and desert, and in time the desert flowered like a rose.

Less well known is the contribution which the religious houses made to our towns. When the monks had saved Christian culture by withdrawing behind their walls in remote places, the friars moved into the towns among the poor and the lost, converting the heathen at home and reaching out to those beyond the borders of Christendom. The friars, the begging or 'mendicant' orders, who started by going as poor to the poor, had to take what sites they could. For example, Norwich Blackfriars expanded into the town as it grew from across the river, and had a ferry of its own to link the two parts of its house.

On the whole, the friars' sites are unusual, adapted to fit into the odd-shaped pieces of land that were donated in built-up areas, or developed for special purposes like establishments of higher education in Oxford and Cambridge which needed lecture halls and large libraries. At first the friars took ordinary small houses in poorer areas, using the local parish churches for services. As they became popular, increased in membership and became recipients of pious endowments, they were able to obtain better sites and built large 'aisled halls' for preaching churches.

Their predecessors, the monasteries, became their rivals, however, and did not leave the towns alone. As well as enjoying their incomes from agricultural interests, the great monasteries played a leading role in the urban real estate speculation of the thirteenth century. The best example of this in the region is Bury St Edmunds.

BURY ST EDMUNDS

When St Edmund's bones were brought to Bury in 908 and a monastery founded at his shrine, the re-planning of the modest market-village began. The monastic precinct was laid out on the west bank of the River Lark with fishponds to the south and a vineyard on the eastern bank. The old main road which had continued between Northgate Street and Southgate Street was diverted and the new town developed on

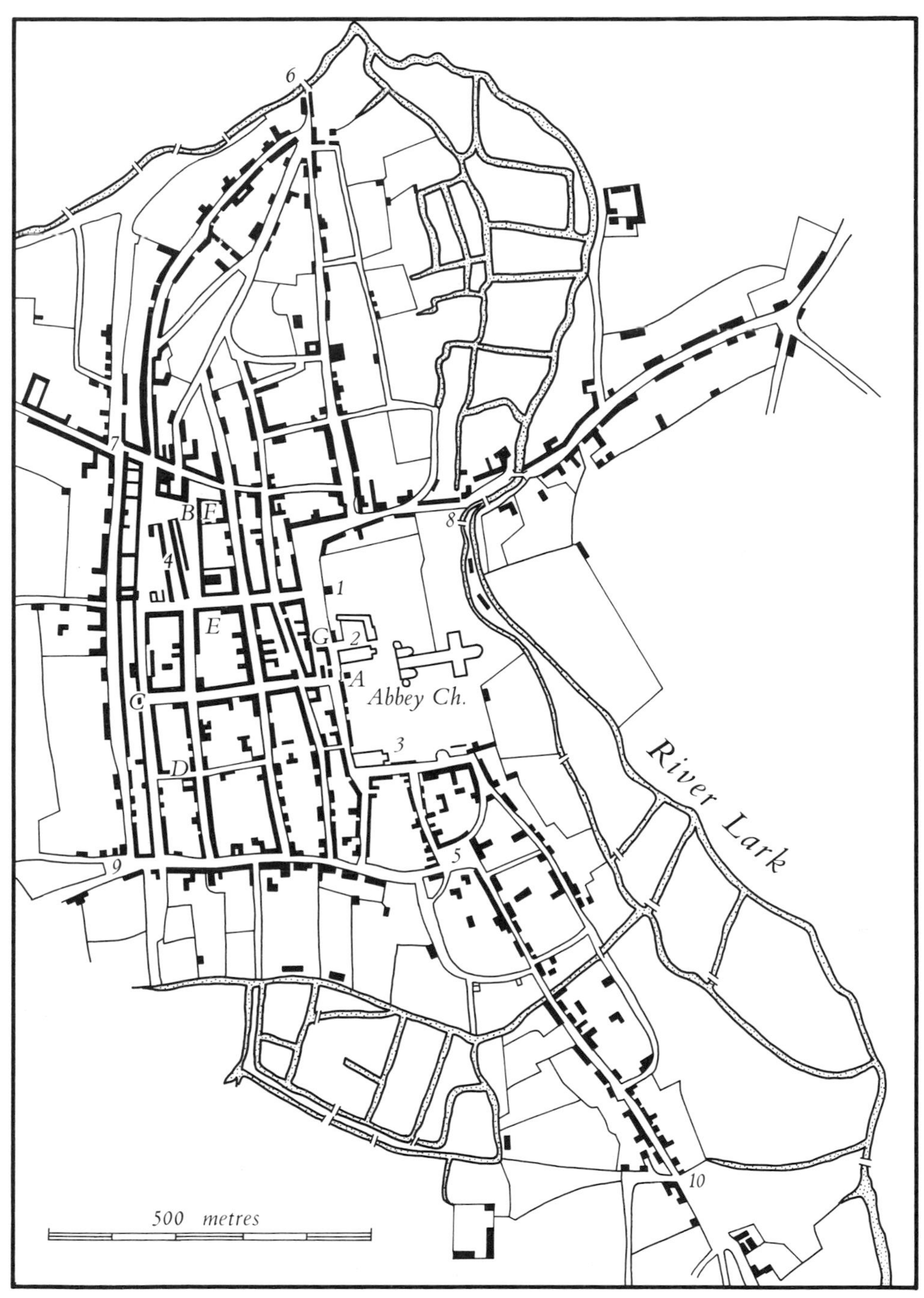

FIG. 2 BURY ST EDMUNDS

A St James' 12th-century steeple gateway leading to west front of Abbey Church **B** Moyse's Hall, 12th-century **C & D** Remaining parts of Norman houses **E & F** Possibly Norman remains **G** Angel Hotel, 13th-century **1** Great Gate **2** St James' Church **3** St Mary's Church **4** The Great Market **5** St Mary's Square (the Old Market) **6** North Gate **7** Risby Gate **8** East Gate **9** West Gate **10** South Gate (AFTER T. WARREN'S MAP OF 1747)

a grid-iron formed by four furlongs taken out of the old west open fields. Between the new town and the precinct is a long narrow triangle of open land, now a car park, but not one in the tenth century when, according to Professors Beresford and St Joseph, it was the late-Saxon market, planned along with the new Abbey grounds. There had already been an earlier market-place down by the old parish church. Norman Scarfe reports the clearing of this long triangular space on Angel Hill at a later date for a fair ground. The Normans planned a new, much larger market which (as in Norwich) is still mainly open today. Inside this, the Buttermarket, which fails to keep the main alignment, and the blocks of buildings above it, clearly represent considerable encroachment on the open trading area, as often occurred when temporary market stalls became permanent buildings.

On the edge of the market is Moyse's Hall, a stone 'first-floor hall' from the twelfth century. Miss Lobel found documentary sources concerning the building for letting of such halls at the side of the market in that period. Such houses, alien imports in style from the stone country of the northern and western counties were, because of their fire-resistance and potential strength against a mob, ideal for medieval bankers. Because of the religious taboos against usury, Jews could only be bankers at that time. The association of such houses with Jewish bankers is quite firm in Norwich and Cambridge. Wensum House in Norwich was built by Jurnet the Jew whose son became the richest man in England. (Lincoln and Stamford have similar Jew's Houses, but they are in stone country where this masonry building style more properly belongs.)

Bury St Edmunds is particularly well served by Domesday Book of 1086, fittingly so as, by contrast with most other towns, it was developing fast when most of the others, such as Norwich, record partial devastation. Domesday reported:

> Here are 30 priests, deacons and clerks together, 28 nuns and poor people who daily pray for the king and for all Christian people; 75 bakers, ale-brewers, tailors, washerwomen, shoemakers, robe-makers, cooks, porters and agents . . . Besides whom are 13 reeves over the land of the abbey who have a house in the town, and under them 5 bordars. Now 34 knights, French and English, with 22 bordars under them. Now altogether there are 342 houses on the demesne of the land of the abbey which was all under the plough in the time of King Edward.

At the time of the Domesday survey, Bury was fast developing into a large medieval town. Suppliers of provisions gave their occupational names to many of the streets around the market, leaving the medieval flavour which is so strong even today.

Bury was one of many medieval towns where a big religious corporation – sitting on the edge of the town it owned, eager to exploit all the possibilities of increasing its income, and reluctant to grant a charter of freedom to its villein townsmen or the privileges of self-government to its free burgesses – lived in a state of intermittent war with its citizens. (To judge by the Cambridge example, a university might be a peculiarly

---

OPPOSITE: *The ruins of the nave at Bury St Edmunds afford an opportunity to inspect the Norman method of building – rubble set in mortar as cores, and finished with a surface of dressed limestone. The Normans relied greatly on the sheer weight of the structure to keep it stable*

ABOVE LEFT: *Moyse's Hall on the edge of the market at Bury St Edmunds was well placed for a medieval bank. The original entrance was at first-floor level, giving some protection from looting mobs*

ABOVE RIGHT: *This medieval undercroft in Wensum House is typical of a very large number found in Norwich where they seem to be more common than anywhere else. This house also has a Norman undercroft beneath the original hall of Jurnet the Jew*

LEFT: *The magnificent main gate into the Abbey at Bury St Edmunds was built by the townsfolk as a replacement for the gatehouse which they had burned down in 1327. It shows very early traces of the Perpendicular style in a building substantially of the previous Decorated pattern*

noxious privileged religious corporation in the eyes of the town. Quarrelling between Town and Gown was endemic.)

The finest surviving piece of architecture from the monastery at Bury St Edmunds is the Great Gate in the western precinct wall. This building shows how splendid the Decorated style became in its full mature glory. We owe it to the rioting townsfolk of 1327 who burned down the old one, and had to rebuild at a time when mature Decorated style was just showing touches of the delicate early Perpendicular style. Its completion in 1353 was the perfect moment to produce the best of both.

Bury St Edmunds has one of the outstanding civic buildings of all times. The Town Hall (called Market Cross) was built by Robert Adam between 1774 and 1780. A superb Classical piece, it was intended as a market hall and little theatre. The trophy panels in the rusticated ground floor represent comedy and tragedy; round-headed niches above carry urns. A most elegant Venetian window occupies the south end of the upper storey, and the architect's ingenuity was called into play to get a flue almost invisibly past this to a stack hidden behind a pediment. There it stands on the edge of the market out of place in its exquisiteness, diagonally across from the Norman banker's house, Moyse's Hall.

Bury is one of the few towns that can rival the Assembly Rooms in Norwich. In the Atheneum, a modified Queen Anne building at the south end of Angel Hill, is a ballroom attributed to Robert Adam, and its quality is almost as good as a signature. At one end, a delicately curved divided stair sweeps up to a small balcony over the main entrance. On the side away from the street is a low platform in a recess for the orchestra masked by a pair of columns. Details such as the chandeliers, fine plasterwork with typical Adam motifs, and a gilded mirror in the entrance portico enhance the breathtaking effect.

IPSWICH AND THE GROWTH OF TOWNS

When Roman rule left Britain, the imperial cities and towns seem virtually all to have disappeared as fully functioning urban centres. When we get an overall view again via the Domesday Book, there is once more a fair sprinkling of towns over the country. Very little is known about what happened in the intervening centuries and how most towns were founded or grew; however, Ipswich possibly has many relevant hints for us.

In the time of the Wuffings dynasty, we can perceive elements of what would later become a town as settlements scattered over an area but functioning together, something that might perhaps be described as a 'non-nuclear proto-town'. There was the hall at Rendlesham, a royal residence which proved easier to discover in field names than by archaeological traces. There was something of an industrial settlement to judge from the kilns under the later town site; they were producing the new pottery, Middle Saxon Ipswich Ware; and there was also an active port. Then, what we all know best, a few miles downstream was a royal necropolis, Sutton Hoo. On the banks of Deben river is Kingston, which was a royal manor and quite literally the king's 'tun', or farm, before that word came to mean 'town'.

Late Saxon Ipswich can be traced in outline from street- and place-names. There seems to be no doubt that the settlement was recognisably a town before Domesday,

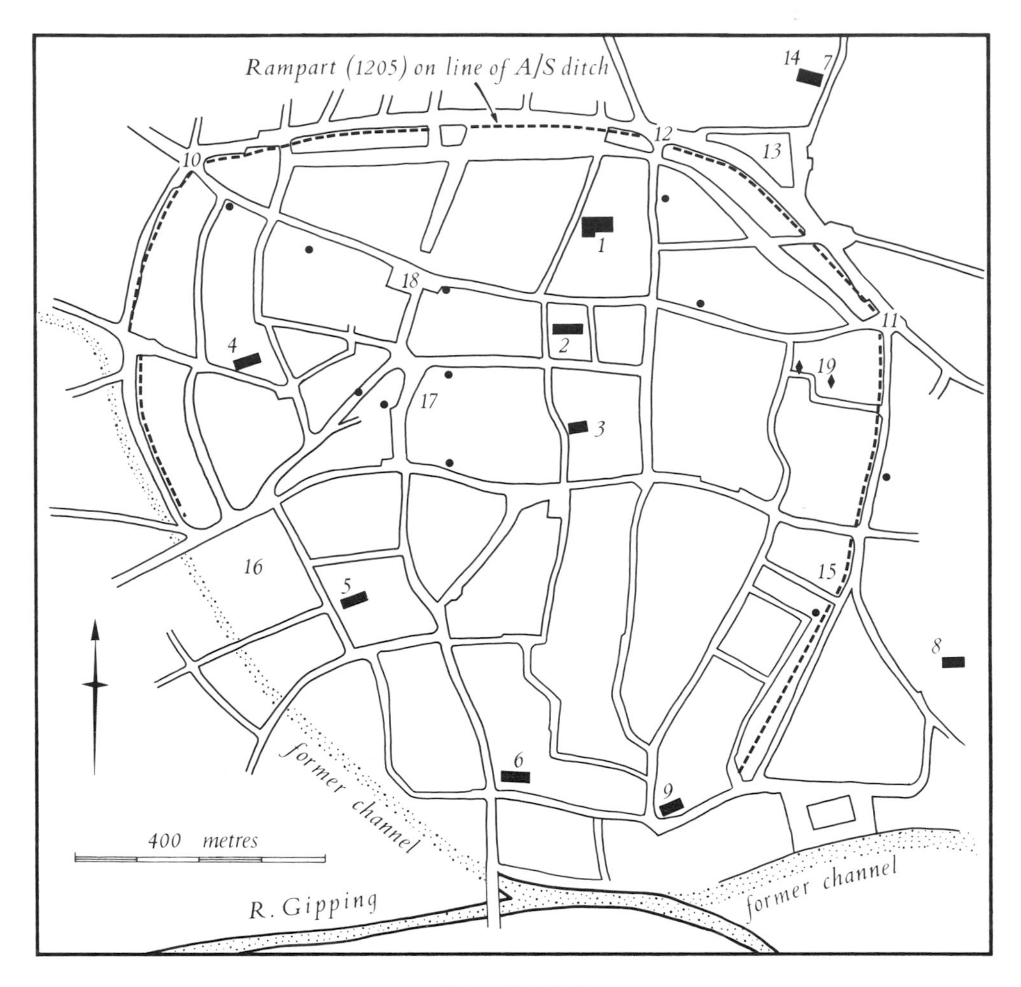

FIG. 3 IPSWICH

● Finds of Ipswich Ware 'Middle Saxon' potters (625–850)

1 St Mary Tower **2** St Lawrence **3** St Stephen **4** St Mary Elms **5** St Nicholas **6** St Peter **7** St Margaret **8** St Clement **9** St Mary Quay **10** Westgate **11** Eastgate **12** Northgate **13** Thingstead **14** Priory of Holy Trinity **15** Blackfriars **16** Greyfriars **17** Whitefriars **18** St Mildred's Chapel (site) **19** Cox Lane, Ipswich Ware kiln sites

A recent aerial photograph shows that the early Saxon people's choice of a river estuary deep in southern East Anglia for a commercial settlement still has much to recommend it (© Cambridge University Collection)

although it may not have been so large as it seems at first sight: with a recorded land-holding population of 538 in 1066, which must represent a total population of from two to two-and-a-half thousands, we cannot be sure how many of these people, if any, were living outside the built-up nucleus. By 1086, the catastrophe of the Conquest had reduced these numbers to much less than half.

By 1200, when Ipswich received its charter, it was still well-integrated with the surrounding countryside. Locally, it was the market centre of four 'hundreds' or divisions, and had numerous burgesses who were resident outside the borough. By the early fourteenth century, it seems to have fallen into the hands of a rich oligarchy of merchants. There were a few industrial craftsmen, and wool woven in the countryside came into the town for finishing, but Ipswich was essentially a port and commercial centre. Local inhabitants of all classes invested in shares of boats and ships. At that time most of Ipswich's sea-borne trade was coastal, trade with the Continent being still mainly in the hands of the Flemish and Dutch. Already in the reign of Edward I, both Ipswich and Dunwich had their constitutions temporarily suspended as a result of disorder arising from the struggles between the poor craftsmen and the rich oligarchy. These struggles, renewed, were to play a major part in the violence associated with the Peasants' Revolt in the Suffolk towns. Already they were encouraging the weaving of broadcloth to migrate from the corporate towns, where gild regulations were becoming increasingly difficult to circumvent, to the rural centres which became the special glory of medieval Suffolk.

EAST COAST PORTS

The violence was not just restricted to the towns, however; ships from Great Yarmouth and the Cinque Ports fought at sea when they met, and piracy of all kinds was rife. As George Unwin wrote: 'Gorleston and Yarmouth are in a constant state of civil war. A fleet of privateers from Harwich lays siege to Ipswich for ten weeks, sinking, burning and pillaging. Walberswick, aided by a convulsion of nature captures the river and port of Dunwich, putting to the sword its protesting customs officers.' He goes on to cite the Inquest Rolls of Ipswich for 1330–40. The decade produced seventeen cases of murder and manslaughter. Accusations against the monks of Bury included, 'rape, adultery, highway robbery, perjury, simony and usury'. Torrid times indeed.

The history of the East Anglian ports has been bedevilled by coastal erosion and silting, as described in more detail in the final chapter. On the north coast of Norfolk, the movement of eroded material is mainly from east to west, resulting in spit formation such as Blakeney Point. Many tiny ports have silted up but some can still be traced in the edge of the salt marshes by the remains of landing stages. On the east coast, the movement of eroded material is mainly north to south and spit formation, across the mouths of the rivers Blyth, Dunwich and Minsmere, resulted in the rivers turning right before reaching the sea. Further north, something similar happened where the rivers Bure, Yare and Waveney join and flow south for three miles through Great Yarmouth to the sea at Gorleston. As with draining marshes, the problems of a silting channel in the late sixteenth

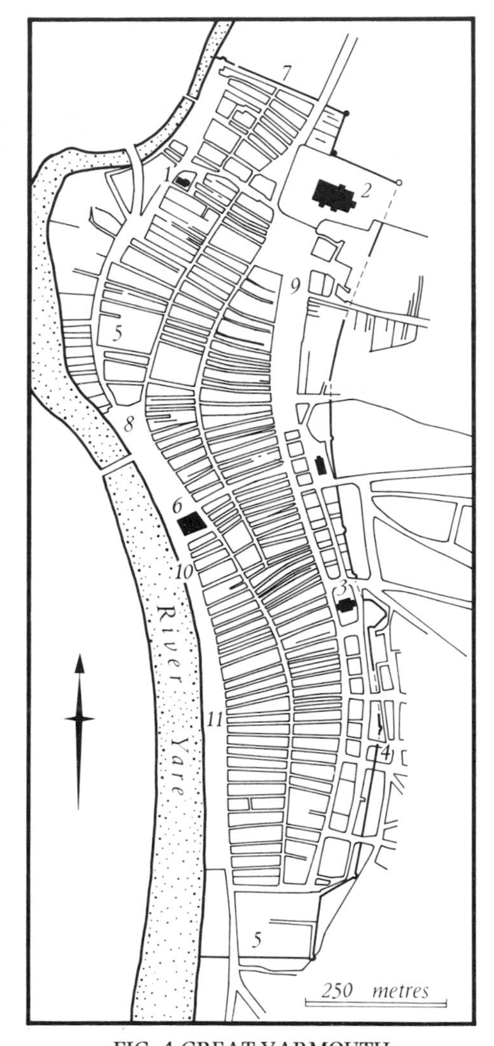

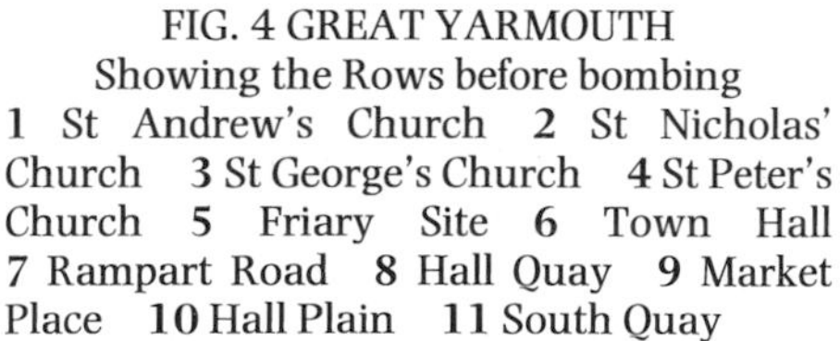
FIG. 4 GREAT YARMOUTH
Showing the Rows before bombing
1 St Andrew's Church **2** St Nicholas' Church **3** St George's Church **4** St Peter's Church **5** Friary Site **6** Town Hall **7** Rampart Road **8** Hall Quay **9** Market Place **10** Hall Plain **11** South Quay

century required the help of an engineer from Holland. Joost Jansen came to fill the need.

Before the Norman Conquest, Great Yarmouth was built on the offshore spit. Five parallel streets ran roughly north and south, cut by 156 alleys running east and west, forming The Rows; some of the alleyways were extremely narrow. A.P. Baggs, who had seen similar settlement patterns in Malayan fishing villages, explains it as a natural result of the river shifting westwards in stages as it silted, creating new streets and building lines, but the alleys enabled access to the sandy beaches on the eastern side of the spit where net-drying could take place and boats could be beached.

It was as late as 1347 that the silting joined the island on which Yarmouth was built to the mainland. The Cockle Water, which had taken river-water to the sea through the present North Denes, was sealed up in a storm. On this coast, tempest was not the only danger and 1285 saw the beginning of a stone town wall, a curtain wall with a sentry walk, and eighteen large towers. Some parts are still intact, in spite of the bombing in World War II which reduced The Rows to three.

All the ports on this coast took up herring fishing and flourished but Great Yarmouth, with its hinterland active in the manufacture of worsted, also became involved in the export of its cloth. It began to branch out as a resort in the eighteenth century and it has maintained and increased its accommodation as a resort, particularly on the eastern side which has always been open to the sea, while fishing has declined as over-fishing impoverished the herring's old feeding grounds.

Lowestoft followed Great Yarmouth, and its peak of importance was probably in the fourteenth century. It was a fishing town; less dependent than Yarmouth on the herring, its white fish industry lasted longer. Old Lowestoft had its own characteristic pattern, different but with functional similarity to The Rows of Yarmouth. Lowestoft High Street ran along the cliff edge, and was connected with the Denes (the beaches) and sea by the Scores (steep passages). What was probably the pioneer of lighthouses in post-Roman England, the Lower Light, was recorded in 1609.

Great Yarmouth and Lowestoft had a medieval rival in Dunwich, the leading port on the Suffolk coast in the thirteenth century. Probably the seat of a bishop for some years in the Saxon period, at its peak, it had eight or nine parish churches, two friaries, a preceptory of the Templars, and Maison Dieu, a hospital. All are gone now, lost beneath the sea; gone too, are the gates on its main entrances. Once its markets were held every day of the week and in the reign of King John it acquired a borough charter.

By 1300, St Leonard's church appears to have gone, and thereafter loss by erosion seems to have been almost continuous – and it is not yet finished. In 1968–9, the remains of the Middle Gate went down the cliff. In a clearing at the top of the cliff edge, set in close cropped springy turf, is a boy's gravestone dated 1826. This is the last of the graveyard that is steadily crumbling away, as the sea continues its work of undermining the cliff. As well as suffering from erosion it was also involved with the problems of shifting shingle and consequent struggles with other east coast ports.

Of the ports and towns that survive, it is possible to follow the shifting pre-eminence from archaeological studies of pottery. Thetford Ware, made on a fast wheel, replaced Ipswich Ware, made on a slow wheel, and paralleling the fashions in pottery, the leadership of East Anglia passed from Ipswich and the Sandlings to Thetford. Excavation of the site of part of the ancient city of Thetford began after the Second World

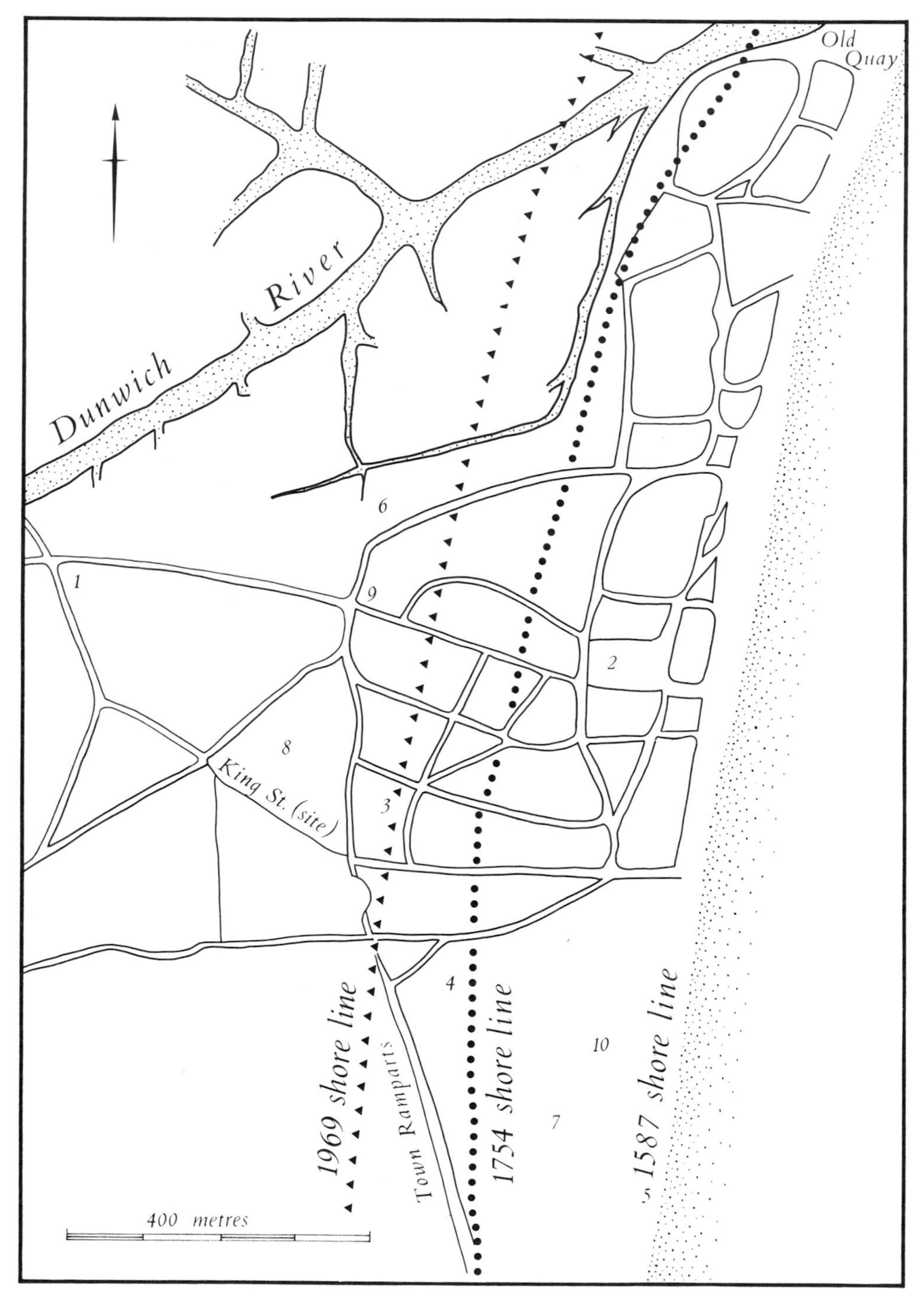

FIG. 5 DUNWICH

1 St James' Church **2** St Peter's Church (site) **3** All Saints' Church (site) **4** Templars' Church (site) **5** St Nicholas's Church (site) **6** Maison Dieu Hospital (site) **7** Blackfriars (site) **8** Greyfriars Monastery **9** Bridge Gates (site) **10** Windmill (site)

On the other hand, Dunwich proved to be a most unfortunate choice in the long run as it crumbled away into the sea

---

War. The first impression was that the most important town in East Anglia was a slum, a shanty-town of hovels. The second group of excavations changed all this, as they uncovered the foundations of substantial stone-built houses, well planned and laid out in streets. At that time, very little excavation of Saxon towns had taken place in England so there was a complete revision of archaeological expectations of such sites, and a good deal of sophistication is looked for nowadays beyond what is accepted as industrial slum and workshop areas.

From 1075–1091, the cathedral of East Anglia was at Thetford. There were four monasteries and, appropriately in a cathedral town, a friary and several hospitals; it was a mint town, and had eleven parish churches. By Domesday, it was overtaken by Norwich which had scarcely unified its various components at the time of the Conquest. The building of Norwich Cathedral and the development of Norwich as the Norman administrative centre meant that Thetford was left behind as a country town of some charm and interest, rather than as a centre of power.

THE GROWTH OF NORWICH

For what was soon to become one of the biggest towns in England, Norwich was surprisingly unformed in late Saxon times; it was still in the process of formation from the growing together of a number of small settlements on gravel patches. A defensible market and administrative centre of the name Northwic can be presumed from the coins of Aethelstan dating between 920 and 940 AD. Only burhs (fortified towns set up by Alfred and his sons and also by their Danish enemies) could have mints. Norwich may have been turned into a burh by the Danes who lost control about 920, having ruled it for forty years, or by Edward the Elder who regained it from them.

Archaeological evidence suggests that there was an early Saxon settlement north of the river in Coslany, across a marshy area; Westwic, at the western edge of the later walled city, seems also to have been one of the very early settlements. What later became the Cathedral Close and Tombland was the settlement called Northwic, and at first it probably had a bank and ditch protecting it. Rather more of a ditch discovered on the far side of the river to the north of this site indicates a defended suburb, probably used for trading. Here excavations have revealed berths for the ships, which were run up on brushwood over the bank of sand. In Pre-Conquest days, Tombland was already the market for an international port. By the end of the tenth century, industry was established. Pottery manufacture had begun at Pottergate and spread westwards to advance the joining-up process. Iron-smelting and -working were active north of the river. By the Conquest, Northwic and Westwic had met.

At the time of Domesday, Norwich was already large by the standards of the time. Earl Ralph had built a new French borough and the new provision market. As in so many other towns, evidence of empty houses, ruined houses and empty sites caused by fire, suggest that the drunken soldiery of the army of occupation had done their worst, and Norwich would have suffered further in the Earl's revolt in 1075. Beccles seems to have been the most popular place to which to flee. One sentence in the survey is unusually eloquent among the jargon of the clerks: 'Those fleeing and the others remaining are altogether ruined partly owing to the forfeitures of Earl Ralph, partly owing to a fire, partly owing to the king's geld [a tax], partly through Waleran.' Waleran had 'farmed' the taxes: this is to say he paid a lump sum to the king and extorted what he could, keeping the difference, just like the Biblical publicans.

As elsewhere, rents and dues were lost from a number of houses (nearly 100) cleared to make way for the Norman royal castle. By Domesday, population seems to have been reduced. The English 'burgesses' suffered particularly, their numbers falling from 1,320 in 1066 to 665 in 1086. Over the same period, it is estimated that total population of the city went down slightly from about 5,500 to 5,000. The market and castle were well-established, however, and in about 1094 the see was moved to Norwich. Two years later, Bishop Herbert de Losinga began to build the cathedral.

The Normans were consolidating civil and church administration. The Norman bishop was very much a feudal lord rather than the man of God of earlier times who walked out from his country church like North Elmham, knocking on the doors of

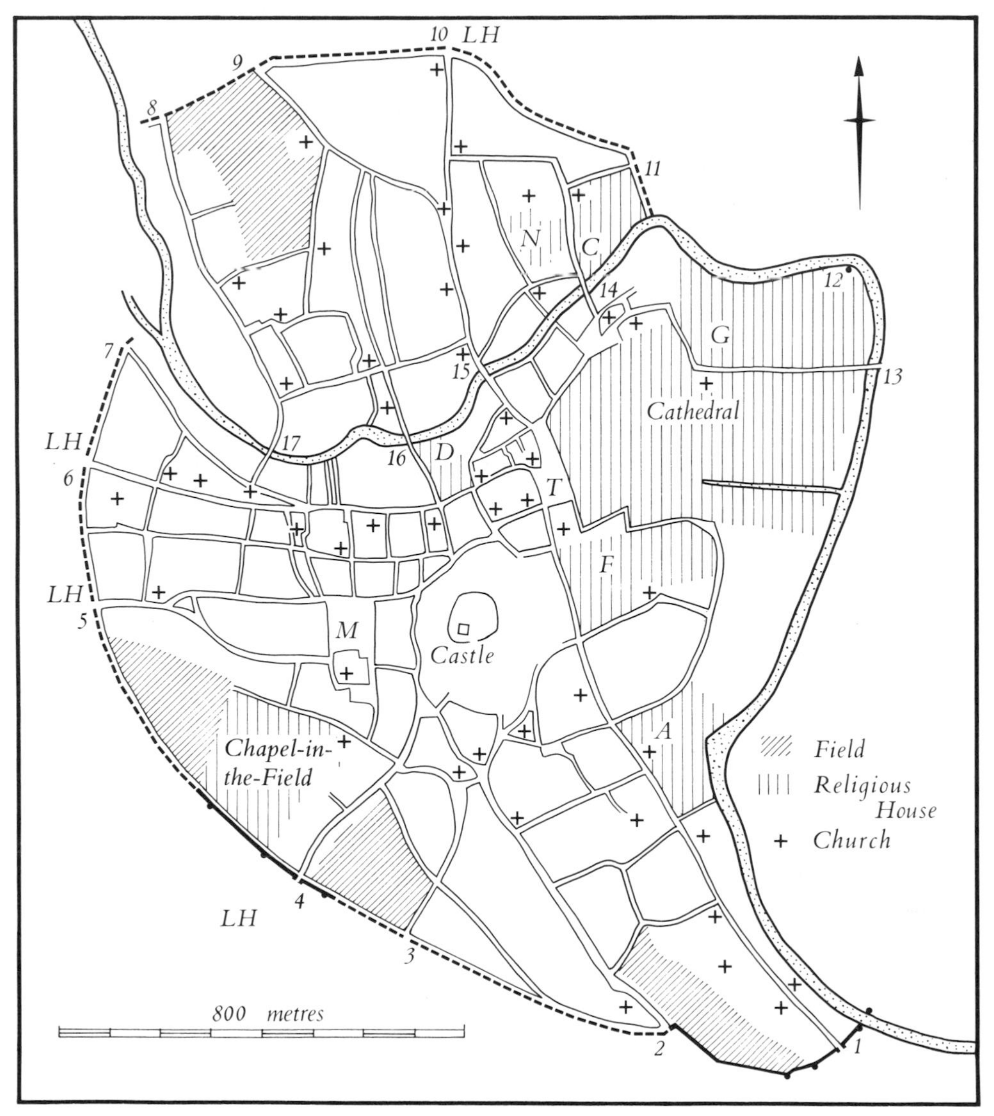

FIG. 6 NORWICH

A Austin Friars **C** Carmelite Friars **D** Dominican Friars **F** Franciscan Friars **G** Great Hospital **M** Provision Market **N** Norman's Hospital **T** Tombland **1** King Street Gate **2** Ber Street Gate **3** Brazen doors **4** St Stephen's Gate **5** St Giles' Gate **6** St Benedict's Gate **7** Heigham Gate **8** St Martin's Gate **9** St Augustine's Gate **10** Magdalen Gate **11** Pockthorpe Gate **12** Cow Tower **13** Bishop Bridge Gate **14** Whitefriars Bridge **15** Fye Bridge **16** Blackfriars Bridge **17** St Michael's Bridge **LH** Leper Hospital

his priests, giving them fatherly advice, but the colossal amount of building must have injected some economic opportunities into the borough. Before his revolt, Earl Ralph had built a church, probably the ancestor of St Peter Mancroft, and the amount of devastated housing must have meant another building boom as population increased. Long-distance trade still centred on the old Saxon market-place in Tombland, while the local trade was accommodated in the new provision market.

By 1144, to oil the wheels of commerce, a banking community was established in Norwich: the Jews. Taking of interest was forbidden to Christians (except for such bankers as the Pope himself needed), yet feudal lords and governments could not survive without borrowing, and practically everything else but money-lending was forbidden to the Jews. Unlike most European cities, there were no restrictions in Norwich as to where the Jews lived: there was no ghetto. In practice, most lived quite near the market.

In the Norwich which we glimpse through Domesday book, there is much mention of 'land' (i.e. arable land) and meadow. In the south-west, the ploughed open fields extended across the line of the future city wall and over a substantial part of the future city. Agriculture must have provided not only the vital food but also much of the employment in the town.

The city was governed as a separate county, but within its circuit the Castle Fee and the cathedral precincts were exempt from the town's jurisdiction. The Priory had control of the Tombland market, and the church of St Michael and Earl Ralph's palace were cleared to enlarge it. With up to sixty Norman monks in the Priory, the Norman garrison at the castle, and the polyglot collection of foreigners in the new borough down by the market, there was constant possibility of Anglo-Norman hostility and friction unless the two main elements combined to attack their bankers, the Jews. A notorious example of an occasion when they succeeded in such an attack was in 1144 when fervid imagination accused the Jews of the ritual murder of a boy, afterwards canonized as St William. It is surprising what an overdraft will do.

Probably even more than the hostility to the Jews was the hostility towards the Normans at the Priory. In 1272 the townsmen attacked the Priory, and had to rebuild the Ethelbert Gate as their penance. They seem to have anticipated the good citizens of Bury St Edmunds in the same course by about fifty years, although with less cause. For in 1194 the citizens of Norwich had been able to buy a borough charter from the ever impecunious Richard I and this had given them a considerable measure of self-government. They were to have their own reeve and a 'fee farm' (a fixed cash payment instead of uncertain petty dues and charges). This really meant the central government and feudal overlords could not interfere. The violence in Bury aimed at achieving what Norwich had already been granted.

In spite of the odd bout of mayhem when the medieval equivalent of football crowds broke loose, Norwich prospered as Normans became English. It is possible to spot some of the main subsidiary markets in place-names. In Rampant Horse Street was a horse fair, and St John Maddermarket speaks for itself in the key town of the most densely populated and heavily industrialised part of the country: its staple industry, cloth manufacture, guaranteed a market for dyestuffs such as madder, a plant whose root produced a red dye. By the Subsidy of 1334 (the national tax based on property), Norwich was the sixth richest town in the land, and climbing. Already, in the 1250s, the construction of a rampart around the city had begun and in 1297 a masonry wall was started. It was completed before the first great visitation of the plague, and by the time Norwich had recovered sufficiently and had expanded, English towns needed no wall.

In the Domesday survey, 480 bordars (low caste peasants) too poor to pay rent were recorded, a reminder that the poor are always with us, especially in medieval towns. One of the most typical kinds of foundation, although most untypical in its powers of survival, is the Great Hospital in Norwich. This was first set up as a house for poor chaplains by Bishop Walter de Suffield in 1279. Originally it was intended to house up to thirty aged or infirm clerks without a living; in addition, thirteen poor people were to have one meal a day and were allowed to warm themselves at the fire in winter. There were special benevolences for the casual visitor, and for the poor of Norwich generally on the Bishop's anniversary. But in addition there was one very special good work: seven poor scholars, nominated by the master of the Grammar School, were to be given a daily dinner. The hospital was important enough for the Bishop's own brother to become the first Master.

Some of the original building survives, but externally it is at first sight very strange to see a chimney coming out of the ridge at the east end of the church and clearly going up inside, behind the east window. The amazing thing is that in spite of the unwelcome attentions of Henry VIII and Hitler, the hospital is still doing its intended work today. The church is divided into three: the centre part is still the parish church; the east end was given a floor halfway up to make two wards for women, and the west end was nominally for the men but they are now housed elsewhere.

The key year in the hospital's history seems to have been 1383 when Richard II and his queen visited Norwich and became interested in the re-building of the quire. The roof has 252 gilded panels with a black imperial double-headed eagle on each, traditionally in honour of the queen, Anne of Bohemia. Medieval social services may have been motivated by the sentiment, 'It is more blessed to give than to receive', their purpose being more to acquire merit for the benefactor than the transient good they did to the poor. The fate of one's soul was taken much more seriously.

By the time the Black Death arrived in 1349, there were already four friaries in Norwich: Blackfriars, astride the river in the dock area, symbolises their mission to the poor and outcast, deprived folk whom the church so far had not reached.

Even in boom times, as in most of the thirteenth century, the city had its share of troubles. At Bury St Edmunds, in the ruins of the old Abbey, there is a plaque commemorating the Assembly of the Barons there to issue the Articles, a fore-runner of Magna Carta, before they went on to Runnymede. It does not commemorate the fact that the French king's son, Louis, was also fishing in these troubled waters or that he seized Norwich in his attempt to wrest the throne from the child king, Henry III. Later, in the Barons' Wars (*see* page 159), the desperate raids on the countryside by the 'Disinherited', who had taken refuge in the Isle of Ely, reached Norwich. The city was sacked and prominent citizens borne off and held to ransom.

In the next century, we know little of the effect of the Great Famine on Norwich, but the city was certainly hit hard by the Pestilence. All the three early major outbreaks, 1349, 1361–2 and 1369, took their toll, but, according to the tax returns, it looks as if the population had recovered by 1377. The natural increase was probably surpas-

LAFAYETTE
FURS AND LEATHERWEAR
ROYAL ARCADE
Harwayes

OPPOSITE

ABOVE LEFT: *Tombland Alley in Norwich is one of the best surviving examples of a 'plain' (open space for social and commercial purposes) attached to a parish church*

ABOVE RIGHT: *This shopping arcade between the market and the castle in Norwich illustrates how easily a grid-iron plan develops in a commercial area*

BELOW: *Another view of an area where open doors offer glimpses of medieval courtyards*

RIGHT: *This church demonstrates one of the happier attempts to find an appropriate use for one of the city's many redundant churches. It has been handed over to the Greek Orthodox Church and remains a place of regular worship*

BELOW: *Perhaps the most famous view of old Norwich: the façades of the shops and houses hide much older medieval courtyards and gardens running back behind narrow frontages*

sed by the settling there of runaway serfs, peasants taking the opportunity of the lords' weakness to escape to the freedom and opportunities of the towns.

Medieval Norwich is a byword for its galaxy of parish churches. The claim of fifty-two, 'one for each Sunday in the year', is probably not exaggerated, and already by Domesday there appear to have been twenty-one churches and forty-three 'chapels', presumably parish churches and lesser foundations. The filling up of the space within the city walls seems to have been the result of two main processes. On the one hand, the religious houses moved in, established precincts and effectively sterilized their little patches of the city from development. On the other hand, developers built a few houses and a church, usually with a 'plain', an open space by the church with the houses around it. The plains were of great social, economic and aesthetic importance, being useful for games and entertainments as well as little local markets. From the old street names as well as local specialized markets, the names of occupations recorded imply a zoning of the crafts was in practice, similar to that suggested earlier in Bury St Edmunds. Where the group went to the same local church, it is easy to see how the voice of a trade could only come from the religious fraternity, the only existing common association.

As was mentioned earlier (*see* page 47), churches were very close to the civic buildings of the Middle Ages, so what could be more natural than for Norwich Guildhall to be built of knapped flint flushwork in the late Middle Ages, just as contemporary churches were? Across the top of the market, St Peter Mancroft outshone it, but at first glance the Guildhall is so often taken for yet another church. The east end was renewed after the previous one collapsed early in the sixteenth century, and the attractive Classical turret came only in the mid-nineteenth century.

Norwich has a gem of urban provincial architecture in its Assembly Rooms. These were built in 1754 and replaced a mansion constructed out of parts of a religious college of the thirteenth century. The grand entrance leads into the middle of three rooms, ballroom to the right, and banquet hall to the left. Great care has been taken to retain harmonious colours, and the decorative detail has been preserved. The current use would probably please its builder: the banqueting room houses an excellent cafeteria restaurant, and the ballroom regularly has concerts and lectures. It is one of the city's most valuable assets.

ELY: A CATHEDRAL CITY

In Ely, the abbey that was to serve the cathedral was already well established when it was decided to set up a see there. Tradition claims that Etheldreda, the twice-married virgin princess of East Anglia, set up and endowed a double house for monks and nuns at Ely in 673, which she then ruled as its first abbess. In 870, it was sacked by the Danes but the survivors, after a short break, re-established some sort of religious life there. In the great period of monastic refoundation and reform, the Rule of St Benedict was established at Ely about 970, and the Black Monks moved in. In 1108 a diocese centred on Ely was set up, and the monks' church became the Cathedral. The property of the house was divided between bishop and monks, and Ely soon became one of the richest sees in the country.

The bishop's palace was built outside the precinct of the Abbey, where it now stands, and originally, so tradition has it, was connected to the conventual buildings across the road by a bridge

Both bishop and monks had their vineyards in the town, and both had their hithes down at the river bank. There were hithes for general use like Castle Hythe, overlooked by the castle which seems to have guarded the way to the bridge and Stuntney Causeway; along the eastern side of Broad Street ran merchants' houses with rows of cottages behind, leading down to the riverside hithes. The 'Three Black-birds' is a survivor from this development: where it now has a short cross-wing at the street end, it probably had a longer block of shops. At the rear end of the large merchant's house, which made up the rest, was probably a counting-house, the medieval term for 'office'. Down by the hithes, a substantial brewing industry was established in very early times and Ely Ales became famous, distributed often via King's Lynn where so much Ely produce went. Some was trans-shipped across the sea.

On the western side of Broad Street, opposite the merchants' houses, were houses of textile workers and other craftsmen. Further development took place above and below the Market Place which stands outside the old main gate to the precincts. Out beyond the town to the north was St John's Hospital, and to the south Barton Farm, the monks' farm. The development of a religious house as rich as that in Ely, could have a decisive influence on the development of a town.

There is a problem when describing medieval town-planning in East Anglia of choosing the criteria. At Bury St Edmunds, the Norman planning strikes us immediately because it has a decisive grid-iron pattern, but this is derived from the layout of the pre-existing open-field 'furlongs'. The Norman new French borough in Norwich, substantial if not quite on the scale of Bury, must have been a piece of major planning, yet its layout is not apparent to us in any clearcut geometrical pattern. But some of the fortified medieval towns are unequivocally new planned creations, 'bastides' in French terms. Examples of this are Castle Acre and New Buckenham.

CASTLE ACRE

Castle Acre in Norfolk must be one of the richest historical sites in the kingdom. As well as one of the finest groups of Norman castle (page 128) earthworks and a superb ruined priory in a perfect setting, it has a remarkable parish church with an interesting two-storey priest's house (page 56). The whole of the old town, apart from the priory and churchyard, was included in earthwork defences which formed the outer bailey. Both castle and priory are still yielding more and more of their past to the archaeologists.

The town is built where a chalk bluff on the north-west side narrowed the flood plain and marshes of the River Nar. This crossing-place had long been used by the Peddars Way, the prehistoric trackway already mentioned which had been adopted by the Romans. It used to be thought that Castle Acre had been a Roman camp which had left its earthworks to be incorporated in the castle and town defences: old maps bear the legend, 'Roman Station'. Such finds of Roman pottery as have been made, however, could be rivalled in most East Anglian villages and have very little significance. They certainly do not indicate a Roman town. The big problem is that (in reality more than on the O.S. map) the north-east corner of the ramparts is oddly detached

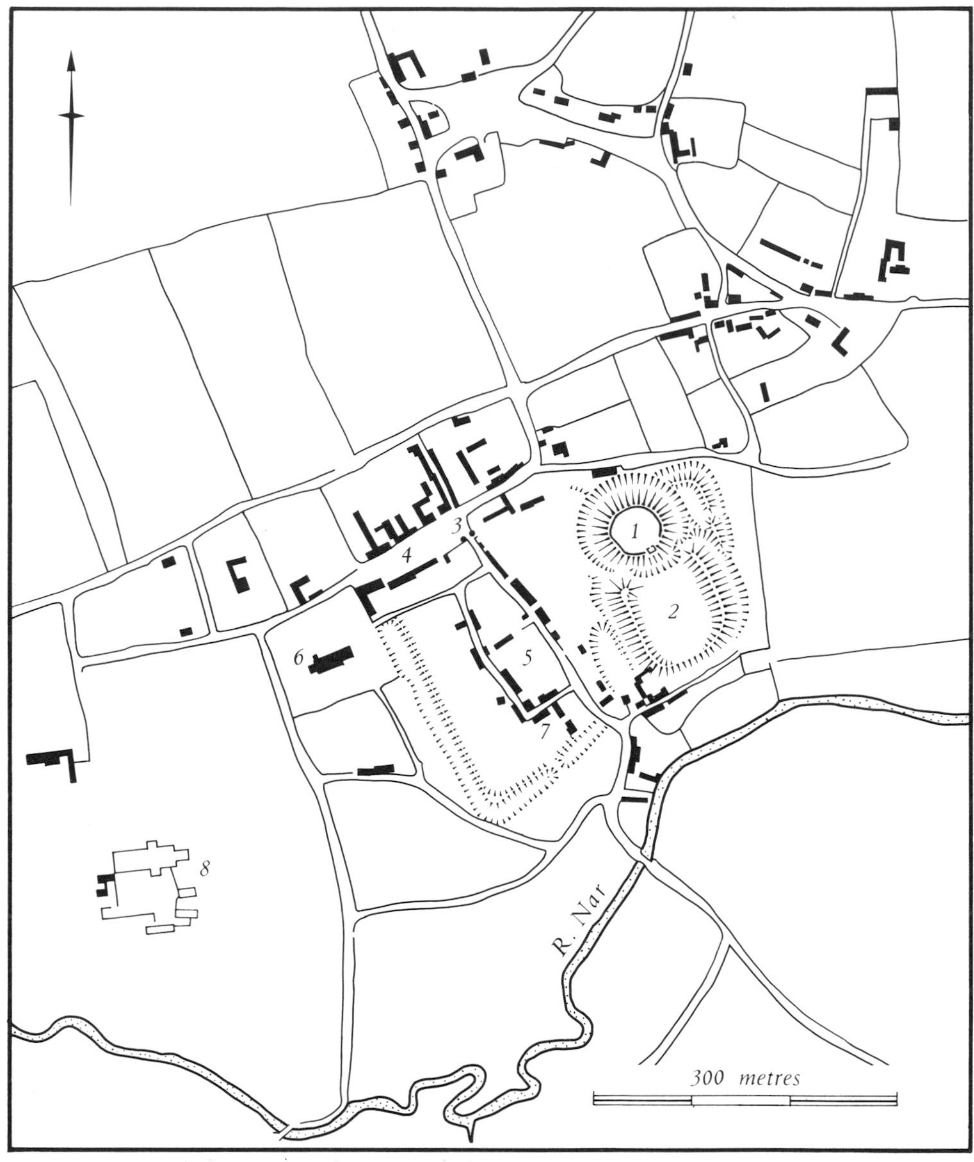

FIG. 7 CASTLE ACRE

1 Motte **2** Bailey **3** Bailey Gate **4** Stocks Green **5** Pales Green **6** St James' Church **7** Tudor Lodgings **8** Priory (PREPARED BY BERNARD THOMASEN)

from the main fortifications of the castle, and looks uncannily like part of a pre-existing structure that the Normans had taken over but failed to absorb completely. After recent excavation it has been interpreted as a barbican entrance on the opposite side of the shell-keep from the newly exposed gatehouse. The castle seems to have had a very complex history, in some ways without parallel (*see* page 128).

The street running uphill from the bridge passes through the massive wall guarding the lower side of the town. This wall, or earthern rampart, turns through a right-angle to defend the town on its boundary with the priory and churchyard. The layout suggests that the whole of the town was built within the defensive walls of the outer bailey of the castle. The road up the hill, as it emerges on to Stocks Green, passes through a thirteenth-century gatehouse with round flanking towers. The slots for raising and lowering the portcullis and the hinges for the gate itself are still in place, but a similar gatehouse at the bottom of the hill was demolished in modern times.

A journey on foot to explore all the planned part of the town gives a much better impression of medieval planning on a grid-iron pattern than does the map. Centuries of slight deviation by walkers who cut corners whenever they had the chance, preserve the spirit, even if they lose the exactness of the lines of the man who first laid it out. Not only the priory but also the parish church stands outside the defensive town wall. Stocks Green has the right alignment to fit the grid-iron of the town plan, but appears to be the fruit of levelling the section of the bank and ditch which must have run from the gatehouse in front of the present row of houses to join the western wall by the churchyard. In the heart of the town, Pales Green is the traditional site of the market, now mostly built over. It was probably superseded by Stocks Green at some unknown date.

NEW BUCKENHAM

New Buckenham, north of Diss, is a fine small example of a grid-iron planned medieval town whose original layout can be traced almost in its entirety. It was founded in the twelfth century by William Daubigny II who built the castle (*see* page 131) and replaced the one he had inherited from his ancestors in Old Buckenham, perhaps to take advantage of its ability to command the old Norwich–Bury St Edmunds road, at that time the main one. The site was carved out of two adjacent parishes, Banham and Carleton Rode, and now consists of three main elements: the large common where rights of pasture for eighty cattle have been perceived by Professor Beresford as a hint of the original eighty house-plots in the town; at the other end is the castle and its works, separated from the town across a field a furlong wide, and between the common and castle is the grid-iron square of town and market. To the west of it was added a parish church, the earliest parts of which are thirteenth-century.

On the way to the castle after passing the old Guildhall on the edge of the town and almost on leaving the road, a red brick barn is passed. It is in fact the old chapel for the castle and was used by the townsfolk as well until the parish church was built. Inside, the main doorway is revealed as good Norman work and there is an Early English doorway in the west end. The jambs or sides of the Perpendicular windows show that the building has been truncated by the loss of its east end.

The Market House at New Buckenham stands on pillars; the central pillar was used as a whipping-post with fetters to suit miscreants' varying wrist sizes. Beyond, the open market green has suffered relatively little encroachment

The little market square has great charm in spite of an out-of-place Victorian mock-Jacobean porch on the largest house. The main road, as so often happens, takes a short cut across the green near the old blacksmith's forge, one of the few pieces of encroachment. It has a focus of interest in the timber-framed, seventeenth-century market-house. This stands on wooden pillars which have cast-iron capitals and bases. The central part is a whipping-post, with fetters for wrists of assorted sizes. At the opposite corner stands a pair of cottages which look as if they have been created by dividing a medieval house of the 'Wealden' type. The original rectilinear pattern still completely dominates the layout. Around each corner, the explorer finds streets and alleys with much good (if often disguised) housing of the seventeenth century and later. Yet it has grown very little, and the old town ditch is still trickling behind gardens and tofts, just where it was diverted to flow and edge the pattern of the square in the twelfth century.

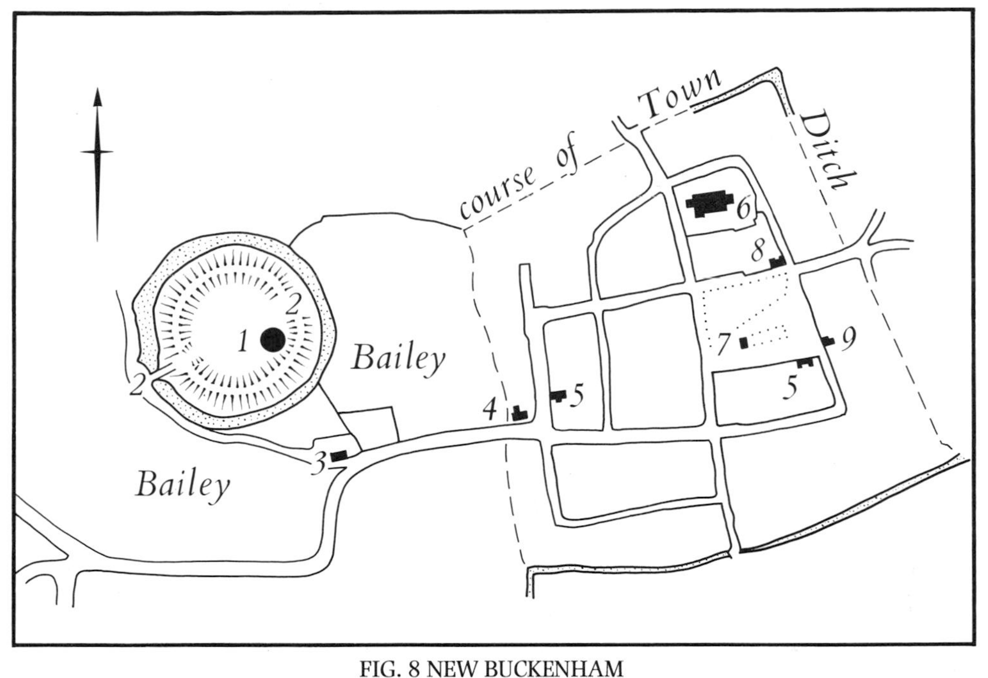

FIG. 8 NEW BUCKENHAM
1 Keep 2 Site of Gatehouse 3 Chapel 4 Guildhall 5 Jettied houses 6 Church 7 Market House 8 Wealden House 9 Blacksmith's (BASED ON FIRST EDITION, ORDNANCE SURVEY, 1884)

As a market town, New Buckenham has never expanded in spite of its position. The housing suggests that it was still doing quite well in the seventeenth and eighteenth centuries and it is still doing quite well today in its sleepy way, basking in the sun and history, although one would hardly call it a town.

KING'S LYNN: BUILDING ON THE SANDS

The founding fathers of some big East Anglian towns had a talent for choosing the most difficult sites imaginable. They did this at Wisbech, Great Yarmouth and at King's Lynn. In considering how much medieval planning there was in the foundation of East Anglian towns, King's Lynn is especially interesting and relevant. In the first place it is often claimed as *two* planned new towns not merely one and, secondly, it is a remarkable success story. By the tax lists of 1334, it had grown to become eleventh in the list of the richest provincial towns. Early in King John's reign, only London and Southampton paid more customs than Boston and King's Lynn.

This remarkable story apparently began in 1101 when Bishop Herbert de Losinga, Bishop of Norwich, granted to the monks of his cathedral the church of St Margaret together with the land between two of the streams running from the higher ground in his manor of Gaywood. The Millfleet and Purfleet streams became the southern

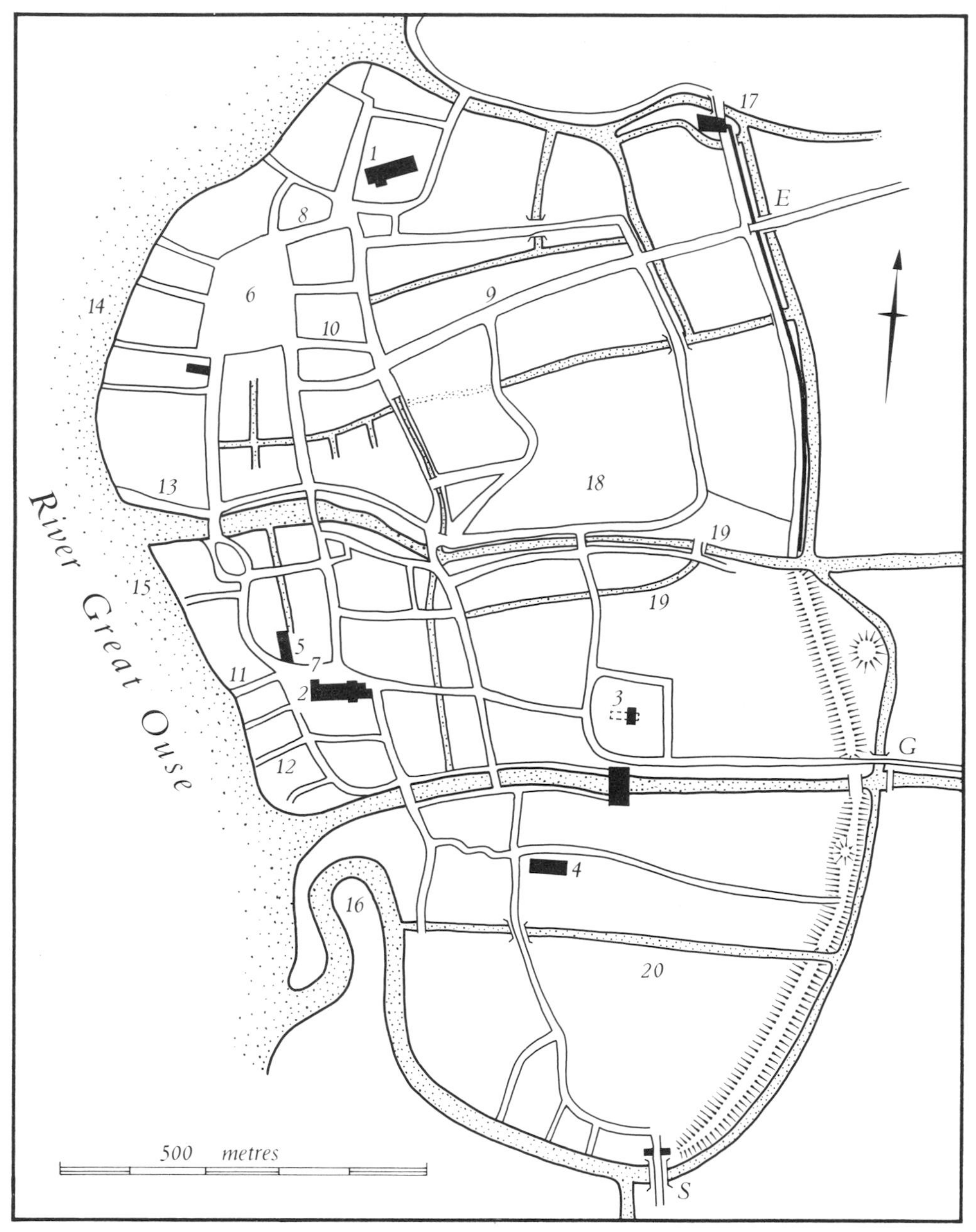

FIG. 9 KING'S LYNN

1 St Nicholas' Church **2** St Margaret's Church **3** St James' Church **4** All Saints' Church **5** Guildhall **6** Tuesday Market **7** Saturday Market **8** Woolmarket **9** Damgate **10** Jews Lane **11** College Lane **12** Muckhill Lane **13** Purfleet Quay **14** Common Staithe **15** King Staithe **16** Fish Drying Ball **17** Kettlemill **18** Blackfriars **19** Tenters **20** Rope Walks **E** East Gate **S** South Gate **G** Gannock Gate

St Margaret's church in King's Lynn is now suffering the effects of having been built on the sands of a disused saltern, and is facing severe structural problems

and northern boundaries of the first town of Bishop's Lynn. The site ran from the Gannock Bank in the east to the River Ouse in the west. The Bishop gave them the right to the Saturday 'Sand Market' and an annual fair on the feast of St Margaret. It was here that the flourishing town began.

When William Turbe was Bishop (1146–74), land called Newlands, to the north beyond the area of the previous grant to the monks, was granted its own chapel of St Nicholas, a market on Tuesdays and a fair. At the beginning of the thirteenth century, the then Bishop gave the monks other land in exchange, and took Newlands back again. Thus when he obtained a charter from King John in 1204, he was able to include Newlands in the limits of the town. The name 'Newland' and the near gridiron plan seem to be the source of the idea that Bishop's Lynn and Newland were two planned towns. Topography, with the Ouse running north and the drainage of the higher ground of Gaywood taking its streams (the 'fleets') west, was almost bound to produce something like a medieval approximation of a grid. The settlement immediately south of Bishop's Lynn, South Lynn, seems to have remained rural, although it had a church older than St Margaret's, and a number of merchants.

The name Lynn (or 'len') means a lake, and sounds scarcely promising as a site for town-building. Miss Parker* pointed out how rapidly salt-marsh can grow in the Wash, but salt-marsh alone can hardly do as a building site. By close study of the salterns and the salt industry among other things, however, Mrs Owen* solved the problems of how a town could grow so successfully on such a site, and proved the antiquity of Lynn before the Charter.

Mrs Owen discovered that 'dead salterns' could raise the ground level as much as 20 ft, and was able to identify such spoil heaps in an industrial estate at the north end of the town, and also under St Margaret's church. In Domesday survey, there was a large but diminishing number of saltings on the east side of Lynn and this suggests that the town was growing back towards the Gannock Bank. Although there was already a prosperous community in need of a parish priest and church when Herbert de Losinga made his grant, the number of saltings still working in the whole area was far and away beyond local needs. Very early on, much of the production of salt must have been for export from Lynn, probably mainly to the east-coast fishing ports.

Medieval salt-workers normally combined their industrial work seasonally with sheep grazing, and Domesday and the other evidence suggest that the Lynn area was no exception. Thus wool would become available for export and, after a time, as reclamation progressed, corn could be grown. Already in Domesday times, the value of land seemed to be rising, particularly between Millfleet and Purfleet. Here, away from Gaywood at the end of the low ground, the salt-making and trading parish that was to be St Margaret's was already growing up. The Bishop as landlord seemed to see more opportunity to levy tolls than to go in for full-scale real estate development. Lynn's growth is more like that of earlier towns rather than those planned in the thirteenth century. Its charter of 1204 gave it the usual rights granted to boroughs of that period.

It was to be a free borough, could have a gild merchant and its own courts, market, fair and so on. The Gild of the Holy Trinity was only recognised as the Gild Merchant in the early fourteenth century, but there is every sign that it was fulfilling such functions right back to the charter, and probably before. It included all the traders in the town, and probably spoke for them in the negotiations that resulted in the original grant of the charter. It was the oldest, largest and richest of Lynn's gilds – of which there were over thirty at the peak. The man most frequently mayor in the reign of King John, Sunolf, heads, the list of the gild members of the time. All the twenty-four 'jurats' who elected the mayor were members. Thus it seems to have been the town government in another dress. It built the biggest and best Guildhall, which still stands on the Saturday Market facing St Margaret's in the old and original commercial centre. It assumed special responsibilities for the good of the whole town, such as a large

* Mrs Dorothy Owen, Keeper of the Archives of the University of Cambridge and eminent medieval historian, and Vanessa Parker (Mrs Vanessa Doe), formerly of the King's Lynn Archaeological Survey, on whose work the author has relied very heavily for the history of King's Lynn.

The Saturday 'Sand Market' outside St Margaret's church was an ancient privilege and the heart of the commercial town. The earliest guildhalls were built there on the opposite side to the church; this guildhall was built in 1421, in flint and stone, and is the core of a fine sequence of public buildings

share in building the defences.

The nature of King's Lynn's trade shows something of England's place in the world economy in the Middle Ages. In the thirteenth century, it exported bulk foodstuffs and raw materials, grain, wool, salt. It imported timber, iron, fish (the Baltic herring), and also luxuries: wine, furs and fine cloth from Flanders. The royal household purchased fine cloth from Lynn. The trading partners most deeply involved with the town were Iceland and the Baltic countries in the north and Gascony to the south; there was always a substantial coastal trade up and down the east side.

Naturally Lynn suffered during the English government's trade wars in the fourteenth century, and it also suffered in the falling demand for grain as population generally decreased after the famines and plagues. When tariff policy encouraged the home manufacture of wool instead of its export in the raw state, Lynn shared the losses without the gains. The first two decades of the fifteenth century saw her exports of wool fall from something substantial, one or two thousand sacks a year, to nothing. Exports of cloth rose, but by no means in proportion. The struggle with the German Hanseatic League for the trade of the North Sea and Baltic forced the English government to give way. The Hanse had established its steel-yard at Lynn early in the fifteenth century.

Salt for the fisheries was still in demand along the east coast, but salt from the Bay of Biscay and Portugal replaced that produced in Norfolk and previously exported in large quantities from Lynn. Climatically, the English industry could not compete with hot countries in the evaporation of brine. The Norfolk saltings went out of business.

The foundation, expansion and stagnation of the town of King's Lynn took place against this economic background. Originally St Margaret's church was practically on the waterfront, but excavation has demonstrated how successive reclamation has moved westwards from the priory, with wharfs, warehouses, little piers and steps all extending out further and further behind the merchants' houses. A timber wharf of the thirteenth century was discovered under the courtyard at Thoresby College, probably nearer to the church tower than the present waterfront. The western side of the waterfront beside the Tuesday Market was always a public landing stage, although it suffered some encroachment as time went by. Moorings for barges, and piers and staithes for loading and unloading, appeared on the waterfront and on these fleets which were navigable when interest revived in the dock area in the later Middle Ages.

By 1557, there were the Common Staithe or wharf, the Bishop's Staithe and twenty-seven public quays. This area, and the whole of Newland to the east, had developed and built up, probably out-doing the earlier part of the town, the original Bishop's Lynn. Residential zoning, as in most medieval towns, was by occupation so long as the gilds were active, but the old craft compartments faded away after the Dissolution of the Gilds and Chantries in 1547. Thirty gilds in the late fifteenth century were reduced to five by 1562. Miss Parker worked out some of the shifts in social zoning in the seventeenth century: silting in the south caused many merchants to move up to the northern fleets and waterfront near Tuesday Market; buildings on the old, southern water-front near St Margaret's were split up and let, or taken by members of the professions, or gentlemen from the countryside. The reverse flow came later. Until the eighteenth century, merchants lived 'over the shop'. Only then did they go out of town to live as country gentlemen.

The long narrow plots in which merchants' houses were built would have a house, and (before the rebuilding in the late sixteenth or early seventeenth century) probably a shop or shops on the street frontage. Behind or over these would come a hall. Between the buildings on the street and the quay would be the kitchen, warehouses, office or 'counting-house', possibly bakehouses and breweries for the household, or even for provisioning the master's own ships. Gardens, orchards and yards were usually slotted in among the buildings. The yards were not wasted spaces but very necessary adjuncts of merchants' establishments, as timber-stacks, tenter-yards for cloth finishing, rope 'balls' or rope walks, or fish- 'balls' for drying fish. Rights of grazing and arable holdings were usually further away, often in the town fields. Lower down the social scale were rows of 'shops and solars', one-up one-down buildings, without any provision for heating during the Middle Ages, and they may never have been intended as dwellingplaces. The rural equivalents for the same period have all gone. From the sixteenth century, there survive documents indicating single-roomed cottages, either heated or unheated, let to waterfront workers. From the seventeenth century, more cottages survive, probably because of the increasing use of brick and other superior materials, and they show the use of the downstairs chamber as a sitting-room rather than a workshop. Heat could be provided from a gable-end chimney. Norwich and other towns have produced similar types of these cottages.

Miss Parker found a major re-building of medieval town houses occurred from 1560 onwards. There was relatively little complete re-building, mostly modernisation up to the new standards. The changes were much the same as Professor W. G. Hoskins taught us to look for in the same period of the 'Great Rebuilding' in the countryside: brick chimneys, glazing of windows and accommodation arranged on the upper floors. Any room could be provided with a hearth, and more rooms became used for special purposes. The revolution in domestic comfort seems to have taken place in town as well as country. A special feature of the re-building in King's Lynn is that virtually all the warehouses were rebuilt between 1550 and 1700.

As befitted a good market town, Lynn was well provided with inns. In the Middle Ages, there were concentrations of inns near the entrance to the market, in the Tuesday Market itself, and on the north side of the Saturday Market. Early in the modern period, they spread also to all the main streets and, eventually, by the nineteenth century there were over 400 public houses and inns in the town.

As well as private enterprise, the town government (and before 1547, its *alter ego*, the Holy Trinity Gild), owned and let property, and the Common Staithe was so owned; it was rebuilt by the town in the late sixteenth century. Warehouses and business properties were even built especially for letting; for example, the coal and timber yards on the King's Staithe. Purfleet Quay had a stone wharf and ship's berths for letting. In 1517 the town had a fulling mill for rent on the Gaywood River. The medieval corn-mill belonging to the Bishops of Norwich had been on the Gaywood River, but in 1448 the Holy Trinity Gild bought one on the Millfleet for town use. Even with supplementary water-courses to increase the flow, however, it failed and was replaced by several windmills. During the sixteenth century, a water supply was literally laid on to the doors of the brewers. A kettle-mill pumped the main water from the river for the town. An early nineteenth-century painting of it survives, but the mill has long gone.

In 1524, the town received a new charter of incorporation. The constitution provided for the annual election of a mayor from twelve aldermen, who also nominated burgesses to the Common Council. This closed oligarchy was swept away when nineteenth-century reformers began the attack on 'rotten boroughs' of which Lynn was by then clearly one of the more notorious, or perhaps we should say 'famous' since it had provided Sir Robert Walpole with a safe seat. Corruption flourished in 'pocket boroughs' where a handful of tenants held all the votes. In this sense, the borough was in the landlord's pocket. A 'rotten borough' was where relatively few remaining votes were freely bought and sold.

The new council soon acquired extra powers. In 1536, it acquired the 'fee farm' (lump sum rents) from the bishop, and thereafter let and supervised the town fields. With the Dissolution of the Gilds and Chantries in 1547, it acquired their property. Its fire precautions, apart from a ban on thatch, amounted to little more than provision of a few leather buckets; sanitation was a constant bugbear in such a low-lying site with miles of open ditches. This was tackled by setting aside places near the larger fleets and waterfronts for muckhills where rubbish could be dumped until it was taken away by the barge, and thus a new profession, 'muckhill fower', was created. The council took over the charitable responsibilities which had become heavier since the days when the Gild of St Giles and St Julian had built an almshouse.

In face of the collapse of the broadcloth market after the devaluation of sterling in 1551, the authorities attempted to begin a local textile industry. Such revival as there was in East Anglia in the second half of the sixteenth century came with the expansion of the 'New Draperies', brought in by refugee craftsmen from the Continent. In less than a generation, the failure at Lynn was complete.

With the destruction of medieval social services, almshouses, hospitals and schools in the Dissolution of the Monasteries, wise town government moved in to claim at least some of the resources thus released. Therefore at Lynn, in 1538 the new Grammar School was founded to replace the old monks' Charnel School. One of the best public buildings of any seventeenth-century town was a private venture of Alderman Sir John Turner, who acquired from the town, the site for a new Exchange. The result was the masterpiece which survives as the Old Custom House – in spite of its not being popular as an Exchange or convenient as a Custom House.

Most of the layout of King's Lynn was complete early in the thirteenth century. From the first, it had town walls derived from the old sea-banks. These were reinforced by the addition of four wooden towers, 'bretasks'. The walls, with their controlled points of entry, were probably a great deal more help in controlling those who broke market regulations by forestalling (selling before getting to market) or committed other economic sins of the time than they were for defence, except at rare intervals. Only two main gates were built, the East Gate and the South Gate. The old entry at the Gannock was shut by a locked bar at night and the East Gate keeper was armed with a club. In the late thirteenth century, Lynn received a grant of murage for the repair of its walls. The eastern boundary of the recently-developed Newlands was defended by an ashlar-faced rubble wall with crenellations and firing slits, much of which survived to its full height into the eighteenth century. The East Gate was demolished in 1890 and the remaining South Gate, which still dramatises the entry to the town, was last re-built in 1520. The town's fortifications, which appear to have been built

The Custom House at King's Lynn was built in 1683 with an open ground floor as the Merchants' Exchange. Free-standing on the quay, it makes a splendid focus

earlier and to have lasted and been restored much later than normal, are probably due to the town's importance as a sea-port and the attractions of its harbour to overseas raiders. It was put in readiness for the rumoured Spanish Armada in 1587, and maps from the seventeenth and eighteenth centuries show the walls as re-established in the Civil War, 1642 and 1643, with the typical earth ramparts and corner bastions of that period.

CAMBRIDGE: A SPECIAL CASE

The local topography almost forced the town of Cambridge into existence, but at the same time kept it modest. It was the first bridgeable point up the River Granta or Cam where the flood plain and marshes narrowed as bluffs of chalk and gravel approached from either side. Iron Age man had his village on top of the hill before the Romans, and when they arrived soon after the Claudian invasion of AD 43, roads were constructed radiating off in four directions and a small Roman town was built on the higher, more substantial chalk bluff, Castle Hill, commanding the river crossing. The bridge has been important ever since. Cambridgeshire is the only shire that takes its name from a bridge.

In common with so much of the Roman Empire, Cambridge seems to have been through a very difficult period in the third century. This must have been made worse by the collapse of the canal system, the Car Dyke, and the flooding of the Fens. In the reconstruction that followed, the town was reduced in size, brought back inside a smaller perimeter, and this shorter wall faced with stone.

The little town, which probably housed few people beside the tax collectors and their protectors, seems to have lasted as an inhabited place until after the withdrawal of the legions in AD 410, but it scarcely deserved the name of a town; rather it was a squatters' camp in its last years. Mercenaries from the Continent were established outside the town and they used a cemetery where Girton College now stands. Probably by the beginning of the fifth century, German was the main language in Cambridge. Then the Dark Ages descended.

When the history of Cambridge re-emerges, Saxon settlements and cemeteries were established on both sides of the river, with a concentration around the present market, and another among the ruins on Castle Hill. The old geographical forces which had made the Romans build a town there, operated to revive it in Saxon times. But these forces also attracted the raiders. At one time in the tenth century there were three Danish kings in Cambridge at once. But the Danes brought not only fire and the sword; Irish traders who are known to have visited Cambridge were probably drawn there as a result of Danish connections.

Attempts to show that Cambridge at the time of Domesday was squeezed entirely into the Castle Hill site have been disastrous as contributions to its history. No scholar living in Cambridge itself could have made such a suggestion, with the splendidly Saxon tower of St Benet's church testifying to what must have been a substantial and prosperous settlement. Some suspect the influence of Christian Danes is revealed by the dedications to St Botolph and St Clement – St Clement being a common Danish dedication. There is a strong probability that in late Saxon times, there was a minster church (a church with a group of priests living together, serving the churches of a wide area) on Castle Hill where a house of Canons Regular was founded in 1092 before it moved out to Barnwell. This was a common development for Saxon minsters after the Conquest. All Saints' Church-in-the-Castle disappeared long ago, as did All Saints'-in-Jewry, except for its churchyard opposite St John's College. In this area were several stone houses like the Jews' houses in Lincoln of which only one outlier, the School of Pythagoras, still survives. This one was held for a time by the first known mayor of Cambridge, Harvey Dunning, who rented it for twelve years from Baldwin Blangernon. The Dunnings were an English family whose holding of an estate in Cambridge possibly preceded the Conquest, and they seem to have been social rivals of the Blangernons (the name means 'white whiskers'), who appear to be a Norman military family. Another of the Norman stone houses had been the property of Benjamin the Jew, and became the City Tolbooth.

The early phases of post-Conquest development in Cambridge can be established by the founding of the parish churches. The document of 1279 called the Hundred Rolls gives a more thorough and detailed account than Domesday. Its survival is most important for Cambridge and it gives a good base for examining the growth of the medieval town. It mentions All Saints, St Peter and St Giles all north of the river, and fourteen parishes south of the river. At this date the town has filled the space inside the problematical earthwork known as the King's Ditch and suburban development at Barnwell and Newnham has begun. The King's Ditch was possibly a Mercian construction, possibly tenth-century, but certainly re-furbished in the thirteenth. It begins roughly along the course of Mill Lane, and re-joins the river downstream of the Great (that is, Magdalene) Bridge. It is now completely underground and the only visible trace is some unevenness in the Fellows' Garden of Sidney Sussex College. Within these bounds, Cambridge flourished as a modest market town, though its Stourbridge Fair became one of the greatest international fairs with buyers arriving from all over Europe.

Then came the foundations of the religious houses at a time when the town had very little good building land left. The Friars of St Mary settled at the foot of Castle Hill; in 1226 the Franciscans gained a tiny foothold where Sidney Sussex now is, and in 1290 the Austin Friars acquired a site between St Benet's and the marshes. The rest of the houses were outside the old town: the Dominicans were outside the Barnwell Gate (Emmanuel College's site), and outside the Trumpington Gate were the Friars of the Sack and the Sempringham Canons. In 1112 the Augustinian Canons migrated to Barnwell and, in 1134, the Benedictine Nunnery of St Radegund settled on the site now taken by Jesus College.

It is difficult to find evidence of when and where the University came to Cambridge. Roger of Wendover tells the story that a group of scholars moved from Oxford to Cambridge in 1209, with a similar defection to Paris taking place twenty years later. For a time there were rivals like Stamford which might have developed into a new university town as easily as Cambridge. Very little information is available from these early years.

The University, as distinct from the colleges, needed few buildings and little land. In the middle of the fourteenth century, it built its first lecture room, the Divinity School. With later additions this site became the Old Schools. The townsfolk soon realised that the shortage of accommodation for students provided the opportunity to fleece them. Students responded by clubbing together to take hostels of their own. Later, masters set up halls in which students were boarded as well as taught. Then came the colleges.

Peterhouse was the first, coming in 1280 and moving to its present site four years later. The Chantry of St Peter, from which Peterhouse took its name, was rebuilt and dedicated to St Mary, and because of the earlier use of that dedication in the town, this was distinguished as 'St Mary the Less', or 'Little St Mary's', or 'St Mary without Trumpington Gates', or simply 'St Mary without'. Across the road and still outside the King's Ditch, Pembroke found a good building site.

The next group were set on the little ridge of gravel owned by the University where the Old Schools had begun: Clare, Trinity Hall, Michaelhouse, King's Hall, and Gonville Hall. This all took place in the heart of the commercial town, and the new colleges acquired the hithes running down to the river at the same time.

In the 1440s, Henry VI set out to build the country's largest educational institution, King's College. His ambition may have o'erlept itself, as his plan is not yet complete. The medieval Milne Street ran straight from Silver Street, past the Carmelites, through

OPPOSITE: FIG. 10: *By about 1380, the city had grown up from the early settlements on both sides of the river, around the castle in the north and around the commercial district inside the King's Ditch. After the parish churches and the religious houses came the first colleges and university buildings. New development was spilling over the old boundaries*

Two views of what Henry VI intended to be the largest educational institution in the country, King's College Cambridge. The first emphasises the chapel which constitutes the most famous building in the University, the second the collegiate notion of the plan.

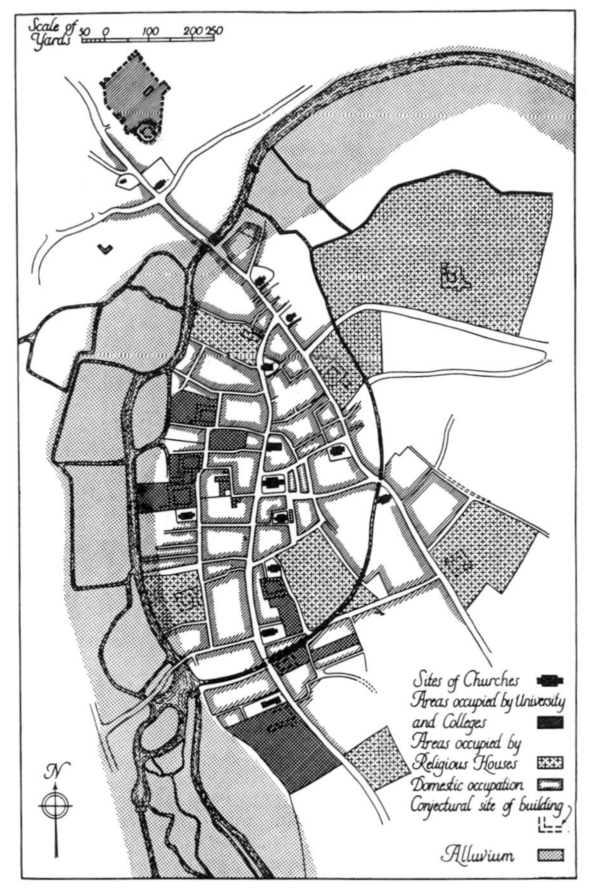

the parish of St John Zachary to what is now Trinity Lane. Henry acquired and cleared all the land along it between the Carmelites and Clare. God's House was moved to where it continues as Christ's College. From the roof of King's College Chapel, in very dry summers, the layout of the streets and houses of the former parish can be seen as parch-marks in the lawn of Great Court. With this great clearance went the Salt Hithe and other riverside wharfs. As development of colleges progressed along the river, the banks and tow-path became private property. A gravel pathway, which any punter on the Cam will know, was laid down the centre of the river for horses pulling barges, and this they continued to do, walking in the water, until the First World War. Along what was left of Milne Street, Queens' (1448) and St Catharine's (1473) were founded.

A different kind of foundation had appeared in 1352 when, under the patronage of John Duke of Lancaster (John of Gaunt), the Cambridge Gilds of Corpus Christi and the Blessed Virgin Mary founded their own college in the heart of the town. Although it was the townsmen's college, it still suffered in the Peasants' Revolt alongside Great St Mary's Church and the Carmelites when the mob burned the University Archives stored in these buildings. Resident tax-gatherers in the town suffered too.

Would-be founders of colleges began to cast envious eyes on the sites of some of the religious houses. In 1496, Bishop Alcock claimed that the nunnery of St Radegund was in decay, and that the nuns had great difficulty in keeping to their vows 'on account of the proximity of the students of the University of Cambridge'. He founded Jesus College there, using a ready-made chapel and other venerable buildings; it is the only college to have its playing fields at home, thanks to its origins as a nunnery with its early spacious enclosure. The Hospital of St John became St John's College in 1511, and in 1546 Henry VIII amalgamated Michaelhouse and King's Hall to form Trinity College. The old Dominican site became Emmanuel in 1584 and that of the Franciscans, Sidney Sussex in 1594. The Dissolution of the Monasteries had freed several attractive sites.

Back in 1428, the Benedictine monasteries which sent scholars to Cambridge had founded Buckingham College in the hope of keeping their men from the kind of problems that were to beset their sisters at St Radegund. In 1542, Magdalene was founded on the Buckingham site and some of the older college's buildings were incorporated in the new. During a renovation, a set of rooms for a master and students was found under later plaster, and was restored. A large square room, which would have been common room and the master's sleeping quarters, has study cubicles at its corners, complete with piscina-like wash-basins. Grafitti on the walls are preserved under glass, looking quite fresh.

Dr Caius in the 1570s recalled a remarkable change in Cambridge compared with what he had known forty years before in his previous spell of residence. Hostels were on the way out: of the eighteen he had known, a few had been absorbed into colleges, and the remainder 'for the most part deserted and given back to the townsmen'. This meant that more pensioners (students who paid for themselves) were living in college, and the second half of the century saw a good deal of improvised accommodation to take them, and some symptoms of the social change in new amenities. The colleges along the river began to reclaim swamp ground towards the Cam, and then to acquire property on the far bank where King's seems to have been the first in the race with its acquisition of Long Green; the college probably surrendered nearby land in exchange. In 1613 Trinity acquired a share of the Backs from the town (which never really owned them) in exchange for Parker's Piece. St John's followed with land leased from Corpus Christi, while Clare made arrangements with King's for its Fellows' Garden.

The ground level was mainly raised by using the dug soil from the town graveyards, and anyone digging in the lawn behind Gibbs Building is likely to find medieval items like buttons – as well as trouble. The result of these activities was the creation of the Backs, with gardens, avenues, bowling greens and pleasure grounds, such as would befit the fashionable idea of regarding the universities as finishing schools for the sons of the gentry.

During the seventeenth and eighteenth centuries, the number of students dwindled. When the revival came, as it did quite sharply, Cambridge had difficulty in adapting as it still wore its old medieval straitjacket of two sets of open fields and one large swamp, Pembroke Leys (formerly St Thomas's Leys) where undergraduates went wild-fowling. First the swamp was enclosed in 1801, enabling Downing College and some of the science block to be put up; enclosure of both the West Fields (Act 1802) and the Barnwell or East Fields (Act 1807) followed quickly. The landowning colleges as immortal corporations were in no hurry, and, apart from particularly handy artisan-type cottages for college servants, preferred to hold off, and when values rose sufficiently superior houses were built and let on long leases.

Thomas Panton, lord of the manor of Barnwell, successor to the Prior and the biggest landowner in the East Fields, died before receiving his award. His executors felt obliged to sell as soon as possible. Blocks of his land could be developed rapidly, even if the colleges' waiting-game made the overall picture of development patchy. The Panton Arms and Panton Street, one of the roads laid down by the Enclosure Award in one of Panton's blocks, still commemorate his name. The area east of Panton Street, in what was called New Town, was a prey to speculative jerry-building and is all now demolished. This gratuitous intervention of fate, the timing of Panton's death, has done more than any other event since to shape the Cambridge townscape. One possible exception is the coming of the railway. The University, moved by mixed motives such as the danger of lowering site values or the moral dangers to undergraduates, managed to keep the noisy, dirty thing away from the colleges. Station Road was not available as a site for the railway workers' houses: the colleges were holding on for higher values, and the workmen's cottages were built away out of sight in Romsey town, tucked into the area of fast development, south and east over the old East Fields. Chesterton Fields were enclosed in 1840, and enough land close to the town was in private hands to force rapid development. University reform allowed dons to retain their posts after marriage, and so there arose a sudden demand for large houses suitable for fecund academics and their domestic staff. The colleges therefore now began to build on the land on which they had held back, such as Hills Road, Harvey Goodwin Road and Station Road.

College development had by no means ceased. The 1820s saw a spate of enlargement in the accommodation ranges in a number of colleges. But new foundations were possible: Selwyn was started in 1881 to help supply sufficient ordinands for the Anglican church, with special interest in the mission field. The spirit of the age hovers here. It was surely a bold innovation not merely to have colleges for women, but to site one almost between an evangelical men's college and an evangelical theological college. Perhaps it was already realised that siting Girton (1869) at such a punitive distance from the men's colleges was carrying an old Cambridge tradition to a *reductio ad absurdum*. It certainly was old. In the fourteenth century, when houses of ill-fame were ordered to avoid the precincts of the borough, a new place-name appeared in two places just outside the boundary of its jurisdiction, to the north where Mount Pleasant emerges into Huntingdon Road, and to the south off Trumpington Road – 'Hor Hil'. In Tudor Cambridge, an undergraduate could not get a game of bowls nearer than the Traveller's Rest for fear of depravity. But the late Victorians did carry things too far.

When Newnham, Ridley Hall, Clare Memorial Court and the University Library had moved across to the west of the river, it was virtually inevitable that colleges and the University would look to this last area (preserved by large houses for dons' families) as a site for expansion. What may not have been quite so inevitable is the architecture. The post-war growth of the numbers of students, creating the demand for more teachers, added to the pressures on the available sites for additional undergraduate college accommodation. but even more for teaching space and graduate colleges. A century and a half since the struggle to keep the railway away, the shift of gravity of the university is still further in the opposite direction, and yet it needs the railway more than ever.

4
THE EXPLOITATION OF THE LAND

Throughout past history, the majority of the inhabitants of the region have depended on farming, and so the whole way of life has centred on what kind of farming is appropriate to their own particular locality. Farming patterns and ways of life can change and change again within a very short distance.

OLD FARMING REGIONS AND SYSTEMS OF EAST ANGLIA

The soils of East Anglia vary and contrast so much that settlement patterns, density of population, and farming types are very diverse. In the north-west of the region, where, in the days before the great draining of the Fens, a small extent of higher land stood out above the general water-level, settlement would take place and the tofts and crofts (little fields and gardens) of the houses would be surrounded by small arable fields which might be added to by reclamation. Beyond, in the areas liable to flood, a series of very valuable specialised zones would develop. First were the 'hards', pasture ground which normally was dry and which would be reserved for dairy cattle, especially cows and calves. There might be outliers of such lands, detached islets: these, if used for pasture, might have milking-places deep in the Fen which would be used as long as the cattle could safely stay out. Slightly larger islets, relatively free from flooding, might attract settlement and constitute the 'necklace' hamlets which formed beyond the arable in many Fen parishes. Where settlements were placed on the sea-bank between the silt fen on the seaward side and the peat fen behind, parishes could be divided as more dry land was won and here population and prosperity grew. In marshland, parishes often became detached from their Fen which was apportioned in a patchwork, until the tidying-up of parish boundaries in modern times.

The region's different soils – ranging from the thin dry sands and gravels which lie directly on the chalk in the Breckland to the heavy glacial boulder clays that defy draining and run across much of the region – have produced different types of farming and patterns of settlement. Following Joan Thirsk, the eminent historian who anatomised the agriculture of the area, many historians commenting on East Anglia group its major farming regions into 'sheep–corn' and 'wood–pasture'.

The soil of the sheep–corn region is mostly loams and sands. Even the sands of the Breckland could be made fertile by sheep. Eventually the sheep turned some Breckland soils into gold, producing the finest malting barley in all England. In the Middle Ages and early modern period, a version of 'infield-outfield' farming was practised,

RIGHT: *King's College, Cambridge, viewed from across The Backs*

BELOW: *John's College, Cambridge*

LEFT: *The ruins of Egmere church mark the site of a deserted village*

BELOW: *Castle Acre Priory*

POSITE, ABOVE: *The medieval tile village of Kersey*
POSITE, BELOW: *The village nd at Great Massingham*

LOW: *The well-preserved forti- ations at Castle Rising*

Framlingham castle, in its day an advanced and formidable fortress

similar methods being used on poor soils from Scotland to Devon; some historians think that this was a common stage from which more intensive farming of the two- and three-field types, familiar in the Midlands, developed in the more favoured areas.

Near the nucleus of the village, next to the tofts in which the houses stood, was the 'infield'. This was ploughed in ridge-and-furrow, cropped (in most places) every year, and given fertility by having all the household and farmyard manure spread on it. The infield would usually be divided into 'furlongs' (bundles of ridges running parallel to each other) and tenants' holdings would be intermixed. Between the infield and the heath would lie the 'outfield' and from this a number of 'intakes' or 'breaks' (the probable source of the name Breckland) would be taken out and cropped with the infield. The fertility of these would have been built up by folding all the beasts of the village on them at night during the previous year. After a few years, the fertility of the intake would fall and it would revert to pasture in the outfield until its turn for cultivation came round again. Professor Darby and John Saltmarsh described such a system on the Norfolk manor of West Wretham, and found that the intakes from the outfield were manured for seven years at a time and cropped for two to three years.

Some East Anglian villages had common field systems such as are familiar in the English Midlands and which are frequently described in the classroom. Some had an East Anglian variant in which what looked like great fields were more often called 'precincts', and what looked like furlongs were often called 'stadia', in which the strips making up a holding or tenement were separate but tended to be concentrated in part of each precinct. Rotation, if there was any, seems usually to have been within the precinct rather than between them. But the most characteristic feature of East Anglian farming in the Middle Ages and beyond, was the foldcourse.

Under this system, the lord of the manor had a monopoly of the right to pasture sheep, and the fields, meadows and commons were divided up so that the foldcourse took in a different sector each year until it came to start again. A frequent arrangement was that the lord, or his lessee, would pay compensation for any disturbance to the tenant's cropping from the exercise of foldcourse. Often this took the form of 'cullet' right, by which the tenant was allowed to put a few sheep in with the lord's flock. Sometimes also, the tenant paid to have the flock folded on his land in order to get the dung. Marling was used extensively on the light soils in Norfolk (*see* page 104), but even with this and the manure produced by the tenant's own horses and cattle, much of the Breckland went out of cultivation when population pressure ceased with the Black Death of 1349 and many little villages on the poorer soils were abandoned.

In the sheep–corn areas, settlement tended to be clustered in nucleated villages with the manorial institutions long remaining as the effective power of control. By contrast, the wood–pasture area was a country of few villages, but with numerous hamlets and dispersed farms in between. The land had been enclosed in family farms from earliest times so that the manor had little significance except as regards rents and land title. The ploughland area was minimal but the pastures and meadow large; it was a countryside that was devoted to beef and dairy. The owner-occupiers in the south-west of the region showed their independence in the survival of early inheritance customs: 'partible inheritance', or Borough English whereby the *youngest* son inherited all.

VILLAGE INDUSTRY AND WEALTH: THE WOOL VILLAGES

It was in the southern half of the area that the development of the cloth industry in the fourteenth and fifteenth centuries produced and bequeathed to us the evocative timber-framed villages like Lavenham, Long Melford, Kersey, Clare and Cavendish. (In Norfolk, too, the industry migrated into the countryside, but it was a different countryside, and the inheritance of buildings is not the same.) Yet it is odd to us that the Suffolk textile country, unsurpassed for rural loveliness in the whole region, grew because it could supply industrial power from water-wheels, had a substantial labour force that was not too well organised, and became beautiful because of the abundance of building materials in the form of oak and clay. It is hard for us now to realise that

OPPOSITE: *This timber-framed barn re-erected at the Museum of East Anglian Life illustrates how this traditional method of construction for farm buildings paralleled and outlasted the timber-framed houses*

BELOW: *At Lavenham, so many timber-framed houses survive that the world we have lost seems to come back to us*

these villages grew as part of the most densely populated and highly industrialised region of medieval England, or to appreciate how closely medieval industry and agriculture grew alongside each other symbiotically, breathing life into each other. Here prosperity spawned a tradition of successful families that were prepared to spend heavily on the creation of beautiful buildings – even if sometimes one is tempted to wonder if the soaring unfinished tower at Lavenham is not a shade too much dedicated to the greater glory of the Spring family, and whether the failure to complete has a faint hint of the Tower of Babel!

In the mid-sixteenth century, the weaving of broad-cloth collapsed. East Anglian cloth manufacture survived by turning to the manufacture of Worsted in Norfolk and the New Draperies in Suffolk, but by the turn of the century it was again unmistakably ailing.

MAKING NEW LANDS: THE DRAINING OF THE FENS

The north-west of the region seemed a place of opportunity for those who desired to get rich quickly. The promotion of schemes for draining the Fens at the beginning of the seventeenth century ranked alongside the notorious get-rich-quick schemes of the period – the formation of companies for colonisation of the Americas, the speculative and hard-selling of schemes for perpetual motion, or petitions for monopolies which would make the monopolists' fortunes. Families like the Cromwells had an eye to the main chance. Oliver was a would-be Fen drainer until the King moved in with the hope of taking the profits for himself. Then Oliver became 'King of the Fens', undertaking to keep the drainers tied up in law suits for five years, the commoners paying Cromwell a groat per beast on the common. It was hoped that by bringing the Fenland under cultivation, the tremendous reserves of natural fertility, built up over millennia, could be tapped and exploited by the landowners. The 'ignorant' opponents at this time – the Fenland peasantry – had evolved their own way of life, dependent on the wealth of diverse common-rights in the Fens, and resisted drainage. In 1618 at Cottenham, in Cambridgeshire, the inhabitants complained that recent local embanking and drainage had forced them to staunch the drains with barn doors in order to get moisture to their grass.

Payment for the work was to be in grants of newly-drained land to the men who put up the money to pay for the works, the 'Adventurers' (hence the common name Adventurers' Fen), and to those who actually made the cuts and banks, the 'Undertakers'. Vermuyden, the great Dutch engineer who finally did the work, had his own arrangement and his own quarrels with the Bedford Level Corporation. Sir Miles Sandys was another Adventurer, and he had mapped out the land he wanted, but made the mistake of taking on the Fenmen of Willingham. The very idea of draining the Fens seemed, to Fenmen, to go against Nature: 'Fens were made Fens and must ever continue such, and are useful in multiplying fowl and fish producing, turf etc. . . . The people think that the Undertakers will work by witchcraft, no persons of experience supposing their designs possible.'

In the discussions, much was written about the problem of the silting of the rivers because there was not enough gradient for the rivers to run fast enough to scour their own beds. One party called for the removal of all obstructions, weirs, shallows, gravels, ponds etc, in the hope that this, together with straightening their courses, would improve the gradient and so the scour. Those with vested interests in river transport and barge traffic were much against this and, in fact, against the whole idea of draining, because in summer there would not be enough water to float the barges clear over the shallows. Mills produced a similar problem because when they stopped, the main river emptied as the ponds filled and it became too shallow again for the barges. Thus there was another element in the struggle between the interests in draining on the one side and commoners and navigation on the other: the water-mills.

The University at Cambridge was wholeheartedly on the side of navigation. It objected to the proposed new cut at Stretham, saying that such an additional channel would drain the Old West River and the Cam so fast in summertime that they would cease to be navigable. The University itself had become dependent on water-borne supplies from King's Lynn and the Fens. After charcoal timber had become scarce, fuel proved a big problem 'so as most colleges are driven to use sea-coal provision for their meat, as well roast as boiled, which in former times they were not wont.'

But in spite of political intrigue, the great work was begun by Vermuyden under the aegis of the Bedford Level Corporation, the Bedford family being the largest Fenland landowners with the most to gain.

The problems that Vermuyden had to tackle are essentially those which current schemes may have solved. Danger is particularly acute at the time of the spring tide. A normal spring tide will rise to about fourteen feet above sea-level. Unfavourable wind conditions (as in 1941 when the wind drove the tide down the North Sea and, then changing, piled up the water in the Wash), may increase the height to as much as seventeen feet above sea-level. Under such conditions, the upland water, from a very large catchment area, cannot drain away to the sea and has to be held within its banks or bursts them until the tide falls again.

In 1630, by the so-called 'Lynn Law', Francis, 4th Earl of Bedford undertook to drain the southern Fens. In return, he was to receive 95,000 acres of the land reclaimed by this process. Although resumed under the Commonwealth after interruption in the Civil War, his engineer, Cornelius Vermuyden's scheme was never completely carried out. An important part of his final design was very much like the cut-off and relief channels dug between 1954 and 1964.

Although Vermuyden appeared to be having some initial success, complaints came in very early on. There was much argument as to whether Vermuyden had turned the Fens into 'summer grounds' only when he should have made them 'winter grounds' as well. Trouble was looming ahead, but the Commissioners of Sewers hoped it would go away. At a Session of Sewers at St Ives in 1637, the complaints were set aside and it was declared that the work had been done according to the true intent. But the disputes got worse rather than better, and were perhaps exacerbated by Vermuyden being too grasping for what he claimed as his due. The King intervened and took over the work, retaining Vermuyden. Civil War interrupted progress.

In 1649, when the fighting had ended with Parliament's victory, a Drainage Act (often referred to after the Restoration as the 'Pretended Act' because the authority of the Commonwealth Parliament could not be acknowledged) was passed and the old drainage works were repaired and new ones carried out. The most important of

These photographs of the Fen near Benwick emphasise the flatness of the ground and the straightness of the drains dug by Vermuyden

these was the cutting of the New Bedford River, or Hundred Foot Drain (its width was a hundred feet) half a mile to the east. Barrier banks were made outside the two Bedford rivers, and the space between, known as the 'Washes', formed an enormous receptacle for flood waters which would have to be held until the tide allowed them to be got away through the river channels. The use of the New River and the Washes was controlled by the Hermitage Sluice at Earith. The tide had to be prevented by Denver Sluice from flooding the whole system, and if necessary, the Washes could hold surplus tidal water. The Old Bedford River, although straight, had been closely confined between banks which could not contain the excess floodwater. There were new ideas about since this failure, and Vermuyden's *Discourse* emphasises the use of Washlands and banks set back to act as reservoirs for flood water, the use of the Bedford rivers and the sluices.

Vermuyden's early work might have been carried out by any competent drainage engineer of the time. Straightening, deepening and embanking the watercourses to increase the gradient, speeding up the flow, and increasing the scour of the rivers to their outfalls, seems to have been the general prescription. However, when this was carried out, tried and tested by the first flood, banks broke in complete failure. Vermuyden had to devise his new scheme, which held the flood water until it could be sent out with the tide.

In 1653 the Final Adjudication declared the work done, and ten years later the Drainage Act settled the constitution and powers of the Bedford Level Corporation. What had previously been thought of by agriculturists as a desert now blossomed and became unbelievably fruitful. Dugdale's diary shows crops of the highest quality growing on the newly drained land. On the one hand he saw flax, hemp, oats, wheat, cole-seed and woad; on the other, onions, peas and hemp. Near Thorney he saw rich crops of all kinds of corn and grass. But still there were floods, and still the vested interests in navigation criticised the work of draining and its results.

As draining became effective for a time, and the drying Fen was cleared, so the peat shrank and wasted. As the water content of the peat reduced, it shrank physically; oxidation, bacterial decomposition and soil erosion all took place and played a part in lowering the surface. For a time, Fenmen thought that their water-courses were growing from the bottom. Vermuyden's draining started and speeded processes by which the drainage of the Fens ultimately divided in two, a low-level series where the water had to be lifted from the field ditches into the drains, and the high-level trunk system for getting the water away and out to sea.

Surveying the Fens in 1604, Hayward saw an engine for lifting water – presumably a very early windmill. In the last quarter of the seventeenth century, as Vermuyden's work succeeded, peat shrinkage surely followed, and made the problem of getting rid of the water worse than ever. The solution was the artificial lifting of the water out of the ditches. Windmills harnessed to scoop wheels succeeded in doing this, but did it so well that the peat shrank, and the problem grew worse again. The height of the lift required became greater than a single windmill could reach. Double- and multiple-lifting by windmills solved the problem for a time. At Wicken Fen nature reserve in Cambridgeshire, one of the old drainage mills, brought from Adventurers' Fen, has been re-erected. It is a small wooden smock mill, with weatherboard cladding. It pumps by a scoop wheel which no longer lifts water out of the Fen but conversely in dry weather lifts water into it to keep it moist, so that it remains as Fen.

When windmill drainage was at its height, the enormous number of mills then operating included some very tiny ones, much smaller than Wicken. It also included a large number of brick tower mills, and these can still be seen in the wetlands of east Norfolk and Suffolk. In fact, on the journey from Norwich to Great Yarmouth, for mile after mile the only relief from the flatness of the country on either side is derelict towers of mills in various states of decay, with a miller's house alongside some of them. Ironically, it was the coming of the Industrial Revolution to the Fenlands that saved the day.

As Arthur Young pointed out, windmills had been known to remain still, becalmed, for as much as two months. As peat shrinkage made the problem of drainage worse, so the windmill ceased to be able to cope with the task reliably. The steam-engine came to supplement the wind at first, but remained to take over. The first steam-pump in the Fens was erected in 1817 or 1818, and others soon followed. A number of the simple functional brick engine and boiler houses, with slim, square tapering chimneys, still survive.

Stretham steam-engine survives intact. It was rescued after the acetylene torches and cylinders had arrived to cut it up for scrap. It had last worked in the great 1941 flood – to such effect that the boiler then in use was strained at the seams. Another had long been converted to a fuel tank, for the diesel engines had taken over from it for normal purposes. These early diesels are in a smaller additional house nearby. The engine at Stretham is typical of the Fen steam-engines, a Cornish-type beam engine driving a large scoop wheel. Preserved, and to some extent restored by voluntary enthusiasts, amid a collection of engineering and Fenland bygones, it gleams inside walls that still bear the original decoration with classical Greek motifs.

At Cottenham, as in other nearby Fen-edge villages, the Enclosure Act was also a Drainage Act. An old man looked back in 1905 and remembered the biggest change in the village in his life-time: 'Nearly all the old landmarks were removed and a fresh order of things substituted in their place. Three old watermills taken down, Undertakers, Chear Fen and Setchell, and two steam-engines in their place, Smithy Fen and Chear Fen. New drains were dug or made.' Quite often one steam-engine could replace up to ten windmills. Soon the much more effective centrifugal pump was introduced, and one of them was used to drain Whittlesey Mere, the last of the great Fenland meres, in the early 1850s.

Steam-engines take time to get up a sufficient head of steam to drive the engine before pumping can begin. Diesel engines are much better at this, and so are better fitted to cope with any sudden or extraordinary flood. The first one installed for Fen drainage was in 1913. Others followed between the wars, but after the Second World War electric pumps have increasingly found favour. With them, the need for enginemen is reduced by the introduction of automatic control.

Fenland newly drained and broken up needed no rotation to keep it fertile. The normal practice was to plough with a skim coulter to take off the turf, especially the tussocky patches. This was then dried off in heaps and burned. After this, it was usually given a first crop such as cole-seed or oats, and the land would then bear a corn crop for year after year without fallowing. Some farmers undoubtedly repeated the paring and burning too frequently for the good of the land; it wasted the peat. As long as the peat lasts, very demanding crops can be taken, but by the middle of the nineteenth century, the peat was obviously wearing out. The deposits were becoming thinner as the surface sank, the thin marginal deposits disappeared and the area of the peatland contracted.

The situation could be dealt with negatively and positively; negatively by giving up paring and burning, and positively by the process of 'claying' the land. In essence, this is the same process as 'marling' which was in use as far back as the thirteenth century. The idea is very simple. Clay subsoil from below the peat is dug and spread over the field, where it mixes with the peat and reduces all the processes which waste the peat. Although expensive, marling pays for itself handsomely quite quickly. But it can only slow down the wearing out of the peat. Once the wet-lands have been drained, short of abandoning drainage and allowing fresh peat formation in swamps, time inexorably leads towards a top-soil of clay which is infertile in itself, and results in a change in farming methods from the highly intensive cultivation with its heavy crops off the peat land to an extensive style based heavily on grass.

The immediate effect of draining the Fens was to decrease their biological potential

Artificial drainage of the Fens has become increasingly reliable. This diesel engine which replaced steam was in turn replaced by electrically-driven pumps

---

and their capacity to support life, in spite of the richness of the crops. The long-term results seem inevitably, sooner or later, to substitute one of the poorest for one of the richest soils. In order to conserve something of the richness of the drained Fens for as long as possible, some farmers have given up ploughing altogether, and go in for direct drilling, relying on spraying for weed control. But the current danger to the Fenland is as serious as any in the past.

IMPROVING LANDLORDS

Nowhere else in East Anglia offered the riches that the newly-drained Fenland had promised. Nonetheless, other opportunities were there for improved methods, and the credit for pioneering these improvements is usually given to Norfolk, and especially to three families, the Cokes, the Townshends and the Walpoles. The great houses, Holkham, Raynham and Houghton, became centres for the diffusion of new agricultural ideas.

The great country houses, which had developed as centres for the intrigue and build-

The splendour of Holkham Hall illustrates something of the wealth that came to both landlord and peasant from the soil of Norfolk in the eighteenth century

ing of 'connection' so necessary to political power in the seventeenth and eighteenth centuries, became centres where the new agricultural methods which were a means of making money for the owners, could be seen to work. (*See also* Chapter 7.) Thomas Coke's 'sheep-shearings' attracted thousands. Holkham displayed what selective breeding could do: Southdown sheep, bred to suit the farming and market conditions, ousted the old Norfolk breed, and the great barn at Holkham model farm indicates what could be achieved alongside the sheep: an increased output of grain. By the use of flocks of sheep, Coke converted what had been a poor barren soil into the best ground for malting barley. Malting towns developed on the rivers running out of East Anglia towards London and on the coast for the export of malt to metropolitan brewers. Certainly Norfolk offered some of the finest examples of what could be achieved by mixed farming that the propagandists of improvement at the end of the eighteenth century could cite.

Sometimes too much credit was given. The name Townshend has become so hopelessly identified with turnips in generations of school textbooks that pupils often seem to think that he invented them! They were being grown as a field crop elsewhere in Norfolk by 1650, and at Abington in Cambridgeshire a large portion of the arable seems to have been set aside out of the rotation of the common fields exclusively for growing turnips, at least forty-five years earlier.

In the Norfolk rotations, which gave up the traditional bare fallows, cropping the land every year, turnips appeared as a cleaning crop. Before this they had been grown as winter feed and so, incorporated in the rotation, did double duty. Clover, artificial grasses and legumes provided more feed, and the clover and legumes 'fixed' atmospheric nitrogen as a fertiliser in the soil. More feed meant that more animals could be kept, and more manure was available for the corn land. By about 1760, such methods produced a peak in the output of corn.

The new rotations could not be implemented on open-field land where the fields were a patchwork of narrow strips, thus adding to the pressures for change from the propagandists like Arthur Young and the other advocates for Parliamentary Enclosures and the repartitioning of the open field. Ancient ill-kept commons were broken up. In the dire need to dig for victory in the Napoleonic wars, even the Breckland came under the plough again.

Probably the best period for East Anglian farming and its landlords was after the recovery from the post-Napoleonic war depression. East Anglia shared the benefits of High Farming with most of the Midlands. New and improved implements were followed by more complicated horse-drawn machinery. Artificial fertilisers came in one by one and imported cattle cake added to the numbers of beasts that could be kept. Then the world's railways began to be completed. First the European prairies were opened up, then, after a brief interruption during the Crimean War, the plains of Poland supplied barley cheaper than the Norfolk grower could get it to market. American farmers with virgin lands easily capable of flooding world grain markets could hardly do so while the armies of the Civil War were marching over the fields, or during the post-war turmoil – called Reconstruction by American historians – but after that, when shiploads of American grain began to pour in, the English farmer hardly knew what had struck.

THE GREAT DEPRESSION IN AGRICULTURE

In the collapse of 1873, the English farmer imagined that the main trouble was bad weather and would pass. In the 1890s, it appeared as if prosperity had gone for ever. As the farmer switched production, so disaster followed. When beef and dairy farming were tried, animal disease and foreign competition struck. Beef on the hoof, canned beef, frozen meat, chilled meat, came from the New World in wave after wave. Cheap bulk imports became more dangerous to the home farmer with every improvement.

Bankruptcy forced many small farmers to give up altogether. Cornishmen and Scots, used to existing on little, arrived from homes even worse hit, and took up some of the farms. Anyone familiar with Cornish names can read something of the effects of those disastrous decades in the pages of current East Anglian telephone directories. The East Anglian farmers who survived best were those near towns and railways, especially if they could expand into horticulture. But there was little general relief until the submarine warfare of the First World War when it became difficult to obtain food. The depression which then followed the war made conditions as bad as ever, and it took yet another war to bring back a relatively stable prosperity. In the post-war decades, the possibility of making money from the incredible farming subsidies on offer led to the entry of syndicates of businessmen and large firms buying up farms to form great estates, and developing large-scale production by bulldozing hedges and filling in ditches to make larger and larger fields. With trees, hedgerows and wetlands destroyed, the modern landscape would make medieval open fields look positively over-grown. In East Anglia, prairie farming seems here to stay and a birthright of lovely countryside has been sacrificed at the altar of profit and greed.

VILLAGES: A MATTER OF LIFE OR DEATH

Norfolk scenes often have, as a focal point, an isolated church standing in the fields, away from all houses. Sometimes an ivy-mantled ruined tower stands alone with a few broken fragments of wall; sometimes the church has gone, and only a bumpy field, ridged and pitted by the abandoned streets and dwellings, records anything of the community which once lived there. A few lost village sites reveal themselves only to the air photographer, through 'crop' or 'soil marks'. Historians and archaeologists have hunted lost village sites for nearly forty years, but there are many more still to be discovered.

Norfolk, which was very densely populated in the Middle Ages, has produced a vast number of deserted villages. Dr K. J. Allison counted 726 settlements in Norfolk Domesday, of which 100 have gone, not including about another 30 minor hamlets. Suffolk has deserted village sites, but not apparently in such profusion. Dr Peter Wade-Martins has shown that the isolated ruined church in Norfolk was only part of the story. Some such churches had bumpy ground suggesting old village sites near them; others were well away from a flourishing modern village that appeared never to have been deserted and had no signs of habitation near the church. By extensive and patient field-walking, he discovered something even more difficult to explain: some villages, to judge from the distribution of the old pottery which was found amongst the plough-soil, moved not only once but several times. Each village had its own story of good times and bad, many villages shifted and drifted or shrank and, occasionally, we can begin to piece together a village biography.

We used to think that most of the present settlements in the east and Midlands were founded after the Roman withdrawal, and were mostly sizable, compact or 'nucleated' villages surrounded by open fields. In the west and more generally hilly stone country, we imagined settlements to be mainly in the form of hamlets and scattered farmsteads. Whenever we get close to a surer knowledge of any particular settlement, it seems to break the formerly accepted patterns.

Thanks to the work of Dr Stanley West and his helpers, West Stow (page 28) has yielded some of the secrets of a very early Saxon village. It was settled before 410 AD, the date usually given for the withdrawal of the Roman legions. Weaving and raising sheep seem to have supported its way of life. For a generation or so, its inhabitants appear to have lived in peaceful co-existence alongside their Romano-British neighbours with whom they traded, and weaving combs of both Romano-British and Saxon types have been found.

The buildings at West Stow were of two kinds with a few 'halls' of up to nearly ten metres in length and surrounded by the smaller 'huts'. These showed a degree of sophistication that we should have expected from people whose boats could make the crossing from the Continent, but which has not always been appreciated at earlier excavations of Saxon sites. Plank floors which covered the excavated cellars beneath

Over much of the area, the village remains the typical unit of settlement, each one with its own shape and pattern: Kersey (right) and Ramsey

West Stow was already here in earliest Saxon times, and young archaeologists have used every possible clue to help them reconstruct part of the village with its houses and its sheds for weaving woollen cloth

walls of vertical oak planks (rather like the nineteenth-century 'slab' houses of the Australian pioneers) and thatched roofs combined to make efficient buildings. Hearths were provided in some dwellings where clay fire bases were placed over the planks. Some of the small huts were obviously weaving-sheds because of the loom weights found there; others were used for sleeping or storage. Although there was no regular lay-out of streets, the earlier small huts appeared to cluster in small groups around the larger halls. The halls seem to have been the venues for family life, while the subordinate huts seem to have been mainly, if not entirely, used as industrial buildings. Since the halls appear to have been in simultaneous occupation, they may well represent separate family homes, rather than the great social halls of larger communities such as we read of in the Dark Age sagas.

West Stow seems to have been undefended, and it is not certain why it migrated to a new site in the middle of the seventh century. Possibly sand blows were beginning to engulf the site as later they did completely. This left a sandy deposit thick enough to be ploughed into ridge and furrow field strips in the High Middle Ages without the plough biting deep enough to destroy the archaeological evidence. So the site was preserved and the information saved; the village has now been partially reconstructed to as it may have been before the desertion.

West Stow should act as a corrective to the common tendency to explain any deserted site as a victim of the Black Death. A careful investigation may establish the date of any particular desertion. It could be as early as the Dark Ages or the Romano-British period or as late as the twentieth century when battle training ranges established in the Breckland in World War II caused the destruction of several villages. The causes may be almost as varied as the dates. The development of monastic granges or large farms for sheep in the Middle Ages, and the formation of parks to give vistas to great houses in the post-medieval period – as at Houghton (page 150), Ickworth (page 152) and Somerleyton – have both added to the number of deserted sites. But probably, when all the controversy has settled, the Black Death will be seen to have played the greatest part in the depopulation of so many villages – although the final desertion of the weakened settlements took place later. Where land was easy to come by after the population decline caused by the Pestilence, the holders of poorer 'marginal' lands might not only have been unable to resist eviction, they might well have anticipated it and fled to take up better land elsewhere. On the other hand, where the soil was suitable for pasture, price movements after 1450 would have encouraged the landlord to evict his tenants where possible and turn over the land to production of sheep for wool which had become more profitable than collecting rents from peasant ploughmen.

In the Breckland, desertion was widespread, nearly thirty of its villages disappearing in the Middle Ages. The expansion of the ploughland in times of population pressure and high demand probably lured many families into unsound agricultural ventures on the Breckland sands, so much so that with conditions deteriorating because of the sand-blows, when the fertile and binding humus was lost with the top-soil, a massive 'retreat from the margins' may have begun here before it became general elsewhere on the poorer soils of England.

Although some deserted medieval village sites are practically invisible at ground level, the majority have at least one surviving building. This may be the manor house, which often survived as a farm house when a village was completely enclosed into one farm, or it may be the church, the best constructed building in the village; sometimes just the church tower remains, as at Pudding Norton. The tower at Godwick, the side of which recently collapsed, stands in what was obviously a church-yard with the main village street – an ample holloway on its northern side – running down a gentle slope between the site of the old manor house and a barn, and on to the site of the old water-mill and mill-pond.

The manor house at Godwick was standing at the end of World War II, but it was finally demolished and the bricks used for building material elsewhere. Amid the vegetation, some broken brickwork survives and a heavy oak beam with Elizabethan 'ovolo moulding' lies among it. In dry weather, the whole house plan is outlined sharply in yellow 'parch marks'. The outer walls of the cross-wings continued forward as garden walls, to complete a square. The barn is a magnificent structure in rubbed red brick, with massive oaken crown-posts in its roof. It seems to date from about the time of the final enclosure of the village, in the very early years of the seventeenth century, when the church tower was also repaired with rubbed red brick. The 'tofts and crofts' or garden plots of the house-sites appear in the turf as roughly rectangular ditches, slightly banked inside on the lines of the old fences or 'muddle' walls (boundary walls made of clay and thatched). The modern farm house stands half-way between the old site and the road. The pool near the north-east corner of the churchyard is probably the old village pond; it was there when a map was drawn in 1596. (The survival of a map of a village that was just about to be deserted is very rare indeed.)

A scatter of more recent marl-pits in the village site as well as in the fields slightly confuses the pattern. Among the village earthworks are those of the manor garden which was extended across the abandoned village. Air photographs reveal its rectangular divisions.

The Godwick enclosure seems to have been for sheep, and a flock is still doing well there although turf-stripping on part of the site may cause concern. A few of these enclosures may in fact have been by agreement of all involved, producing the consolidation of some land-holdings by the exchange of fragmented lands, but most enclosures were for the benefit of landlords who had an eye to the main chance, and scant regard for the peasants whom they probably hardly knew. Some saw enclosure as an opportunity to enhance property values and the squeezing out of smaller tenants is still a feature of East Anglian country life. In the sheep–corn regions with lighter soils where the foldcourse system operated, such practices could give the landlord a virtual monopoly of the means of raising the profitable sheep (*see also* page 98). This was also an area in which manorial control had remained strong and was often at its most oppressive.

The Commission on Enclosures of 1517, set up to investigate and check the flood of evictions, found Sir Thomas Thursby busy enclosing in eight different places in Norfolk; at the same time, his activities extended to Cambridgeshire. At Cottenham, on the edge of the Fens, he was separating a house from its 'sheepgate' (the rights to graze sheep, such rights belonging to the house) and to make sure of success he was allowing the house to fall down. These practices were unmitigated evils in the eyes of the moralists of the time, like Sir Thomas More. Separating sheepgate from land meant enjoying another man's living as well as the one and only one to which it had pleased God to call you. A ruined house meant another homeless family on the road, a possible drain on the resources of parochial charity, and an increase in the vagabond menace.

The second half of the fifteenth century appears to have been the most severe period of enclosure, and the first half of the sixteenth century was the period of the greatest outcry against it. Rising prices from the Great Debasement of the Currency, rack-renting – whereby some rents could be raised to compensate for inflationary losses on fixed rent – and the abuses of landlords who over-exploited the commons, were probably the most serious problems alarming Kett's rebellious peasant followers, who revolted in 1549 (*see* page 162). But they could see the enclosure fences and had probably heard about their evils from their grandfathers. In such desperate times it was natural for them to break the fences down.

Cottenham illustrates the process of the division of commons by agreement and bargain through the Chancery or Exchequer courts. A case was brought alleging illegal enclosure, and was halted when the legality of the enclosures was admitted. After two previous attempts in the 1560s and 1580s, the commoners of Cottenham came to agreement with their lords in 1596. The agreement recognised the lords' enclosures in the Fen, in exchange for their surrender of all common rights and all authority of their courts over such common rights. In practice, this agreement amounted to an enormous extension of village self-government, until the arrival of the Parliamentary Enclosure in 1846 two and a half centuries later. The commoners and their officers took over the regulatory powers of five medieval manors; all agriculture, draining and highways, the town boat, windmills and bird-scarers came under their scrutiny. Archdeacon Cunningham saw in this the preparatory school of American democracy.

5
VERNACULAR HOUSES

The ordinary early medieval houses of the Dark Ages that have been examined by the archaeologists at North Elmham and West Stow have all vanished. At West Stow (*see* page 108), a very serious attempt has been made to reconstruct pioneer houses, following as exactly as possible the structure deduced by the archaeologist from such clues as could be found. Much of the process of reconstruction from this kind of information must be guess-work, but at West Stow the guesses are very well-informed and highly intelligent. At least at West Stow we can get an idea of the sizes of dwellings.

In the period for which standing houses remain in some numbers, structures can be examined as well as plans and we can begin to follow sequences and types. It is also sometimes possible to see alterations and so infer how the original features appeared with a great deal more reliability than one can from archaeological remains which are little more than discolourations in the soil. From the 1530s onwards and for two centuries or more, it is often possible to see in many places something of the house and its household from 'probate inventories'. These were required when anyone with property to be inherited died. Before Probate or Letters of Administration would be granted, two 'honest neighbours' had to produce a list of all the movable property along with a valuation. Frequently they made the list as they went around the house, listing the items room by room. When an inventory is completely specific in this way, it gives a verbal snapshot of the house as it was used on the day when the owner died.

LOCAL MATERIALS

Local house styles were based on the use of local materials. The region as a whole was short of good limestone or sandstone even for its churches, and lesser houses could be spared very little such stone, if any. The great exception to this lack of stone was flint, which in coastal zones was often freely available as large beach pebbles, or elsewhere, as stones turned up by the plough in the topsoil on the chalk. At the Crowland manor of Cottenham in the mid-1450s, payments were made for collecting stones in the fields and also stones from an old well to build a 'kilnhouse'. Glacial erratics dumped by the ice sheets and other stones from the fields, and sometimes even lumps of chalk clunch, were used for plinths before bricks were used; even clunch chimneys are fairly common.

Near to the coast, the abundance of flint is most evident as walling material, with

A house has a history rather than a date. Both of these timber-framed houses have features from the fifteenth century, and later modifications. The so-called 'Plague House' at Landbeach in Cambridgeshire (right), a substantial village house, has a more rustic feel than that at Kersey in Suffolk (below) where wealth flowed with the prosperity of the late medieval weaving of woollen cloth

the more expensive brick being used for the quoins, door and window openings and fireplaces.

For roofing domestic buildings, thatch becomes more predominant the further we go back. It was very widely used for churches: of the survivors, two thatched church roofs are quite close to each other at Rampton and Longstanton in Cambridgeshire and there is a real gem at Woodbastwick in the Norfolk Broads. For preference, the local reed was used if a fen was nearby, and elsewhere wheatstraw was favoured. Roof ridges were made with sedge when it was available while especially stout reeds from some parts of the Fen like Willingham in Cambridgeshire were used as a base for laying plaster to form ceilings or walls, and these were known as 'watling-reeds'.

The bulk of the medieval and seventeenth- and eighteenth-century ordinary houses in East Anglia were timber-framed. For preference, the timber was oak, although elm, sweet chestnut, ash and various soft-woods can sometimes be found as newel-posts in staircase towers, or main ceiling-beams; imported pine sometimes occurs. Hazel and ash were used in walling as a wattle base for plaster.

Brick for humble houses was manufactured and used in the region by the sixteenth century. It can still be seen in plinths, chimneys, and the filling of the timber frames known as 'brick nogging'. The latter was often put into houses when already old and weathered, and may thus give a deceptive appearance of the age of the dwelling. There are some fine examples in very warm pink brick in Lavenham, and also in nearby villages across the Essex border.

CLASSIFICATION OF PLANS

The Royal Commission on Historical Monuments has spent many patient years amassing analytical information about Cambridgeshire vernacular houses, and in its two volumes on *West Cambridgeshire* and *North-East Cambridgeshire* the researchers produced schemes of classification for types of vernacular houses. These plans, though heavily based on Cambridgeshire, are prevalent in the rest of East Anglia. Town plans are less clear at the moment, although the publication of the material gathered by the Norwich Survey is likely to transform the position.

East Anglia has some strong local characteristics, as is to be expected in vernacular style. Some of these are being interpreted as phases of development which appear to be 'syncopated' with pioneering advances or lags in particular areas, but the effort to build all the variations into a general scheme of development, driven by social and economic courses, does not seem to have been accepted. Nor has more investigation changed the picture. Cruck constructions were common in the Midlands, north and west but they still appear to be virtually absent from East Anglia where box-frame building reigns supreme. Crucks are pairs of 'A'-shaped curved timbers, which splay outwards at the base and are pegged near to the top to support the ridge-pole and the weight of the roof. In the box-frame system, heavy posts at the corner of each bay are held square by substantial tie-beams which prevent the weight of the roof from pushing the walls outwards.

Another very useful difference in constructional method in East Anglia is that old roofs have no ridge-piece. If an East Anglian roof has a ridge-piece, then the roof cannot date from before the eighteenth century. Instead, with the East Anglian box-frame

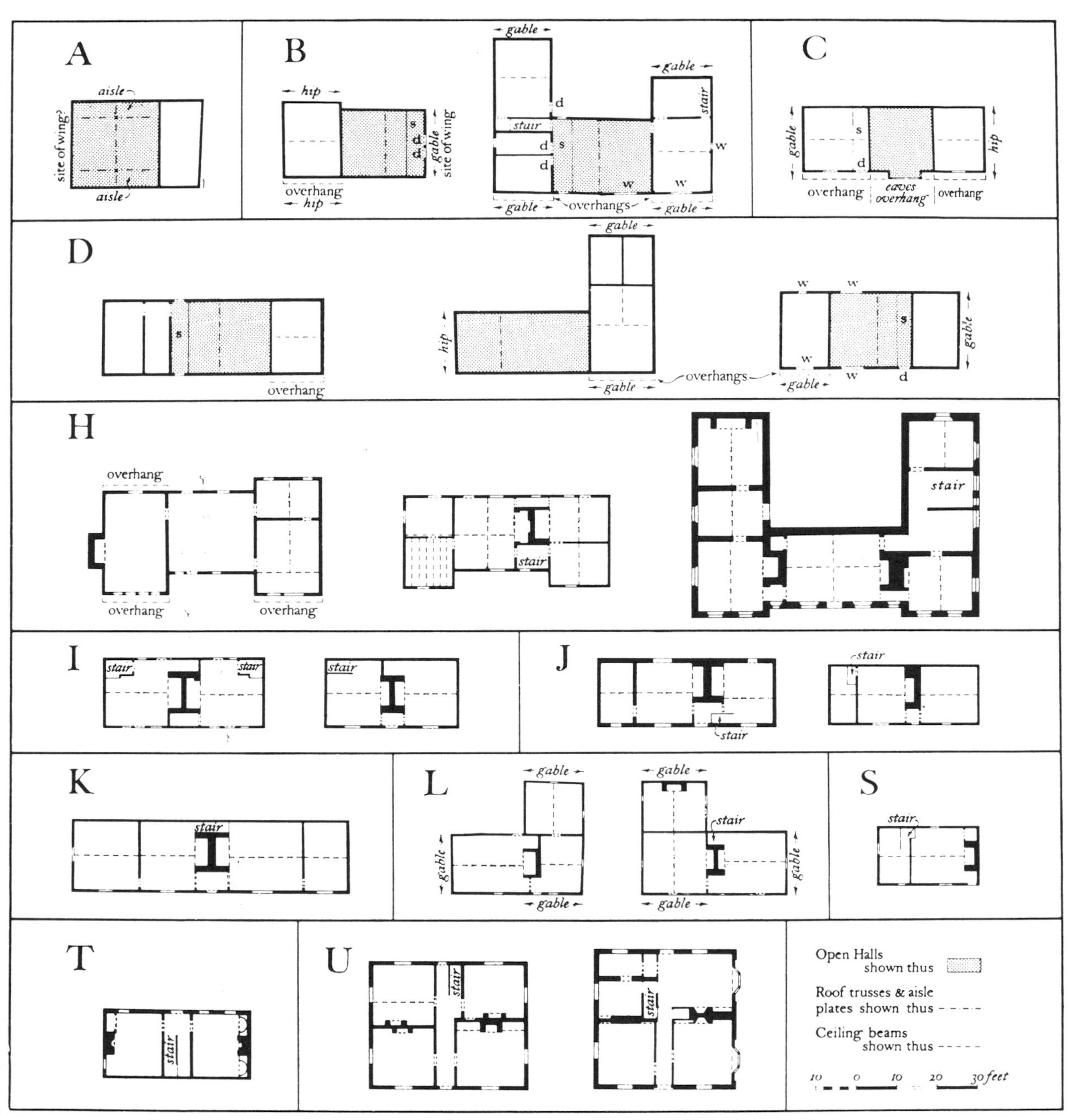

FIG. 11: CLASSIFICATION OF HOUSES

The diagrams illustrating types of houses are based upon existing houses in west Cambridgeshire, but they are schematic in so far as later additions have been omitted. In Classes A to D, door and window openings which are known to be coeval with the building are indicated by 'd' and 'w' respectively, and the position of screens passages, whether existing or inferred, by 's'. In the walls shown without openings, the original features are not traceable.

The following houses have been used as the basis for the diagrams:

Class: A. Barrington; B, Comberton, Croxton; C, Barrington; D, Eltisley, Haslingfield, Eltisley; H, Gamlingay, Great Eversden, Elsworth; I, Gamlingay, Bourn; J, Gamlingay, Elsworth; K, Elsworth; L, Elsworth, Toft; S, Barrington; U, Little Everden, Barrington (TAKEN FROM ROYAL COMMISSION ON HISTORICAL MONUMENTS *WEST CAMBRIDGESHIRE*)

The 'Old Barge' in Norwich shown as it was when it was divided into three – pub, vicarage and butcher's shop. In process of restoration, it appears to have been mainly a very large warehouse and display area for goods. However, the delicately-carved and painted dragon in the spandrel suggests it must have been built for something more than a simple store. The near end had once been a hall house of the fourteenth century at right-angles to the road, running down towards the river. The finely-carved screen of the earlier house is still in place

Edgar's Farm House, now re-erected at the Museum of East Anglian Life, offers a good opportunity to inspect an early fourteenth-century aisled hall house with a crown-post roof, generously carved and moulded

construction, pairs of rafters are half-lapped at the top and pegged. To give the ensemble more rigidity, it was usual to fit wind-braces, curved flat timbers that run from the principal rafters to the purlin (the long longitudinal timber that connects each couple of rafters to the others).

Another difference between East Anglia and western counties lies in the more elaborate, and probably socially superior, roof structures. The king-post is a feature that belongs outside East Anglia: it is a vertical post, often decorated with moulded capital and base and it runs from the tie-beam and ends at the ridge. Usually two curved braces connect it to the ridge purlin, and often two others connect it to the principal rafters. The East Anglian crown-post is shorter and, instead of rising to the ridge, it stops at a high collar to which it sends out curved braces. Its other two braces run to a crown purlin which lies along the centres of the collar.

An East Anglian crown-post that has been preserved and re-erected can be seen in Edgar's Farm House at the Museum of East Anglian Life. This is an 'aisled hall' of the fourteenth century, and is one of the earlier types of building to use this feature; the whole structure is handsomely decorated with mouldings, and is built of substantial, high-quality timbers. It was obviously meant to be seen by visitors and to impress by its quality.

An East Anglian feature almost confined to the southern part of the region, south

RIGHT AND ABOVE: *This house at Clare shows good examples of 'pargetting', a feature typical of southern East Anglia: externally it is decorated with raised panels, sometimes including plant motifs*

Rows of cottages like this one at Ludham often turn out, on close examination, to have a history of extension, followed by sub-division in times of population pressure, and still later restoration to larger units once more. The axial chimney suggests that the building has an interesting past

Fig. 12: A SURVIVOR FROM THE EARLY SEVENTEENTH CENTURY
This is the most frequently surviving type of house from the Great Rebuilding (Class J) and is described below.

Cambridgeshire and Suffolk, and shared with adjacent parts of Essex, is 'pargetting'. This is the decorative treatment of the external plaster of houses. A common pattern involved dividing the surface into rectangular panels by shallow, broad channels; each panel was then decorated. Sometimes each was simply filled with an elementary pattern repeated over and over, such as quadrants of combed marks; sometimes simple geometric patterns were pressed on again and again with wooden moulds, but sometimes one or more of the panels was decorated with elaborate realistic designs, cornucopias, flowers and other motifs. The priest's house at Clare may be the best example.

The great divide in vernacular architecture came with the arrival of the chimney, allowing the installation of a ceiling over the ground floor with space made available for new rooms above. Before the Reformation, to take a well-known approximation for a date, the normal East Anglian house had its main room or 'hall' open to the rafters. The change, with smoke going out through a chimney instead of swirling around the hall until it found its escape through a louvre, perhaps with a smoke bay to help, began the revolution in domestic comfort which transformed the house unequivocally into a home. The probate inventories of the time show a relatively rapid increase in the use of furniture which hitherto had been sparse. This seems to have taken place over a couple of generations in a once-and-for-all fashion, compared with which no other period can quite match the rise in domestic comfort until the electric revolution.

Vernacular house types fall into two broad families. The first and smaller, perhaps more 'peasant-like', is seen where the rooms are arranged in line, with a straight roof ridge over all. These are to be found in two-, three-, and four-roomed versions which fit in with the Royal Commission's plans I, J and K (the plans are really just a kind of short-hand to enable references to be made without tiresome repetition). These are the fully developed seventeenth-century patterns, built or modified up to the new standards of the Great Rebuilding in Cambridgeshire most frequently in the generation before the Civil War – although the real peak of building activity may well be rather earlier as there seem to be technical reasons why the Royal Commission's dates tend to be later.

These types of house are revealed by an axial chimney that has its long side running along the ridge and not through it. The door is normally directly in line with the chimney so that it opens into a small 'baffle entry' with progress ahead being blocked by the brick side of the chimney while doors opening right and left lead one into the parlour and hall. In the dominant type of this period, the three-celled house or the Royal Commission's type J, the lack of symmetry resulting from door and chimney being placed one-third of the way along the ridge makes survivals from this pre-Civil War period very obvious.

It is more difficult to distinguish earlier houses especially as any medieval survivors will usually have been modified to post-Reformation and seventeenth-century standards, and tell-tale detail is often masked by plaster. Roofs, although they are the most likely part of the main structure to have been renewed after neglect, are still the most promising places where evidence of medieval arrangements may have been preserved. Soot on roof-timbers betraying an old open hall is a very common first hint. Other constructional details may also point to the former existence of a hall that was open to the rafters, the sign of the older house: as has already been said, the presence of an integral ridge-piece will certainly disqualify it from the more venerable categories; trimmers, where a pair of rafters have been shortened to allow a smoke louvre to be fitted, are a good symptom of a medieval roof; and inserted ceilings are often betrayed by short triangular fillets nailed onto the ends of the joints to lengthen them, which got over the difficulty of putting them into a wall already standing. The discovery of blocked unglazed windows behind a ceiling and floor can be quite secure evidence of later ceiling insertion. One of the best indications is a medieval hearth *in situ*, with burnt earth and hearth stones. But if one of these is discovered when lowering or damp-proofing a floor, it will have been destroyed in the process for ever.

If such houses, dating from the late Middle Ages, can be discovered under their disguises of more recent years, the peasant houses of the earlier Middle Ages can only be envisaged from their archaeological remains. By the thirteenth century, the pattern found at West Stow, with loose and scattered clusters of single-roomed huts grouped around larger halls, had vanished. Archaeologists have come to expect peasants' houses of this post-Norman period to be two-roomed, and the excavations also suggest that such insubstantial houses were re-built about once in each generation.

Documentary evidence suggests something more complex. Peasants' retirement arrangements which, from as early as the thirteenth century, were supposed to be reserved in a third of a house for the old couple, sometimes mention two or more reserved rooms; in one case, a new kitchen was built when two women could not agree. Perhaps the distinction between house-rooms and sheds was changeable? Perhaps the rebuilding in each generation was sometimes supplementary and temporary? However, the documents usually give us only enough information to speculate, not to prove. For instance, when, in 1353, John Pepys of Cottenham, along with his two sons John and William, bought the lease of a ten-acre plot for twelve years, one of the conditions was that he had to build a complete house eighteen feet by forty. Could these be the external dimensions of a standard two-bay/two-room house with each room a rod each way inside? The court at which this was registered would have known. We do not.

In the late eighteenth and early nineteenth centuries, population rose rapidly. Some cottages were built for the families of agricultural labourers. Some labourers, with help from their friends, built cottages for themselves out of materials like clay bat (large building blocks of clay tempered with chopped straw, not dissimilar in essence from west country cob). But many of the families were housed by sub-dividing peasant houses, or by repartitioning the large old farmsteads which had been forsaken as the more prosperous farmers moved out to settle at the heart of their lands after the Parliamentary Enclosure of the village fields. The two-celled and the four-celled houses could be divided at the back-to-back hearths, leaving a heated room in each house. Similarly, the three-celled house could be made to yield a two-roomed (one up, one down) and a four-roomed cottage (two up, two down) with a heated room in each.

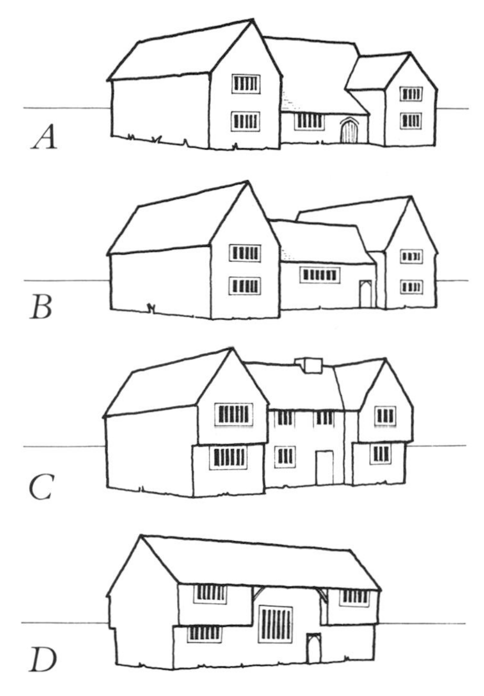

FIG. 13: THE DEVELOPMENT OF THE DOUBLE-FRONTED HOUSE
This type of house shows very characteristic changes through the centuries.
A. The aisled hall with cross-wings is a very early form which ceased to be fashionable in the fourteenth century.
B. A good many of this type of house survive from the fifteenth century. The central range is still a hall open to the roof, but without aisles.
C. The pseudo hall and cross-wings, where the central range was of two storeys, was typical of the form the double-fronted house took in the Great Rebuilding.
D. The so-called Wealden House has jetties on the end ranges, and braces hold the timber that carries the roof in front of the hall. Most common in Kent and Sussex, there are plenty still to be found in East Anglia.

But here the sub-divisions had to end unless a new chimney and hearth were added. This could be accomplished by adding a small square brick stack on to the gable end of a former three-celled house, or to each gable of an old four-celled house. When such houses have been restored to their original state as one dwelling, the small added chimneys may still survive, sealed off, to tell of the house's complicated history.

The other main family of types of vernacular houses in East Anglia are the double-fronted kinds, the hall and cross-wings house and its successors. This consisted of three similar units to those of the class J in-line house and its predecessors, but the components were arranged differently. The two outer units, the cross-wings, have their axes at right-angles to that of the hall range in the middle. Such double-fronted houses are often larger and have superior decorative treatment than the simpler house with a continuous ridge over the three cells.

There is a well-known hybrid type which has a straight ridge over the three units, but often with hipped ends to the roof. The upper storey projects with overhangs at the front on the two outer units, and a plate carrying the eaves straight across is supported by curved brackets in the centre section where the roof stands. The door and chimney are usually in line at the end of the hall. This is known as the 'Wealden house', but it is found far beyond the Weald and many specimens can still be found in East Anglia, including several village inns. There is an interesting one at New Buckenham – *see* p. 80.

The earliest form of hall and cross-wing house had an aisled hall. This form which is reminiscent of the naves and aisles of a church seems to have reached the peasantry after it was disappearing from aristocratic houses. Humbler versions of the aisled hall began in the thirteenth century but fell out of fashion during the course of the fourteenth. There are still a few 'aisled halls' standing (the so-called Edgar's Farm House is one of the best surviving examples), and previously unknown ones can still be discovered. Only last year, one of the authors – Jack Ravensdale – gained access to the roof of a Cambridgeshire house which for seventeen years he had suspected of being an aisled hall. There was a very early crown-post truss with moulded capital and base, and an aisle-post with a moulded capital was found *in situ* under the stairs.

This public house on the green at Barrington in Cambridgeshire is a good example of a house type more commonly found in Kent and Sussex, the 'Wealden House'. The two end bays have jetties although the whole is under a single straight ridge. Between the jetties, the hall range sits back, and the roof is carried on a wall plate held in front of the wall by curved braces. This often has a hipped roof, but here one end is hipped and one gabled

---

What aroused suspicion that this was an aisled hall was the way in which the roof over the central (hall) section came down to just above head height, typical of the 'cat-slide' roofs which often reveal aisled halls. The date of this hall, Ryder's Farm at Swavesey near Godmanchester, would be between 1280 and 1310 so that it is a very old dwelling indeed.

The next member of this family of house patterns is the open hall without aisles, and it generally has cross-wings: Emplins Farm at Gamlingay in Cambridgeshire is a good example. Survivors date mainly from the fifteenth century. As with other variants in the group of double-fronted houses, it may have lost, or perhaps only ever had, one cross-wing, so the plan form may be shaped like an 'L' or ' T' instead of 'E' or 'H'.

The final type is met in examples where the middle range is multi-storey and thus

ABOVE: *This house in Kersey has the typical appearance of a house built or modernised after the Reformation with a two-storey range in the middle*

BELOW: *Ryder's Farm at Swavesey in Cambridge was suspected of being a very early house because of the long 'cat-slide' roof over the middle range. After a wait of seventeen years, access to the roof revealed a moulded crown post and aisle posts typical of the decades just before or after 1300*

its ground floor is thought of as a pseudo-hall: Gamlingay again has a fine example in Merton Manor Farm. Here the chimney (and this is often true of the earlier types where a chimney has been inserted) is at the junction of the hall and cross-wing, with the door directly in line beneath it to produce the 'baffle-entry' again (page 121). Such houses were still being built at the beginning of the eighteenth century, but by then they presented a symmetrical elevation, in keeping with the current fashions. The door and chimney were placed centrally.

Where a chimney was to be inserted in an existing hall-house there was a choice. At the lower end of the hall and leading to the kitchen would be a screens passage (so called because a light partition across the width of the hall created a passage), and the chimney and fireplace could be inserted against the screen. Alternatively, in

Although a town house of very wealthy people and using a large amount of stone and brick, Wensum House in Norwich shares some of its pattern of development with the humbler house in Kersey. The left-hand wing was originally built in the 12th century by Jurnet the Jew, whose son became the richest man in England. It is still over a vaulted Norman undercroft, but the Paston family reduced it to a crosswing, building the present two-storey range in the centre to include a new hall with glazed windows

the rather 'superior' dwellings, the upper end of the hall might be chosen for the fireplace and back-to-back hearths in the hall and parlour could be installed together. When the lower end of the hall had been chosen, a second hearth and a second heated room could be created at the back of the first fireplace at the cost of dispensing with the screens passage. This process is still visible sometimes in the straight joint left where the second chimney has been added on the back of the first. The first part of the house to be lofted over to create an upper floor seems in most cases to have been the servery end, and here it may be possible to find traces of a former ladder-like stair with a trap-door giving access to the upper level.

Corresponding to the dominance of the J plan in the vernacular houses of the region are the room names in the probate inventories: 'Parlour', 'Hall', 'Kitchen' and the 'Chamber'. Favourite names can vary from place to place and even more in time. The greatest change can be seen in the 'hall', which starts off in the earlier Middle Ages encompassing the whole house, and develops as a multi-purpose living-room which slowly loses its functions and prominence as it degenerates to end as the space behind the front door which we still call a hall. 'Chamber' usually means an upstairs room, and very often a bedroom, but a downstairs sleeping room may still be called a 'chamber' or a 'parlour'. In the first generation of the fully two-storey house, the chambers upstairs were often used for junk or servants' accommodation. The master continued to sleep in the parlour or even the hall, conveniently heated by its fireplace. Ursula Priestley and P.J. Corfield, investigating the probate inventories for Norwich, found the term 'great chamber' being used for a dining-room which was usually located upstairs.

In the city itself, the houses were much more complicated, and the general movement away from types based on the medieval hall-house was completed probably a generation before this took place in the countryside where the physical traces of the change are so much more visible in old dwellings enduring in the villages.

The change from the seventeenth-century pattern probably started earlier in the east of the area, possibly due to the availability of flint in Norfolk. Gable end chimneys, which ousted the axial chimney, need to be set in something more substantial than a stud-work end wall. According to Peter Eden, the adoption of stone or brick gable end walls probably marks the beginning of the change to new materials.

6

STRONGHOLDS AND MANSIONS

Castles came to England from France with, or perhaps just before, the Norman Conquest. The commonest form of Norman castle, the motte and bailey of earthworks crowned by a timber palisade, provided a cheap, strongpoint and safe base for William the Conqueror's army of occupation. With a plentiful supply of labour, composed either of prisoners or of pressed Saxon peasants, an effective motte and bailey could be erected in a week, even up to the standard and scale of the royal campaign castles. Many baronial castles were much smaller, and a good example of one of these is at Mileham in Norfolk. Time has taken away its timber furnishings – the palisade around the bailey, the gates and defended drawbridges, and the wooden tower on stilts that surmounted it all. It requires an effort of imagination to picture such a castle as it once was, and to realise that then it was strong.

CASTLE ACRE

What emerges clearly from the study of these smaller castles is that they were only regarded as desirable residences in those first few years after the Conquest, when every Norman needed to guard his back at all times. Even at the opposite extreme, a castle like Castle Acre that was spacious, well built and high, and which used a good deal of masonry in its walls, had more suitable domestic peace-time accommodation in its inner bailey than in the stone-building of the keep. Here, in the years since it came under the care of the DoE, regular cropping by goats and mowing have revealed ever more clearly the outlines of the foundations of a great hall, and those of other rooms, possibly the solar, the detached kitchen, and so on. There was obviously a much more acceptable standard of comfort at Castle Acre than at the petty baron's motte and bailey.

In spite of this, to turn it into a permanent residence, much more substantial building was needed. Originally, the main strongpoint appears to have been an enormous ring bank or 'ring-motte'. At the top of this was built a circular flint masonry wall, with arrow slits in its thickness, and surmounted by a sentry walk. Some signs of crenellations remain. The moat is deep, the sloping sides of the mound very steep and the girdling flint wall (supported by its shadow Norman buttresses with good ashlar corners) is sheer. Inside, not yet fully excavated, is a massive rectangular keep. This has proved to be a most extraordinary feature: originally a residential stone house of two ranges, it was subsequently converted into a keep by the massive addition of stone to the *inside* of the walls.

At the junction of the moat and the ring-motte, the remains of a well-built gatehouse, of good, neatly-cut limestone, has emerged from the excavations. The inner bailey is formed by two massive ramparts – originally with masonry walls on top – which run parallel down the slope until closed by another stone wall with a postern gate set on the edge of what is virtually a cliff above the swampy flood plain of the River Nar.

The north-east corner has an earthwork which stands detached and clear of the ring-motte. This was once considered to be Roman but, in spite of its appearance, opinion has changed since no substantial finds of Roman material have been made here. Excavation has shown it to be a barbican entrance. The outer bailey, with its ramparts and twin-towered gatehouse, embraces the rest of the little town. In scale, strength and impressiveness this castle was worthy of one of William I's most important tenants-in-chief, William de Warenne, who founded the Cluniac Priory at Castle Acre at the same time.

NORWICH CASTLE

Norwich was a royal castle and very grand. The mound, from which the keep dominates the new French market that was set up by the Normans, was given its imposing scale by heightening a natural hill and digging a deep ditch around it. This formed

The defences of Castle Acre were very elaborate. As well as the motte surmounted by a shell keep seen here, there was a rectangular stone keep inside reinforcing an earlier house and an inner and an outer bailey, the later enclosing the town

The Norman market-place in Norwich was dominated by the Norman castle

---

the inner bailey and, in due course, the surrounding outer bailey became a cattle market in more peaceful times and, finally, a car park.

What survives of the castle today is deceptive. Neglect, fire and other disasters reduced the original walls to their rubble cores. A period of service as a gaol added crenellated granite walls at the rear of the building. What is said to have been an accurate Victorian restoration of the Norman masonry by Salvin in the 1830s is very hard to accept as such because of the quantity and minute exactitude of decoration on the outside of what was still, a century after the Conquest, a building made for war. The Bath stone used for the facing by the Victorians lends an unreal fineness to the finish: an old print which shows the lower stage in flint looks much more convincing.

The old interior has gone. It was originally entered, as was usually the case, at the first-floor level by stairs under a fore-building on the outside of the main keep. The floors were divided by a solid wall, not by the present museum's pillars, and the two halls on the principal floor were known as the Soldiers' and the Knights' Halls. It is possible to locate the kitchen and chapel from fragments that remain in the walls, but not much else. If virtually all original detail has gone, its scale and site still make Norwich Castle very convincing as the Norman regional headquarters of a completely militarised society. Today, it is put to better use. It houses one of the museums of Norwich's remarkable Museums Service, including an art gallery which contains among its treasures the world's finest collection of the East Anglian School of water-colourists, the most quintessentially English of all painting techniques.

WEETING CASTLE

At Weeting, near Grimes Graves on the edge of the Breckland, is an interesting small variation on the stronghold theme: it is in the form of a stone castle which was already more of a defensive house than a fortress. Not yet fully explored and expounded, it appears strangely out of time. Probably of the late twelfth century, it has a square moat like many later and many lesser dwelling-houses. The Norman work seems very clear in the part that was probably the crypt of a great hall. At either end of the great hall is a wing, one being three-storeyed and surviving much more completely than the other remnants of the castle. But there are no signs of any surrounding curtain wall which one might expect at a stronghold of this period.

NEW BUCKENHAM

The castle at New Buckenham was a private castle, built about 1140 or earlier. Its ring-motte, nearly 400 feet in diameter, invites comparison with Castle Rising and Castle Acre, and all three are connected with planned towns.

New Buckenham and Castle Rising were built and held by the Daubigny family, but as well as the shared similarities, each has remarkable differences from the others. The astonishing thing about New Buckenham is the cylindrical keep, placed eccentrically in the ring-motte near the gatehouse. Originally about 20 ft higher, it appears to be the first round keep to be built in England. But there is no sign of the original entrance, forebuildings, or stairs and staircase tower. The keep seems completely unbuttressed, and the shape may be due to the same reason as the round towers of so many East Anglian churches: the need to make a strong structure with little stone other than the local flint. At Castle Acre, the walls around the ring-motte are strengthened by shallow Norman buttresses, but even these required a quantity of good limestone for their quoins.

The ring-motte was heightened at some stage in the history of all three castles. At Buckenham, this demanded the construction of a new gate, and this was placed on the opposite side from the keep. A good deal of masonry of this second gatehouse, which operated a draw-bridge over the wide, wet moat, remains. The bank runs very steeply for 40 ft from the water to the rampart walk. It may have had a masonry wall on top of the ring-motte, as the Acre and Rising castles did. Very much smaller banks and ditches formed baileys on the eastern side linking up with the old town ditch on the south-west.

The castle appears to have withstood siege in the Barons' Wars in the 1260s and, in 1461, Alice Knyvett, left in charge during her husband's absence, was able to defy the king's officers who came to seize it. In the Civil War, the castle was slighted. Some ten years before, the current owner mentioned a steel mill in the granary there. This seems to reveal the use to which the keep had been put, and the entrance broken into the basement probably dates from this period of use. There still remains some unexplored brickwork and masonry in the inner bailey; possibly they are from a

This round tower, set eccentrically within the circular rampart at New Buckenham, may be the first circular tower-keep in the country

dwelling-house which seems to have existed there until the Civil War.

William Daubigny II, the Lord of Buckenham – which was one of the most important baronial holdings in Norfolk – had advanced the family fortunes and married the queen, the widow of Henry I. His father founded the Benedictine Priory at Wymondham, while William himself founded the Augustinian Priory at Old Buckenham.

CASTLE RISING

The son replaced his father's stronghold at Old Buckenham Castle with New Buckenham Castle, and also built the impressive castle at Rising, moving the township and church to do so. Both for the massive quality of its earthworks, and the elaborate, fine decoration of the stonework, Castle Rising can be rivalled only by the most splendid castles such as Norwich as it once was. Only a king could surpass Daubigny II: in the disruptive Anarchy (of King Stephen's reign 1135–54) scarcely even a king could presume to do so. The walls of the large oval inner bailey at Castle Rising reach 60 ft above the bottom of the ditch. They seem to have been raised in height (as also at New Buckenham) about 1200. Formerly the walls would have been much more obviously dominated by the keep. Two other outer baileys form rectangles east and west, with walls of lesser height. The stone keep which is massive, broader than it

A view of the Norman keep through the Norman gateway at Castle Rising

LEFT: *The stairs inside the fore-building on the keep at Castle Rising gave the only access, and this was at first-floor level*

BELOW: *This late Saxon, or more probably early Norman church, buried by the rampart at Castle Rising, is now thought to have been a Norman parish church destroyed by the construction of the castle*

is tall and of a type known as a 'hall keep', is superb. As well as having lavishly carved decoration, it has lavish accommodation for a donjon, two great halls and two great chambers as well as basement stores, kitchen, service rooms and chapels. The great hall at first-floor level is reached by a massive stone staircase housed in a forebuilding. As well as the keep, the inner bailey would have contained all the buildings necessary for maintaining several households. Some of these can still be seen in ruins in eighteenth-century prints, though only earthworks are now visible on the site.

In the bailey bank on the north are the excavated remains of an old church. Some herring-bone work in the nave once led people to believe the church was Saxon, but this in fact belongs to a Tudor fireplace, inserted when the floor level was much higher. The church is now reckoned to be post-Conquest, and was the parish church until the new castle was built. Then the church was rebuilt outside the walls along with the houses on the site, while the new castle had its own internal chapel. The earliest phases seen in the present Norman parish church in the village nearby would fit in with this explanation.

Near the gatehouse are remains of a repaired fourteenth-century brick and masonry wall, and what appear to be fragments of stone walls occur from time to time in the top of the bank of the inner bailey. Three mural towers seem to have once surmounted this wall.

Isabella, widow of Edward II and dowager queen, frequently stayed at Castle Rising, and the repairs to the top stages of the keep probably date from her time there. The castle was set in defensive order again when it was in the hands of the Black Prince, and it is possible that the two very early cannon found there (and now in the Armoury of the Tower of London) date from his time.

The dominant theme of the late fifteenth-century and early sixteenth-century surveys is the state of 'evil repair' which seems to have become general and normal. By the last years of the reign of Queen Elizabeth I, the rabbits from the nearby warren had bred, invaded the ditches and banks, and threatened to collapse the walls by their mining – just as medieval sappers might have done.

ORFORD CASTLE

In the Middle Ages, fashions in building lordly residences, whether houses or castles, seem to have spread easily from the Continent to East Anglia. The royal castle at Orford, built 1165–7, marked the change from the square stone keep to stronger shapes. The weakness of the rectangular corner was its vulnerability to mining. Sappers would drive a tunnel under the foundations across a corner; when the pit-props were fired, the whole corner could collapse, and possibly bring down the entire edifice. The remains of Bungay Castle in Suffolk show this process in action: a mine had been ready when the castle was surrendered.

One of the first improvements in design to meet this weakness was illustrated by Orford. The keep here was built as an eighteen-sided polygon, but some of the advantage was lost by adding three square towers, to house the staircase and to serve as buttresses. This type of keep was soon to be rendered obsolete by the design of a circular keep at Conisborough in Yorkshire about fifteen years later.

FRAMLINGHAM CASTLE

At the accession of Henry II in 1154 there were no castles left in royal hands in Suffolk. The Bigod family, the Earls of Norfolk, were fast becoming overmighty subjects. But then in just three years, the king seized all four Bigod castles along with Eye in Suffolk and Norwich. In 1165 Framlingham and Bungay were restored to Bigod, but the king retained Walton and Thetford and began the building of Orford, probably as a foil to Framlingham. (It was at this time that Bigod built the recently mentioned rectangular keep at Bungay that was to prove vulnerable to mining in the next rebellion.) Framlingham castle at this stage had consisted of a motte and a bailey guarded by palisade and ditch and flanked by a mere produced by damming a stream. The castle was dismantled when it fell into royal hands between 1175 and 1177.

The reconstruction at Framlingham brought the greatest revolution in castle-building to East Anglia. Between 1190 and 1200, the great encircling curtain wall with its flanking towers was constructed. With this innovative design, cross-fire from the flanking towers would catch any attackers in enfilade at the bottom of the wall. The concept of the keep as the key strongpoint in the defence was giving way by this time to that of the tower-gatehouse. The entrance to any fortified place had always been a point of dangerous weakness and always required extra strength and elabora-

tion, while a curtain wall furnished with projecting mural towers could, if properly designed and built, remove the need for a central stronghold in the form of a keep.

FROM FORTRESS TO COUNTRY RESIDENCE

In East Anglia, the concentration on the gatehouse marks the beginnings of the shift from serious fortification to residence and display. The gatehouse, with its fancy crenellation and moat lingered on into the Tudor period as a decorative tradition and status symbol. The Edwardian concentric castle so popular in the Welsh campaigns passed East Anglia by: the area had no Beaumaris or Caerphilly. Instead East Anglia has Oxborough and the other red-brick gatehouses (*see* page 145), and the Cambridge colleges. The tradition of the tall strong tower, the donjon, lingers as Spenserian nostalgia. In East Anglia, the change coincides with the increased use of brick. The bank and moat of the castle dissolved into the unbanked, showy, but rather innocuous moat of the homestead. The knight's home had quietly undergone the same sort of change as the title knight itself. The age of Don Quixote and Falstaff had arrived.

One of the most important houses encapsulating this change is Little Wenham Hall in Suffolk. A brick house on flint foundations, its window openings and tracery betray its age: 1270–80. Its plan befits its date: the entrance is at first-floor level, and the undercroft is rib-vaulted with brick. It offers a very early example of the effects of civilising influences on the fortified house. The first-floor chapel and hall are in a clear line of descent from the Conqueror's Tower of London and its contemporaries. The house is still fortified, but its hall windows discard strength for light and elegance. Battlements set off the three roof levels, again using the old traditional elements for decoration following the severely practical dictates of defence.

From Little Wenham on, the story of the development of the English country house is very close to the story of the early use of brick. In the development of national style, East Anglia is important on both counts. Little Wenham was built of brick made in this country, but much early brick and many ideas on its use seem to have been imported from the Low Countries. East Anglia was receiving immigrants from that quarter as textile workers and the region was singularly well-placed to introduce the continental fashions. The Cistercians seem to have been early agents for importing the techniques for the making and laying of brick. In a countryside where good building stone could only be obtained from a distance, the extensive use of brick, strangely neglected since the Roman era, was only a matter of time. For major works, such as town walls, it provided an obvious source of strength in bonding the flint rubble, rather as centuries before the Romans had alternated brick courses with flints at Burgh Castle.

Norwich, Great Yarmouth and King's Lynn all used some brick in their walls, and the gates in Ipswich's old ditch and palisade defences were refurbished in brick in the fifteenth century. In order to create a strongpoint at the end of Norwich's defensive

---

OPPOSITE: *The new form of castle represented by Framlingham, which depended on curtain walls protected by flanking towers at regular intervals, had been introduced into England at Windsor and Dover. Modernisation of Framlingham on these lines reflects its great importance*

When the infertile Breckland sand was given over to the production of rabbits, warreners in fortified lodges were needed to guard against poachers. This one in Thetfort Warren is remarkably well preserved

ring, the astonishing Cow Tower was built entirely of brick about 1378. Completely circular, with worn crenellations and much bigger than the wall towers, it now rises sheer out of a meadow, with spiral staircases set in the 11-ft thick walls.

Brick was used entirely in the building of the fortified Caister Castle. This was built by the old war horse Sir John Fastolf in 1432–6, and it remained a family residence for almost a century and a half. There are fireplaces on all floors except the top, and so it was obviously designed as a residence – but as a residence during the period of gang-warfare of the fifteenth century. Under Fastolf's command, it successfully resisted a French raid, but later, and without a proper garrison, it was no match for Howard's siege guns. Some of the defenders resisted the Duke of Norfolk's forces for five weeks in 1469, only surrendering when food and gunpowder were exhausted.

Genuinely defensive houses were built after this period only in places of special need. In Scottish Border country, the disorders from cattle-rustling produced a type of defensive house to meet its own local needs. This 'bastle' house, had two storeys, the upper for people and the lower for cattle. Although lacking cattle thieves, East Anglia had its poachers – and they were dangerous enough. After the Black Death when population pressure and buoyant markets for grain had both gone, the sandy soil, so light that it blew and engulfed villages and fields, was of little commercial use except for raising rabbits. Much of the countryside near Thetford and Brandon is divided into warrens as described on page 212. If the rabbit was a valuable product for the monks and other landowners, it was valuable for poachers, too. Poachers' ways of dealing with an isolated warrener in the fifteenth century would hardly bear contemplation.

Thetford Warren Lodge stands in isolation, a two-storey stone house, with a garderobe, and a first-floor fireplace and chimney as concessions to comfort, but defensible against a gang, if not an army. Its present surroundings in a dark and dingy Forestry Commission plantation of conifers should not deceive us. In the old open Breckland landscape, its upper storey would have afforded an all-round view over a considerable distance and given an open field of fire.

OXBURGH HALL

By the time that Oxburgh Hall was built in 1482, residential considerations had emerged victorious over defensive factors in the design of big houses. Tradition has it that Henry VII visited Oxborough, and if he did he would have seen a great gate very much as it appears today. The colour of the brick, the delicate mouldings, the width of the moat, the perfect proportions, and indeed the whole setting with its formal

Oxburgh Hall has what is probably the best of all the early Tudor brick gatehouses. It is a country house rather than a fortress, but its wide moat and strong walls were deterrents to bands of thieves

and its informal gardens, must make this a favourite among all the superb country houses that Norfolk offers. The seven tiers of the rubbed brickwork on the gatehouse seem exactly right, whereas often in this period gatehouses of this kind can be over-weening and too tall, or squat and heavy. The great hall and some other parts of this square house have been demolished, but members of the family who acquired the original licence to crenellate still live there: the Bedingfields survived. Having lived through the fifteenth century in disorderly Norfolk, they could probably survive anything.

The alleged royal visitor, Henry VII, preferred not to spend his own resources on defence. His more flamboyant son probably had more trouble over defence expenditure than wives, but his chains of coastal castles did not extend north to the East Anglian coast. These castles were the last castles proper to be built and they were concerned with foreign invasion threats rather than internal conflicts since the Tudors had put a stop to such dangerous squabbles within the nation.

'FORTRESS ENGLAND'

When a final show-down with Napoleon was looming, a similar chain of defences, the Martello Towers, did embrace the Suffolk coast, reaching as far north as Slaughden, near Aldeburgh, where the largest of these towers was built. Visually, the contribution

The last of the many: the American Flying Fortress rests at Duxford Airfield, a reminder of the hundreds that often darkened East Anglian skies towards the end of World War II

to the landscape of these squat cylinders is not aesthetic, but just possibly nostalgic, as the remains of other people's wars can tend to be.

The crude little brick and concrete pill-boxes of World War II were mainly designed for local defence, and their siting indicates something about their own particular military landscape. Far too many still remain for them to be listed. Most of the nissen huts that were grouped in camps and dispersals, at gun-sites and training areas, have gone; most of the hangars have gone, although some farmers still maintain and use them.

World War II saw East Anglia converted into an unsinkable aircraft carrier. The first strike of the war was claimed by the Fairey Swordfish biplanes based at Bircham Newton in Norfolk, although others may also claim this honour. This was a grass airfield from World War I, with good peacetime living quarters. In 1939 there were nearly a hundred airfields in East Anglia, and during the course of the war this number went up to over seven hundred and fifty, and most of them had thick concrete runways, perimeter tracks, dispersals and campsites: an enormous construction job. Nearly forty years on, it seems impossible to recognise and remember the scale of the military works: roads stop in the middle of nowhere and what looks like a concrete taxi-track runs alongside a cornfield. There are now less than a hundred old airfields, and the sites of the others are difficult to recognise or remember. Gorse, heather and ling hide the remaining concrete in the heathlands, and in arable Norfolk most of the concrete was ripped up when the land was restored.

The operational military airfields of today are frightening in their size, the obvious power of their aircraft and the implied power of their weapons. But perhaps that should not surprise us after a glance back to the archaeology of the region so replete with the accoutrements of war, with finds of swords more common than ploughshares, and so much of the landscape a monument to human folly.

7
COUNTRY HOUSES

Being a region lying close to the capital and one endowed with good farmland and empty spaces, it is not surprising that East Anglia acquired an exceptional collection of great houses. The following examples reveal the story of the English country mansion.

MANNINGTON HALL

Oxborough Hall was discussed on page 139, at the conclusion of East Anglian developments of the castle and fortified house as it turns into mansion. But really the battle between security and opulence had already been won. By this time, Mannington, which is south-west of Cromer, represented the triumph of the claims of domestic comfort, blending materials and ideas, old and new – English brick and flint with just a touch of Italy in its terra cotta which is possibly among the earliest in the country. The owner gained a 'licence to crenellate' in 1450, but the house was never defended except by its highly ornamental moat.

The original plan is difficult to disentangle from later work, especially that perpetrated by the 2nd Earl of Orford who lived until 1898. There are architectural details which suggest that the great hall originally ran the entire height of the building, and that the whole layout was designed on traditional medieval lines, but much improved for comfort. A unique feature which Pevsner attributes to the Earl of Orford is a sequence of anti-feminist inscriptions in Gothic lettering on the front and rear walls. In spite of his classical interests, and whatever personal failure lay behind the inscriptions, the Earl satisfied the comfort-loving philosophy of a classicist in an exquisite example of the medieval tradition of the moated domestic house. It is still a house, and still exquisite; it is sometimes open by appointment.

MELFORD HALL

A century after Mannington, and seventy years after Oxborough, came Melford Hall in the heart of what had been prosperous, industrial Suffolk, the area of the cloth villages. It was built, just after the collapse of the export trade in broadcloth, not by a clothier but by a lawyer, Sir William Cordell, who had attained high office, becoming Solicitor-General, Speaker of the House of Commons and Master of the Rolls, in a career of public service under four Tudor monarchs. Its red brick is very typical of so many

This lovely red brick building probably looked even better before so many eighteenth-century window frames had been inserted, destroying the rhythms of the Gothic shapes. Melford Hall was built from profits of office rather than wool by Sir William Cordell a few years after the great wave of country house building that followed the Dissolution of the Monasteries

fine laymen's houses which were built in the reign of Elizabeth I on the site of old religious houses that had gone down in the Dissolution of the Monasteries. Sir William Cordell was able to carry out his designs on a grander scale than most of his contemporaries. It is a red-brick Elizabethan manor house, but was far more suitable for one of the highest officers of the Crown than the farmhouses which commonly answer to that description.

The most favoured Tudor house-plan resembled an 'H' and had an entrance porch in the main range, and cross-wings at either side projecting well forward. This is essentially only an enlargement of the commonest medieval plan for a modest country house, but the first breath of the Renaissance in England froze it into symmetry, with the porch in the centre, balanced bays on the façade and matching gables to the equal wings. The design at Melford Hall is practically a Platonic exercise in simple mathematical shapes. Octagonal turrets of varied girths have ogee caps while the cuboid shapes of the main range and the wings are picked up by the rectangular mullioned and transomed windows. Most of the classical forms are concentrated in the entrance. The two-storey porch has Doric and Ionic pilasters under a round shell, and has a semicircular top to the doorway. This is picked up by the round gable-end lights in the attics. Any uneasiness created by the design (apart from the way in which two-storeyed wings in the front became three at the rear) is due to the later insertion of tall sash windows, destroying the former rhythm. Yet similar new windows in the octagonal banqueting hall fit very happily.

The gatehouse is made of two matching lodges having polygonal turrets and lunettes which echo the entrance to the house. Although Victorian, they follow the earlier style and brickwork very well. Matching the brickwork, and probably once echoing the gatehouses, is the brick conduit, and the hall, gatehouse, conduit and other buildings at Long Melford including the school, hospital and church, join in a remarkable feast of English village landscape.

Now owned by the National Trust, the Hall is open at the usual times.

A few miles north of Melford Hall, but dated a generation later, is Kentwell Hall, again built in brick with stone transomed and mullioned windows; it is almost completely symmetrical in façade, with a pair of square towers turning into octagons, and again with ogee-shaped caps as at Melford and Madingley.

Kentwell is privately owned, and has its own opening times.

MADINGLEY HALL

Nonsuch, the vanished palace of Henry VIII, was just a generation old when Cordell was building at Melford. Sir John Hinde, serjeant-at-law, was only a few months ahead in his building of Madingley Hall in Cambridgeshire. Although he was a lawyer, he did very well from grazing sheep, illegally enclosing common ground in Cambridge, Cottenham, and other nearby villages.

Madingley was not a monastic site, indeed the old medieval manor house is still standing in the village which is just north-west of Cambridge, and on the left as one comes up the drive are earthworks, not from any 'bare, grey, ruined choirs', but from the main street, tofts and crofts, and house-platforms of the medieval village that was swept away to form the new park. The setting was completed by altering the boundary

The final embellishments on Hadleigh Deanery tower, which dates from the late fifteenth century, are the barley-sugar chimney stacks which were added early in the nineteenth century with further additions twenty years ago

---

to bring the pretty parish church inside the hall grounds. Major re-making of the landscape of the different vistas from the Hall has taken place several times. Capability Brown is among the landscape architects who have left their contributions. His work was fully mature when Dutch Elm Disease struck a few years ago. Fortunately, Madingley has a collection of magnificent full-grown specimen trees of other varieties.

Later alterations to the house have kept its asymmetry, and contain added medieval work including materials from St Etheldreda's redundant church brought to Madingley in 1588 by Sir Frances Hinde. The roof of the main east range is said to have come from St Etheldreda's also. Up in the loft, where the heavy mouldings of this false hammerbeam roof can be inspected, there is also a series of frescoes of hawking, hunting and bear-baiting scenes. Madingley cannot be accused of classical symmetry, even though it has later additions with Renaissance features.

The grounds of Madingley Hall are open to the public, but not the house itself.

In the period when the medieval tradition met the Renaissance, some of East Anglia's finest brickwork was laid to build gatehouses (*see also* page 137); sometimes they survive where the house has now gone. As brick was losing its reputation as an 'inferior' material, and becoming the fashionable material of the fifteenth century, the gatehouse – which had become the point of concentration for military power and strength in the castle – was retained in the plans of some superior domestic houses as it offered a great opportunity to make a powerful impression by virtue of its size and lavish decoration. It was a splendid status symbol in a status-conscious age. This was true for collegiate as well as private houses.

Hadleigh's Guildhall is a fine medieval building in a perfect setting. The upper floor is inserted, and a row of crown-posts grow out of its centre like a row of trees

---

A fine example is the Deanery gatetower at Hadleigh in Suffolk. It is situated in an enchanting setting alongside the green with the church, and opposite the three-storeyed guildhall with its double over-hang. It was built in 1495 by Archdeacon Pykenham.

CARDINAL COLLEGE, IPSWICH

A scaled-down version of an imposing gateway is the surviving gate of Cardinal College in Ipswich. Begun by Cardinal Wolsey, the college was never completed and this example was not intended as a main gate. Polygonal buttresses echo the polygonal towers of the larger structures. The door is under a four-centred arch of several receding orders, and above it in a rectangle is a coat of arms, surrounded by niches. On top there are the bases for pinnacles, now missing. As a lesser door, this is small and modest but, nevertheless, fine and it exploits the qualities of rubbed and cut brick. Again it seems to develop from extremely functional beginnings to a highly decorative degree of abstraction.

EAST BARSHAM

The best of all the red-brick Tudor houses in East Anglia is the private dwelling at East Barsham. Driving towards Walsingham from Fakenham, as the road bears left and starts to run downhill, the traveller at first may not believe his eyes. For a few moments before the solid fence obscures the view again and restores privacy, one glimpses a gatehouse and then a whole Tudor house, under a forest of tall barley-sugar chimneys and finials, all in delicious mellow red brick.

East Barsham marks the final triumph of the gatehouse as a decorative feature. It has a royal coat of arms in cut brick over the main entrance of the detached gatehouse, and another over the porch of the house. These are crucial for indicating the date of the building, since the greyhound as one of the royal supporters on the house, along with the griffin, has changed to become the lion in the gatehouse. The royal emblem changed in 1527, so the gatehouse post-dates that year and the porch precedes it.

East Barsham makes some use of flint to give a little decorative relief in colour and texture to the brick which, with its carving and moulding, has reached the decorative limits of the medium. Flint and stone are used in chequer panels on the porch buttresses. Some people have seen Italian influence in the heads in the decorative friezes of moulded brick, and in the terracotta windows. Pevsner in his *Buildings of England* does not.

Since the First World War, East Barsham has undergone several major, and fortunately sensitive restorations and for a time became the home of the famous pop-group, The Bee Gees.

KIRTLING TOWERS

Just inside Cambridgeshire, Kirtling Towers survives in its moated setting, but the house that went with it has gone. The present name, Kirtling Towers, is very appropriate, as the height of the polygonal turrets emphasises that this is a tower-house and not just a gateway. The way in which the oriel window in the second and third stories is crushed in between the turrets exaggerates the height compared with the breadth of the building. Where Barsham used a little stone and flint to add to its decorations, Kirtling uses blue brick in diaper patterns among the red. Italian features in the corbel under the oriel mark one of the first early touches of the Renaissance in the region.

The house and gardens are privately owned, and not open to the public.

ERWARTON HALL

The middle Tudor period has certainly left many monuments where brick is used as brick and not as a substitute for stone. One of the most remarkable, built in 1549, is the gatehouse of Erwarton Hall, itself a slightly later house. It lies west of Felixstowe on the Suffolk side of the Stour. It is built entirely of brick and the entrance is through a round arch and tunnel vault. There are four semi-circular gables, and round brick pinnacles stand on top of the round angle buttresses with others intermediate. The whole forms an astonishing piece of abstract sculpture.

From gatehouses to residences proper. The climax of the tradition developed and handed on from the Tudor period is Blickling Hall which is the first of many such beautiful houses in East Anglia.

BLICKLING HALL

The Hall, situated near Aylsham north of Norwich, is perhaps the most attractive house in the whole of East Anglia. The approach is down immaculate gravel drives between lavishly wide, perfect lawns, flanked by the tallest of yew hedges, with the shaped gables of the buildings at the side taken up by the red and white of the brick and stone of the much higher, shaped gables of the house. After this, it is difficult to be critical, or even to disentangle much of the complex building history. The other garden walks here rival, if not surpass, the first.

Begun in 1616, the year when classical Palladian ideas took root in English architecture in Inigo Jones's design for the Queen's House at Greenwich, it was originally completely Jacobean. Soon it became apparent that it was well behind the new fashion. What to do with the great hall puzzled the architects. Originally the house seems to have had a typical layout for the Jacobean age, one which was much nearer the medieval country-house tradition. The abolition of the traditional great hall to make room for an even grander arrangement of the great carved staircase took place in 1767. The hall was provided with a long gallery, now a library of quite exceptional length and charm. The detailed treatment in the ceilings, for example, is very rich and rewarding; even the central tower and lantern, which are genuine Victorian and not restorations, are remarkably effective. Hannah More, who admitted to coveting Blickling, claimed that its setting was better than that of all its greatest neighbours in Norfolk. It is now in the care of the National Trust and is regularly open to visitors.

Its greatest contemporary, across the East Anglian border in Essex, was Audley End which proved too big for a king although it might do for a Lord Treasurer. These were supposed to be James I's words when he first saw it and was offered the house by its builder, Thomas, Earl of Suffolk. It only survived by selective demolition to reduce its scale.

FELBRIGG HALL

Felbrigg Hall shows the great changes of the seventeenth century, and in fact looks like two houses when viewed from the south-west. The south range is the Jacobean house of stone and brick, with shaped gables, a two-storey porch with classical ornament and projecting bays with stone mullions and transoms. A rather odd feature is the cut-out stone lettering on the south balustrade, *Gloria Deo in Excelsis*

The west wing, of the late 1680s, is a country house of a new age built in red brick, with emphasised brick quoins. The two middle bays project very slightly. The eight

---

OPPOSITE: *Kirtling Towers is a fine example of a middle-Tudor gatehouse. Unfortunately, it is not open to the public*

tall sash windows are matched by only six dormers with triangular pediments in the hipped roof. The eaves are decorated as a dentellated cornice, and a doorway and matching window on the ground floor have round pediments. The façade between the two wings illustrates the effect of Inigo Jones on English houses, and possibly indicates that some Dutch influence was infiltrating East Anglia even before the Glorious Revolution and William of Orange.

A good deal of internal re-modelling and alteration has taken place, particularly about 1750 and in the early nineteenth century. The plasterwork of the ceilings is particularly rich, varying in date from 1687 to 1830. About 1750, the Cabinet room in the north-west corner was enlarged, and a bay window added in order to make room to display the owner's collection of pictures. Elaborate plasterwork, rich silk damask hangings, thick, warmly-coloured carpets all combine to produce a result which is as rich as it could possibly be without cloying. The superb interior must make this house one of the most attractive in the whole region.

A few miles from Cromer, Felbrigg Hall is cared for by the National Trust and is extensively open between April and October.

HELMINGHAM HALL

Helmingham Hall, between Debenham and Otley, is difficult to place in a chronological sequence because it has features from so many periods. It was originally a timber-framed Tudor courtyard house inside a wide square moat. It has brick facing, and includes work from the Georgian, Victorian and modern periods. A forest of barley-sugar chimney shafts and tall brick finials, battlements and crow-stepped gables are mostly from more recent restoration, a good deal of it by Nash in the early years of the nineteenth century. It is still occupied by the Tollemache family who came there by marriage in the late fifteenth century.

The monuments in the church, and in the graveyard which adjoins the deer park around the house, make vivid comments on the society which built and sustained the Hall. Even though the house is not usually open to the public, the superb park and the views of the house on most Sunday afternoons in the summer when the grounds are open, allow visitors to come closer to an important side of East Anglian history. The family brewing business has, by the excellence of its product, been able to sustain and enhance this palatial house.

During the life of Helmingham, the Palladian mansions came to the Norfolk countryside; the fortunes needed to maintain them in the modern day have largely gone, however. The great country house had a significant role in English political life as the place where political power was cultivated and often exercised; it was the centre of intrigue, which was the life-blood of politics in the days of pocket and rotten boroughs (*see* page 88).

HOUGHTON HALL

What could be more appropriate than that the member for the pocket borough of King's Lynn, in effect the first British Prime Minister, the manipulator and master of vote-purchasing, Sir Robert Walpole, should have built Houghton Hall. Even the fashion in architectural style was controlled by connection and faction. Lord Burlington's circle took up the pure classicism of Inigo Jones, and went back to the principles of Palladio. In 1718, Colen Campbell designed Houghton for Walpole in the new 'Italian' style. As was so often the case, a village was kicked out of the park to create the necessary solitude. Its replacement, New Houghton, stands cap in hand at the park gates.

The ground floor is rusticated, and the tall principal rooms on the first floor are reached by a grand twin-armed external staircase which has only recently been restored. A small triangular pediment over the door echoes the bigger one above it at roof level, supported by four attached Ionic columns in front of the floor of parade. At the flanks, this is paralleled by the shape of the cupolas and the Venetian first-floor windows while curved colonnades connect service blocks on the flanks in typical Palladian fashion. The house symbolised dominance, wealth and power. The two principal apartments are fit for an almost perpetual Prime Minister who needed to display the weight of his purse. These are the Stone Hall and the Saloon. The Stone Hall has even the same dimensions, a 40-ft cube, as Inigo Jones used in the Queen's House at Greenwich. But in his treatment, Walpole's house seems deliberately to outdo its model of a century before.

The stable block with carstone facing and a brick interior is spacious and is grouped round a courtyard with a fountain in the centre. Of unfussy, simple bold shapes, it comes almost as a relief after the interior of the house.

Houghton Hall, situated near East Rudham, opens less frequently than most National Trust houses.

HOLKHAM HALL

The greatest East Anglian house, Holkham Hall, bears the date 1734 on a foundation stone. Houghton was then still being built, and Kent, who was working on the interior and furnishings there, became Holkham's architect. Burlington and other members of his group, amateur and professional, played lesser parts.

The design was completely Palladian, executed in a very attractive local brick that looks like stone; it has a rusticated basement, principal rooms on the first floor, entrance by a grand staircase through a pedimented portico, and linked lesser blocks away from the main block at the corners. Externally somewhat severe and pure, according to many tastes, inside it is magnificent throughout. The appearance of the house is enhanced from every point of view by the splendour of the grounds and the trees. Nesfield designed the gardens which were later improved by Kent and Capability Brown.

The 1st Earl of Leicester of the second creation, known to historians as Coke of Norfolk, made the house and estate a centre of agricultural progress and the dissemination of new ideas for farmers. The tenants raised the great monument to him in 1845, but perhaps his best memorial is the Model Farm. Thanks to the example he set in running the estate, his successors have been able to keep the house within the family. (*See also* page 106.)

Holkham Hall, near Wells-next-the-Sea, has restricted hours of opening.

PECKOVER HOUSE: WISBECH

If Holkham shows how nearly perfection can be achieved on the grand scale, its contemporary, Peckover House, shows some of the same elements, achieving this quality on a small scale. A town house in a country town becomes a variant of the country house. Tall, segmental-headed windows reduce in height with each ascending storey. The yellow brick is dressed by red brick. The rear door has a modest straight grand staircase, and there is a pediment over the rusticated doorway, a Venetian window above, and a semi-circular one on the top storey.

Internally the decoration of overmantels, doorheads and coves is superb. In the past, other Georgian houses on this bank of the River Nene probably had something of the same finish although, as a banker's house, Peckover may have headed them all.

The house is now in the care of the National Trust, and open at the usual hours.

HEVENINGHAM HALL

When brick went out of fashion for the building of great houses, the appearance of stone was often achieved by covering brick with stucco. Sometimes, as at Heveningham which was designed in 1778, this enabled a restrained elegance to be achieved, and in this case it is matched by the interior decoration of Wyatt. The setting too, by Capability Brown, is more a natural East Anglian scene than a contrivance. The house is still in the Palladian tradition, with a centre block linked to two pavilions, but the principal rooms are on the ground floor and so there is no grand staircase entrance. Instead, the central block is topped by an elaborately sculpted attic. The result is one of the most elegant houses in the region; it lies between Halesworth and Yoxford in Suffolk.

ICKWORTH

The Hervey family had lived at Ickworth since the fifteenth century, and eventually their line came to be headed by an eccentric, Frederick Bishop of Derry and 4th Earl of Bristol. Ickworth was begun in 1795 but the Earl died in 1803, long before its completion in 1830.

The centre block is a rotunda, elliptical in plan. This is only achieved at the cost of some internal awkwardness. The wing blocks are connected by quadrant corridors to the rotunda. The scale of the whole is much more suitable for a public building than a family house. In fact, it was intended as a home for the Earl's collection of Italian pictures but these were seized in Rome by the French in 1798. Good furniture and excellent displays of silver cannot fill the space intended for the great display of pictures, even on the reduced plan of 1822.

In the matured grounds the house is well displayed, whether seen from across the ha-ha, through the woods, from among the ornamental trees in the park-like approach, or from the trees by the swan-pond. Down beyond the artificial lake, the siting of the house in relation to the church of the otherwise lost village here becomes clear. The walled garden with its early red-brick garden house in the banqueting-house tradition and the dower house use space in the landscape on a scale in keeping with the size of the mansion.

RIGHT: *Peckover House at Wisbech brings the tradition of country house building to town in modesty and elegance*

BELOW: *The house, grounds and buildings at Ickworth are best viewed together, when the assertiveness of the house will seem less important*

Ickworth is well sign-posted west of Bury St Edmunds, and is open during the usual National Trust hours.

SANDRINGHAM

The estate here was bought for the Prince of Wales, the future Edward VII, in 1860. Its extremely turbulent architectural history is partly explained by the widening interests of the heir apparent as these expanded from bowling and billiards to ballrooms. The Georgian predecessor was pulled down. Some of the Victorian 'Jacobean' additions have been demolished, others lost by fire and others added. Red brick is still in favour, but with plentiful use of stone for the quoins and details. It seems strange that the self-confidence of the Victorian Royal Family should express itself in architectural nostalgia and in changes of mind. The real interest in this house is in how it serves as a rather special family home.

Sandringham, which lies just inland of the main road from King's Lynn to Snettisham, has generous opening hours.

8
EAST ANGLIA INSURGENT

Ever since late Roman times, Ely had been an island surrounded by bogs and mires, treacherous thickets and pools. Only the native Fenman was safe among the natural hazards that beset all who sought to penetrate the wilderness, and the enemies of the Fenmen were never safe among the aboriginal inhabitants whom legend credited with webbed feet.

REBELLIOUS LORDS

The development of marshes around the approaches to the Isle of Ely, especially the southern approaches, made it a tempting refuge for any medieval rebels. It was practically impossible for government soldiers to force an entrance when the Isle was occupied by determined rebels unless the attackers could find someone in the Isle to bring them in by treachery.

The men who held Ely during Hereward's rebellion in 1071 probably deserve the name given to their thirteenth-century successors even more than these successors themselves: 'The Disinherited'. The support given to Hereward by Saxons of the highest rank whose lands William had confiscated, made it possible for him to defy the Norman military might. Plenty of lesser followers who swelled the numbers of rebels in the Isle would have come for similar reasons. The oppressive Norman settlement which took away estates from the Saxons, was paralleled among the lower classes by the depression of freemen into villeinage. The number of sokemen (in effect, freemen) in the Isle of Ely was reduced to a fifth by the Conquest.

Hereward's revolt represents, among other things, the last flicker of the idea of an Anglo-Scandinavian Empire based on sea-power. King Harold, in concentrating his military efforts to defeat the Norwegians at Stamford Bridge a few days before the dash to Hastings, probably lost the superiority he would otherwise have had, if all his forces could have been concentrated instead against William. Attempts to secure Danish help against the Normans succeeded in 1069, when Sweyn's expedition arrived on the east coast and moved into the Wash. Local Fenmen brought the Danes to Peterborough where the king had installed a Norman as Abbot. The Abbey was sacked and burned, but William managed to secure an agreement with Sweyn. The Danish fleet sailed away, but the revolt of the English continued. During 1070, reinforcements trickled in by water, and enough rebels rallied to earn William's personal attention.

Belsar's Hill, which bestrides the road to the Isle that runs in by Aldreth Causeway,

has traditionally been the site of William's castle, and on the earliest Fen map, dating from the early seventeenth century, it bears the initials W. C., indicating the folk-lore of the matter. The only piece of pottery found on the site was attributed to the Norman period. Most of the circular bank and ditch still survives today, although the road was diverted in the last century and cuts the banks, probably destroying the entrance.

Discussion as to the location of William's castle of 'Aldreth' has been hindered by ignorance of the earlier course of Cottenham Lode which joined Beach Lode at Landbeach Points, the northern tip of the parish on the present A 10. Drivers up this road today should try to imagine it as it was before, not merely prior to the road, but also before the banks and the Great Draining of the Fens confined the water to the Washes. If it can be imagined with meres, meanderings and reedy pools, it takes only a shade more imagination to see it as William did when preparing for his assault on the Isle, filled with all the little boats of the region, much like the Solent on the eve of D-Day.

The folk-stories and other contemporary accounts of the conquest of the Isle have come down in a highly coloured form, but may none the less be true. There is the tale of the pontoon bridge made of logs and buoyancy bags made from sheepskins which sank as the Normans, eager to get at the supposed riches of the monastery, crowded on the pontoon. Anyone who has walked on a pontoon bridge in a party will recognise a ring of truth. The folk tradition developed centuries after, told of the finding of Norman corpses still in rotting armour. The unfamiliar Fen, with its treacherous 'bottomless' bogs and thickets of reed and brushwood and full of invisible armed Saxons, must have been terrifying; perhaps this explains the proper name of Belsar's Hill, 'Belasise', i.e, a fine place to be stationed! With the help of the wild Fen that has been preserved at Wicken, it is easy to understand William's recourse to the aid of a witch. When she appeared on her wooden tower, given the right wind, the firing of the reeds would have trumped his ace. The most powerful curse cannot quench a fire in dry reeds. In the end, William used what became the royal way into the Isle: treachery from within.

KING STEPHEN'S ANARCHY

During the struggle between King Stephen and Matilda, the Isle again became a rebel stronghold. When Bishop Niel of Ely had had Devizes Castle taken away from him, he went into the Isle and called the local gentry to join him. Alrehede Castle was strengthened and the whole Isle fortified and made ready for siege. After a siege which Stephen came personally to superintend, the royal forces effected an entrance by the treachery of a monk. Bishop Niel escaped from the city to a Fenland hiding-place, and got away to join the Empress in the west country. The property of the bishopric was seized and restored according to the shifting fortunes of civil war and national politics. Geoffrey de Mandeville, the archetypal robber baron with a remarkable capa-

---

OPPOSITE: *The moorings below the towers of the cathedral are a reminder that Ely was once very obviously an island served by waterways*

ABOVE: *At Wicken Fen, the reeds are still harvested annually for thatching. In the past, they made a valuable crop wherever they grew in the wetlands of East Anglia*

BELOW: *The earthworks of the unfinished castle at Burwell. When beseiging it, Geoffrey de Mandeville received his fatal wound*

city for changing sides, had been sent by Stephen to clear the nest of opponents from Ely. He took over the town and fortified Alrehede, Fordham, Ramsey and Benwick. From this Fenland base, Geoffrey could raid all the countryside as far afield as Cambridge and St Ives. Famine arrived.

Stephen found it impossible to force Geoffrey to meet his army in pitched battle, and had to resort to siege again. His investment of the rebels could not be total, but he began the construction of a ring of garrisoned strongpoints. From the earthworks which remain, the one at Burwell can be seen never to have been completed: the great moat, spoil heaps and traces of the dwellings were all removed to make way for the castle. A very similar set of earthworks of an unfinished castle can be found at Rampton at the end of the causeway from Cottenham; this causeway provided a short-cut through extensions of marsh on the southern edge of the Fen. However, Geoffrey laid siege to Burwell (which was to be the key position of the forces attacking the rebels) while it was still unfinished. It was hot midsummer, and Geoffrey removed his helmet to cool off. He was struck by an arrow, retired wounded to Mildenhall, and died there.

In the next few months, under Geoffrey's son, the rebels' power faded away. Bishop Niel was reconciled to the King, and the church at Ely had its lost lands restored.

THE BARONS' WARS

Insurrection returned to East Anglia in the aftermath of Magna Carta when a number of important magnates who were opposed to King John gathered at Bury St Edmunds. When John sent a royal army, they fled to the Isle of Ely, and fortified all the entrances ready for a siege. The Isle seemed again to be playing its old role of refuge for rebels but in the winter of early 1216 the Fen froze over, and the besiegers were able to walk in on the ice at Stuntney and Earith.

Knowing this, the possibility of baronial opposition seizing the Isle as a fortress seems to have caused concern to Henry III's government even before the outbreak of hostilities in the 1260s. While trying to force the king to bargain, the barons, led by Simon de Montfort, began civil war again. Violent expropriation of the lands belonging to the side losing for the moment by those in power at that time, left an aggrieved group who, having lost their land, could not be reconciled. This band of 'The Disinherited' was besieged at Kenilworth in 1266. A raiding party, out plundering and foraging, went on to the Isle and turned it into a base and safe refuge from which they could raid all over Cambridgeshire and into Norfolk, to Bury St Edmunds in Suffolk, and even into Essex. The whole of East Anglia was at risk. The situation was so serious that Henry himself became preoccupied with the rebellion. The barons were summoned to Bury St Edmunds, the lands of the rebels seized and granted out among the loyal nobles, and the army then moved on to Cambridge to plan the attack when the time became ripe. In the meantime, all roads in and out of the Isle were cut. From King's Lynn, a waterborne invasion of the Isle was attempted but it was beaten off with ease, and the rebels made overtures to the men of Lynn, as well as others, to join them.

Before the assault on Ely was ready, disasters elsewhere caused the King and his army to return to London where the rebellious Earl of Gloucester had occupied the city, while Prince Edward with his forces went north since the lord of Alnwick had ridden and endangered the whole royal position there. Left virtually defenceless, Cambridge fell to the raiders who destroyed fortifications and again pillaged royalists' houses. Prince Edward was free to return in the summer when drought made it possible to get into the Isle. Peace was restored although the University seemed to have adapted to the new way of life: 'many malefactors issue out from the University of Cambridge, committing many depredations and other enormities both within and without the town: Wherefore the sheriff seeks an allowance of £40 for his expenses, insofar as, for considerable periods, he was compelled to maintain a large number of men about him equipped with horses and arms.'

THE PEASANTS' REVOLT

Rural disorders were common in fourteenth-century Europe and in 1381 England had its share of trouble, with East Anglia as one of the major areas affected by the so-called Peasants' Revolt. It was short and sharp, but there had been various local disturbances as forerunners, and sporadic local outbreaks followed.

In some ways, the term Peasants' Revolt was a misnomer: towns were heavily involved. Huntingdon alone in East Anglia kept its gates closed to the rebels. Wat Tyler himself bore the name of a petty craftsman rather than that of a peasant. Of the surnames of those accused with Richard de Leicester for the insurrection at Ely, five have such names and another has his occupation as skinner recorded. Probably 'Villeins' Revolt' would be a better description, because where a lord (and this was particularly true of resident ecclesiastical lords like the Abbot at Bury St Edmunds) refused to grant a borough charter to his townsmen, the famous freedom of town air could not be savoured. Petty craftsmen who felt sure they should be free were called the Abbot's villeins and treated as such. The contemporary accounts of the revolt, whenever they mention the happenings at towns like Bury and St Albans, talk of the lord's villeins; many townsmen had precisely the same main grievance as their country cousins. Cousins from town and country would meet regularly at town markets, and share their discontents.

In Cambridge, the University, Barnwell Priory, the Carmelites and Corpus Christi College were all substantial landowners and the University authorities, with their privileged proctorial authority which in many ways extended over townsmen as well as students, were heartily disliked. Town and gown riots were not new. Nor were violent struggles between abbots and their townsmen in Bury and St Albans. As mentioned on page 63, the splendid Abbey gatehouse at Bury St Edmunds is owed to the punishment of the townsfolk who had burned down the previous one. Amongst other things seized by the mob in Cambridge, with the assistance of the town authorities, were the University Archives from Great St Mary's Church and the Carmelites, and also some of Corpus Christi's archives. The rebels burned them in the market square. Rent-rolls, tax-rolls and charters of privilege were very necessary proofs of the rights and feudal burdens of the day, and their loss caused much embarrassment later. Corpus Christi, the college of the town gilds, seems at first sight to have been a strange target for the townsfolk until it is noticed that its patron was John Duke of Lancaster, the most hated man in southern England and head of the government.

ABOVE: *Blickling Hall, a splendid National Trust property*

BELOW: *Kentwell Hall, built around 1564, is one of the finest of the East Anglian moated halls*

ABOVE: *Holkham Hall, one of the grandest of the East Anglian stately homes*

RIGHT: *Part of the Elizabethan mansion of Madingley Hall near Cambridge*

OPPOSITE: *Orford castle, still an impressive monument*

ABOVE: *Oxborough Hall, now preserved by the National Trust*

BELOW: *Melford Hall at Long Melford is now preserved by the National Trust*

Of all the enemies that the mob chose to attack, probably the most generally disliked were the men who had collected, or tried to collect, the Poll Taxes. For instance, the collector Roger de Harleston had his houses at Cottenham and in Cambridge attacked. Thomas Hazelden had been a faithful retainer of John of Gaunt, the Duke of Lancaster: the mob went out from Cambridge to burn down his house at Steeple Morden. Parts of the present house there in the moated site appear to belong to the house that replaced it. On the way was Shingay, Preceptory of the Hospitallers whose master, Robert Hales, was Treasurer of England and so Shingay too was attacked. Lawyers were the butt of peasant hatred at all times. In Ely, where the feeling was quite savage, Adam Clymme proclaimed that, 'no man of law or other officer in the execution of his duty should escape without beheading'. The higher clergy were unpopular, especially among the great numbers of unbeneficed clergy who had been ordained during the shortage of priests which followed the Black Death, and now saw no opportunities for promotion.

At Ely, some of the rebels led by Adam Clymme 'feloniously broke and entered the close of Thomas Somenour [a minor legal officer of the bishop?] and there took and carried away divers rolls, extracts of the green wax of the lord the king and the Bishop of Ely'. The significance of green wax is that they were seals of the Exchequer. The modern equivalent would be the records of the Inland Revenue.

Simple robbery may not necessarily have been important as a motive inspiring many of the insurgents to take up arms, but it certainly emerges in the records. A simple example occurred at Ely when Richard de Leicester had sentenced to death Edmund de Walsingham, a royal justice. John Buk of Ely seized Edmund's purse containing 42½d, paid John Deye of Willingham 12d for the execution and seems to have kept the rest!

One of the remarkable features of the revolt is that there seems to have been no general attack on landlords *as* landlords, and no massacre of prisoners. Adam Clymme again shows how far feeling against lords went: 'No man of whatsoever condition he were, free or bond, should obey his lord to do any services or customs, under pain of beheading otherwise than he should declare to them on behalf of the Great Fellowship.'

In the depositions taken after the revolt were accounts of men who had travelled around as agitators, and also many mentions of the Great Fellowship. Early writers have speculated as to whether this implied an organisation behind the whole rising. Adam Clymme himself behaved in a way that tempts speculation, 'always wandering armed with arms displayed, bearing a standard to assemble insurgents'. John Wrawe, 'a most scandalous priest', was alleged to have come to Suffolk directly after receiving his instructions in London from Wat Tyler himself, and at Bury he led the mob that captured and executed Lord Cavendish, Chief Justice of England, and also John de Cambridge, Prior of Bury, who had defended 'his monastery's rights against the villeins of Bury'. Wrawe had been vicar of Ringsfield, near Beccles: he turned informer in the vain hope of saving himself and, in accusing others, he has left behind an account of his mode of operation and the places in Suffolk where he went gathering support.

George Donnesby of Lincoln made the clearest claim to be acting under instructions from an organisation: 'He said that he was a messenger of the Great Fellowship, and had been sent to the town of Bury St Edmunds to make the commons of that town rise.' The Latin name for this mysterious body could perhaps imply rather more the connotation of the word 'conspiracy', perhaps 'association'. It seems to be used with consistency over a wide area.

For one brief moment at Cambridge, there may be signs of a professional agitator at work. 'John Shirle of the county of Nottingham was taken because it was found that he was a vagabond in divers counties the whole time of the disturbance, insurrection and tumult, carrying lies and worthless talk from district to district whereby the peace of the lord the King could be speedily broken and the people disquieted and disturbed.' He is charged for what he said in a tavern in Bridge Street in Cambridge. He seems to have dropped the pretence (the folk-lore equivalent of the doctrine that the king can do no wrong) that the rebels were acting for the king against traitorous ministers. He said that John Ball '. . . a true and good man, prophesying things useful to the commons of the realm', had been unjustly condemned 'by the said ministers with the King's assent . . .' and further 'of wrongs and oppressions done to the people by the king and the ministers aforesaid . . .'

The end of the revolt in East Anglia came swiftly. On 18 June 1381, Bishop Despenser of Norwich made preparations to return to his see, and with the help of the Abbot of Ramsey dispersed the mob away to Ely. He then moved swiftly to Cambridge, crushing the rebellion savagely. On 24 June, he entered and quieted Norwich; on the following day, or the day after, he met the main band of the rebels and destroyed it. He was the same man who converted the old church or cathedral at North Elmham into a house of ill-fame (*see* page 49); there was nothing squeamish about him, and the rebels could expect little mercy.

KETT'S REBELLION

East Anglia in general and Norfolk in particular were prominent in the turmoil of the reign of the boy king Edward VI. For a time, the discontented men of Norfolk would have held the country in their grip if only they had been able to link with the rebels in the south-west and keep the government over-stretched in a war on two fronts. This they failed to do and so the opportunity passed.

The excessive over-spending by Henry VIII's governments, chiefly on war, which was in turn financed by inflation through the debasement of the coinage, set in motion an underlying trend of rapidly rising prices. Three bad harvests in a row sent the price of food soaring in a way that would make the prices of the 1980s look stable. In the last quarter of the fifteenth century, villages that had been weakened by the Pestilence a century before, were fast failing. Enclosures and evictions by rapacious landlords were blamed, and not always without cause. Speculations in the land-market intended to create large-scale sheep farms which accelerated as former monastic lands became available, added to the instability and provided the government with scapegoats. The debased shillings and rising prices took arbitrarily from some and gave arbitrarily to others; some peasants and some landlords did well, others badly. Those who did well saw how they might have been able to do even better had the government not tried to protect the poor. All were aggrieved.

The government tried to treat the crisis by punishing the unemployed, by sending out commissioners to stem the waves of agricultural change, and to denounce greed, but this failed to bring universal content. Riots against local landlords and local grievances erupted sporadically. The enclosure of agricultural land was an outward and very visible sign of the causes of discontent, and indeed it did play a significant part in the troubles, but the great struggle of 1549 was the battle, or series of local battles, between peasant and landlord for the commons. These commons could be exploited to take advantage of the boom in the manufacture and export of woollen cloth by landlords who overstocked them with their sheep and drove off or impounded the peasants' animals, as well as by those who actually enclosed the pasture with hedges or fences. In Norfolk, the foldcourse system often gave the lord a monopoly of the grazing of sheep on the stubble and commons. His peasants must have seethed with frustration as the price of wool rose sharply while they were unable to share in the bonanza.

The uprising which was to engulf East Anglia and threaten to bring down the government began with attacks on enclosures of common pasture. Yet in the long list of demands drawn up by the rebels, the only direct mention of enclosure was a request that men might be allowed to keep their saffron ground enclosures, and that henceforth no one would enclose any more. (Saffron is a form of crocus and was used in the manufacture of a yellow dye.) On the other hand, they demanded that lords should be deprived of their ancient rights and leave the peasants free to enjoy them: 'We pray Your Grace that no lord of the manor shall common upon the commons.'

The riots and uprisings in Devon and Cornwall were concentrated against religious changes and the new English Prayer Book. By contrast, the East Anglian rebels liked the 'new preachers' and the English service. The Cornish had expressed their economic discontents to the Lord Protector Somerset before they took up arms for religious grievances. In East Anglia, only slight, fading hints of Catholic sympathies appeared early on. The first riots of the eastern rebellion came on 20 June 1549 at Wilby, only two or three miles from Kenninghall where the Princess Mary, the focus of hope for the adherents of the Old Religion, was staying on her manor there. She was able to clear herself of all complicity in these troubles.

During the first week in July, Wymondham was accustomed to hold its annual fair of two days and one night in honour of the Translation of Thomas à Becket; popular features were a procession and mystery plays. Henry VIII regarded the cult of St Thomas as specially worthy of destruction since it made a saint of a priest who had defended the church against his king. There was at that time (and still is) a chapel dedicated to St Thomas in the town. At the end of the Fair, amid the bustle, jollity and headstrong gossip, some strong words were spoken. A party got together and went off to Morley, two miles away, to break down the enclosures that had recently been made there.

Two families of local landowners were rivals competing for the profits deriving from the Dissolution of Wymondham Abbey: the Ketts and the Flowerdews. Heading the Flowerdew family was one of that hated clan, a lawyer, and among the other perquisites which evolved from the Dissolution, Flowerdew had the job of demolishing the church and selling the materials. For centuries, the monastery and parish had disputed how far the other's rights in the fabric of this peculiar church extended, so Flowerdew's activities aroused considerable opposition. As the party of enclosure breakers returned from Morley, the suggestion was made that Flowerdew's enclosures at Hethersett might repay attention. Flowerdew met the marchers and, with the help

OPPOSITE: *Double use of parts of the church by the parish of Wymondham and the Abbey lies behind the rivalry which produced these over-weening towers. Kett was hanged here after the rebellion. Wymondham is one of those rare parish churches where too much money has been available for restoration*

ABOVE: *Contrasting with the church, the simple market cross at Wymondham is most effective in its modesty and dignity*

of a modest bribe, persuaded them to return to Wymondham and concentrate on the Ketts' enclosures there.

Kett listened to what the rioters had to say, was apparently convinced by their arguments, and agreed to help them level his own enclosures, and then became their leader in a second march to Hethersett to deal with those of the Flowerdews. From there he launched the march on Norwich. Gathering supporters as he moved along the road to Norwich, Kett crossed the Yare at Cringleford, turned left, and began to circle the city to the north. Camp was made at Bowthorpe, still two miles from the City Wall. Sir Edmund Wyndham, the High Sheriff, appealed in vain for the rioters to disperse but was forced to take refuge inside the city. Thomas Codd, the Mayor, was no more successful.

On Wednesday night, the rebels camped in Eaton Wood. Kett asked for a safe passage through the city to Mousehold Heath and after this was refused, he crossed Hellesdon Bridge over the River Wensum, and camped at Drayton. Here Sir Roger Wodehouse arrived with two carts of beer and one of provisions, in the hope that he might persuade the rebels to disperse. They took his provisions, stripped him, and kept him prisoner in a ditch.

The following day, Kett completed the march around the city to Mousehold, and the Earl of Surrey's palace was requisitioned as a prison. For a week there was something like a *de facto* truce; the rebels came and went in the city, while the mayor and some of the aldermen paid visits to the camp. On 13 July the Herald, Grove Pursuivant, had arrived with a commission to Dr Watson, an eminent Protestant divine, to preach against rebellion. This may not exactly seem to have been a robust way to handle a major uprising, but the government had already raised and despatched two other armies to different parts of the country, and the JPs of Suffolk and Essex had dealt with their own rebels without an army. Watson was able to get the rebels to accept Thomas Conyers, one of the 'New Preachers', as chaplain, and one of the favourite pastimes of the rebels seems to have been listening to inordinately long ultra-protestant sermons. Matthew Parker, a Norwich lad and currently Master of Corpus Christi College who was unwillingly to become Queen Elizabeth's first Archbishop of Canterbury, seems to have been one of the first visitors to the camp. He too tried to disperse the rebels by preaching.

Kett had made an administrative centre at the camp by laying planks across the lower boughs of an oak tree. This, the famous Oak of Reformation, provided for what have less happily been called 'People's Courts' in recent years. Alternatively, a preaching platform was ready for open-air exhortations to the rebel army. Parker preached a sermon against intemperance and blood-shedding and urged them to disperse and be patient. As the sermon became less to their liking, the crowd began to murmur, grow restless and sought to prick his feet with their pikes. Conyers, the chaplain, created a diversion by striking up with his choristers the Te Deum in the New English fashion. The crowd joined in, distracted, and Parker escaped into the city.

On the following day, he preached at one of the city churches, St Clements, where he had grown up and where his parents were buried. Rebels in the congregation warned him that his horses were to be requisitioned, but he had them doctored so that they appeared lame and were rejected. The next day he walked through the fields to Cringleford where his servant and his very fine horses were waiting to take him back to Cambridge. It seems strange that he should apparently have expected to be able to stop a rebellion with a sermon. He was more successful in Landbeach, in Cambridgeshire, where his college held one manor; he restored order by supporting the village peasants at law against the violent lord of the other manor.

Meanwhile, the rebels' supply problem seems to have been solved by 'requisitioning': they sent out gangs to seize supplies and take them to Mousehold. In view of the rebels' attitude to the landlords' flocks – Sir Roger Townshend of Raynham had 4,200 head – sheep figured largely on the menu. For the rebels to eat sheep was practically the performance of a symbolic duty in helping to restore the social balance.

On 15 July, Leonard Sotherton rode to London to get help from the King's Council. All available forces had been detached to other centres of rebellion so Sotherton was sent back with York Herald to try persuasion once more as a means of dispersing the rebels. On 21 July, with the City Sword Bearer, York Herald approached the camp and gave the offer of pardon. When this was not accepted, the Herald ordered the Swordbearer to arrest the rebels, a rather difficult task in view of their numbers. Mayor Codd ordered the city gates to be closed, and preparations began. Cannon set up on the castle rampart exchanged fire with Kett's guns on Mousehold, but the range was too great. Kett had obtained artillery from King's Lynn, Great Yarmouth and probably from other Norfolk towns; he captured some from Paston Hall as they were on their way to the city authorities. It was obvious that action was tending to concentrate on the city's weakest entrance, the Bishopsgate Bridge.

On 22 July, the guns on both sides were brought into closer range. Kett asked for a safe passage through the city to provision his army and when he was refused an artillery duel began. Attempts to cross the bridge were checked by the city archers until rebel parties swam the stream to outflank the defenders on the far bank. Then Kett entered Norwich. The City Chamberlain was forced to hand over his arsenal and supplies for the guns. The rebels were ready when the Marquess of Northampton arrived with his army, which included a contingent of Italian mercenaries. At once, the Herald called for the surrender of the city. To this the Steward, Mayor and deputy Mayor agreed. The City Sword Bearer led in the new army and Kett's forces withdrew back to Mousehold. Feelings began to worsen: an Italian captain who strayed the wrong side of the lines was hanged by the rebels in sight of the city.

On 1 August, after a night of bombardment, the rebels again refused the Herald's offer of pardon. Then they broke in across Bishopsgate and Northampton left a burning city behind as he withdrew to Cambridge. Sheer numbers had told against him in the street fighting. Heavy rain put out the flames.

Kett set up a new camp in the Cathedral Close, installed his own officers to run the city, and had Alderman Steward organise a watch. What he now needed above all was for the uprising to spread. In the event, even reinforcements from outlying Norfolk could hardly reach him. A camp of rebels at Castle Rising moved by stages under attack from the gentry, prominent among whom was Sir Edmund Knyvett based at New Buckenham Castle. The rebels' attempt to take Great Yarmouth was a minor military disaster; under a smokescreen which they produced by firing haystacks, the townsmen captured thirty rebels and six guns.

In mid-August, the Council had an army ready: Somerset had intended to command it himself, but, unfortunately for him as it turned out, he gave the command to

Warwick. On 24 August, the new army reached Norwich and Warwick set up his headquarters at Intwood Hall, belonging to Sir Thomas Gresham. When he marched on towards Norwich, he sent a herald ahead to parley with an offer of pardon before beginning the assault. Kett and his lieutenants allowed the herald to speak, and in fact conducted him around the separate groups to make his speech to each of them. But when a boy made a filthy gesture and shouted insults at the herald, a harquebusier shot the boy and tumult erupted. Kett, who seems to have been specifically excluded from any offer of pardon, was prevented by his own men from accompanying the herald back to Warwick.

The assault on the city began again, and Warwick broke the St Stephen's Gate with artillery. Steward advised assault on the Brazen Gates, a lightly-defended postern, and had St Benedict's Gate opened; Warwick's troops poured into the Market Place, which became their headquarters. Street fighting was fierce and, in the confusion, Warwick's train of military stores passed clean through the city and into rebel hands. Gradually Kett's men withdrew to their camp. The government forces established a bridgehead with artillery on the camp side of Bishopsgate. A good shot by Myles, Kett's gunner, killed Warwick's master gunner, and in the alarm the guns and supplies were taken by the rebels. Myles then brought down a tower with a lucky shot on Bishopsgate. During the night, rebels broke into the part of the city north of the Wensum, while Kett's guns bombarded Bishopsgate and the eastern defences. Under this pressure Warwick ordered the bridges to be broken, but three were left.

The expected final assault on the city never came. The following day, the reinforcements of fourteen hundred German mercenaries arrived. Kett decided that he must now attack and the camp and stores on Mousehold were burned, and the rebels moved at night to Dussindale, which seems to have been north-east of the city. As Warwick's cavalry approached, the rebels left their newly-prepared positions and, having refused the last offer of pardon, they advanced, driving their prisoners chained together as a screen in front. Myles, the gunner, now managed to pick off the King's standard bearer, then a volley from the harquebusiers broke the van of the rebels, whose prisoners escaped. At first, bands of Kett's men fought back in groups as the cavalry charged them, then news began to spread that Kett himself had ridden away. Warwick made a personal offer of pardon on Tuesday 27 August, and this was accepted.

Kett's flight ended when he stopped to rest in a barn at Swannington, only twelve miles from Norwich. He was recognised, and held until a detachment of troops arrived to take him back to Norwich as a prisoner. Dussindale was filled with slaughtered bodies, three thousand five hundred of them. The rhyme which prophesied this had been taken by the rebels to mean the bodies of their enemies, not their own. Folk-lore had proved to be as two-faced as the classical oracles.

The country gnoffes
Hob, Dick and Hick
With clubs and clouted shoon
Shall fill the vale of Dussindale
With slaughtered bodies soon.

Thirty-nine leaders were hanged, drawn and quartered and three hundred others hanged on the approaches to the city. Now Warwick's badge, the ragged staff, was displayed alongside the Royal Arms. He left for London on 7 September taking the Kett brothers and other rebel leaders with him to the Tower. On 14 September, Somerset arrived there too, now a prisoner himself. The Ketts, both Robert and his brother William, were sentenced to be hanged, drawn and quartered at Tyburn but, in fact, Robert was hanged in chains from Norwich Castle, and his brother from Wymondham church tower.

The rising was over. What more could the men of East Anglia do? Worse economic troubles were to come. The peak of inflation was soon to be reached, followed by the violent deflationary calling down of the value of coinage, the bursting of the export boom and collapse of the cloth industry. Depositions taken by the Norwich magistrates in the next few years, mostly telling of seditious chatter in taverns, show the survival of bitter hatred. But there was little that could be done. Kett had been beaten.

'BREAD OR BLOOD': RURAL DISORDER IN THE NINETEENTH CENTURY

By the second half of the eighteenth century, East Anglia had become the most important source of grain and many other foodstuffs for the London foodmarket. The golden hoof of the sheep and the new methods of Coke had turned the barren sands of the Breckland into gold-dust, producing the best malting barley in all England. Down the rivers flowing south to London, East Anglia's barley left the malting towns of Suffolk and Essex as malt for the capital's enormous brewing industry. At the little ports around the East Anglian coasts, up all the estuaries as far as light coasters could penetrate on the tide, were to be found granaries and maltings. Aldeburgh, Snape and Ely have concert halls where the name 'maltings' is the last testament to a very ancient trade and industry. The Maltings at Snape are still a superb collection of industrial buildings.

Already by the sixteenth century, in times of dearth, the London merchants cast their nets wider and took more grain. If famine was near, Norfolk was one of the first places to feel it. Disorder could easily start at the transhipment centres if, following any sudden sharp price rise, the activities of the 'foreign' merchants and local dealers seemed calculated to exacerbate the shortage.

Kett's Rebellion had been the last great peasants' revolt in the tradition of 1381. As described earlier, their grievances were largely about land, particularly the commons and rents. By the late eighteenth century, rural disorder had become more a matter about the scarcity and price of food. By the nineteenth century, it was much more a matter of jobs, the fearful consequences of mechanisation and low wages. East Anglia, which became so much a centre of agricultural advance, was in the forefront of the manufacture as well as the use of agricultural machinery; it witnessed the whole gamut of violent reactions posed by the condition of the agricultural labourer.

In the food riots of 1795, the worst hit places were the ports with coastal grain trade – Wells-next-the-Sea, Wisbech and Boston – the inland ports like Ipswich, and malting towns like Hitchin on the roads or rivers leading to London. The Fenland towns found their own rioters augmented by 'bankers', labourers working on the drains and banks. In some places, notably Wells, the military joined in. There seem to have been few landless agricultural labourers involved in the bread riots of 1795–6

Snape Maltings were converted into a concert hall and cultural centre for the Aldeburgh Festival some twenty years ago. Rebuilt after a fire, this success has inspired similar conversions of redundant maltings elsewhere, as at Ely

and 1800–01, but matters were very different in 1816 at Littleport, Ely and Downham, where nearly all of the eighty arrested appear to fit into that class. Unemployment and low wages were general grievances; the Poor Rates were swelling alarmingly and the magistrates were meeting increased poaching with increased severity. At Downham, an *agent provocateur* had been insinuated into a poaching gang. The labourers involved were sentenced to a year's imprisonment, and one of the objectives of the Downham rioters in 1816 was to secure their release. But the whole country was disturbed after the introduction of the Corn Bill in 1815, designed to keep the price of corn artificially high, as in wartime, to favour the big landowners, and there is little doubt that a sudden price rise was the immediate cause of the outbreaks of 1816.

The disturbances started after a meeting of the Littleport Benefit Club in the Globe public house. At that time, the village benefit clubs were as near as one could get to an organisation of labourers and the story of the riot has been well told by A.J. Peacock in his book *Bread or Blood*. After leaving the Globe, they went to demand increased wages from the JPs and the farmers. This easily subsided into extortion, riot and plunder. Having gone to Ely with such arms as they could muster, including punt guns used for duck shooting mounted on a cart, they returned to Littleport again. It was here that the Dragoons caught them when they were drinking the remains of the money which they had taken from local farmers the day before, and in the skirmishing there was one man killed and several wounded. Eighty of the rioters were arrested and sent for trial at a special assize. In the meantime, with trouble in other Fenland villages, as well as in Essex and Huntingdon, the government began to treat the affair seriously. The Home Secretary sent a detachment of horse, foot and artillery, and three hundred special constables were sworn in at Cambridge. The Vice-Chancellor and Heads of Houses were prepared to arm the undergraduates if needed.

After the trial of the rioters had lasted a week, it was considered that enough had been found guilty to act as an example and the rest were bound over: twenty-four were sentenced to death but nineteen were reprieved. Of the five who did hang, Dennis, the only restraining force during the riot, was cited as the leader. Over a century and a half later, the feeling is still bitter in the Fenland townlet of Littleport and the victims are remembered as the 'Littleport martyrs'.

Much of East Anglian agitation in the early nineteenth century concerned opposition to threshing machines and mole-drainage ploughs, both of which meant seasonal unemployment, as well as campaigns for higher wages. Some outbreaks were aimed at the reduction of church tithes in order to pay for wage increases, thus uniting the labourers and farmers against the church. But it was an unstable combination. Part of the objection to machinery may have been transferred from the resentment felt by workers at the way they were 'stood off' with the decline in annual hirings and in 'living in' accommodation. Even as mild a man as John Denson in his book *A Peasant's Voice to Landowners* could be very bitter about the gulf thus created between the farmer and his labourers.

The centre of the disturbances of 1816 were quiet in 1830. The savage repression sent resentment underground. The rick-burning long outlasted the disturbances associated with the followers of the perhaps mythical 'Captain Swing', and in fact arson went on sporadically in most of the countryside through the 1860s into the period when the farmworkers' union began to organise. Hobsbawm and Rudé, the historians of popular revolt, report that 'thirty-nine per cent of the rural prisoners in Bury and Ipswich jails in 1848–52 were there for incendiarism'. This seems to have been more common in East Anglia after, rather than during, the 'Swing' riots of 1830–2.

For a time it was thought that Captain Swing himself had been arrested in Suffolk. John Saville, who came from Luton where he was a straw plait merchant, was taken in his green gig with £580 and a large quantity of barely literate 'Swing' letters, threatening missives to landlords. These suggest he was probably a Ranter (primitive Methodist) local preacher. He was sentenced to £50 fine and twelve months in jail. After this set of disturbances, the solitary fire-raiser continued to leave his mark on the countryside, but independent organised action by the labourers tended to find other channels. The revolt was followed by a primitive Methodist revival of substantial proportions, and the Baptists also made progress in East Anglia.

There is only the slightest hint of any continuity between the riots of this period and the appearance of Trade Unionism some forty years later. Joseph Arch in 1870 appeared to be breaking virgin soil. The first attempts to organise the East Anglian agricultural workers could, in retrospect, have hardly happened at a more difficult time. The great slump in agriculture was just ahead and brought dire trouble in 1873. Effectively the union had gone by 1878. Some branches appeared again in the 1890s, but the real beginnings of continuous organisation date from the appointment of George Edwards in 1906 as Secretary of the Eastern Counties Agricultural Labourers' Union. At the end of the Second World War, in the heady days of the 1945 General Election, a local organiser of the agricultural workers was elected to the House of Commons.

PART II

THE LANDSCAPES OF EAST ANGLIA

by Richard Muir

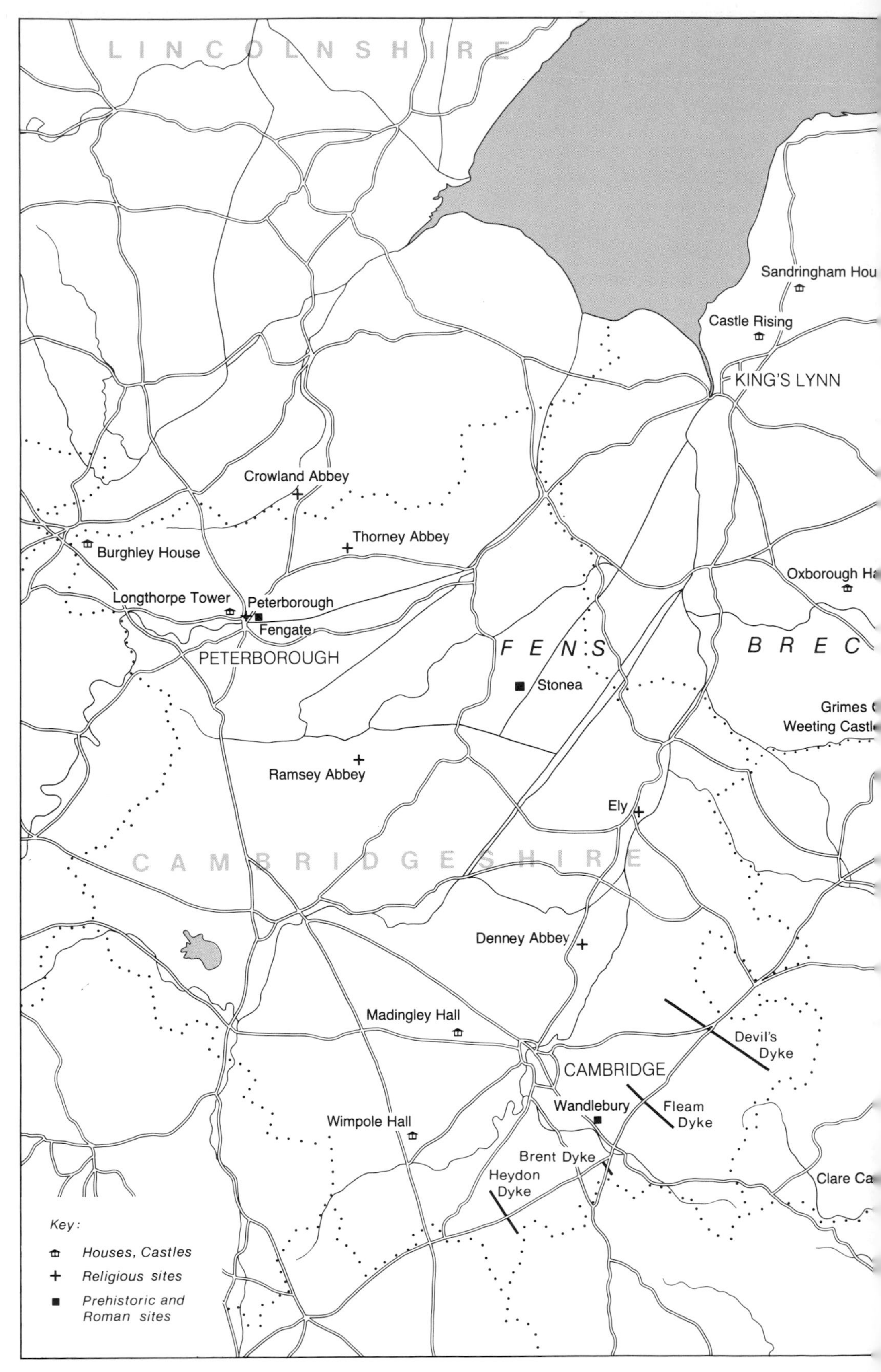

FIG. 14: EAST ANGLIA

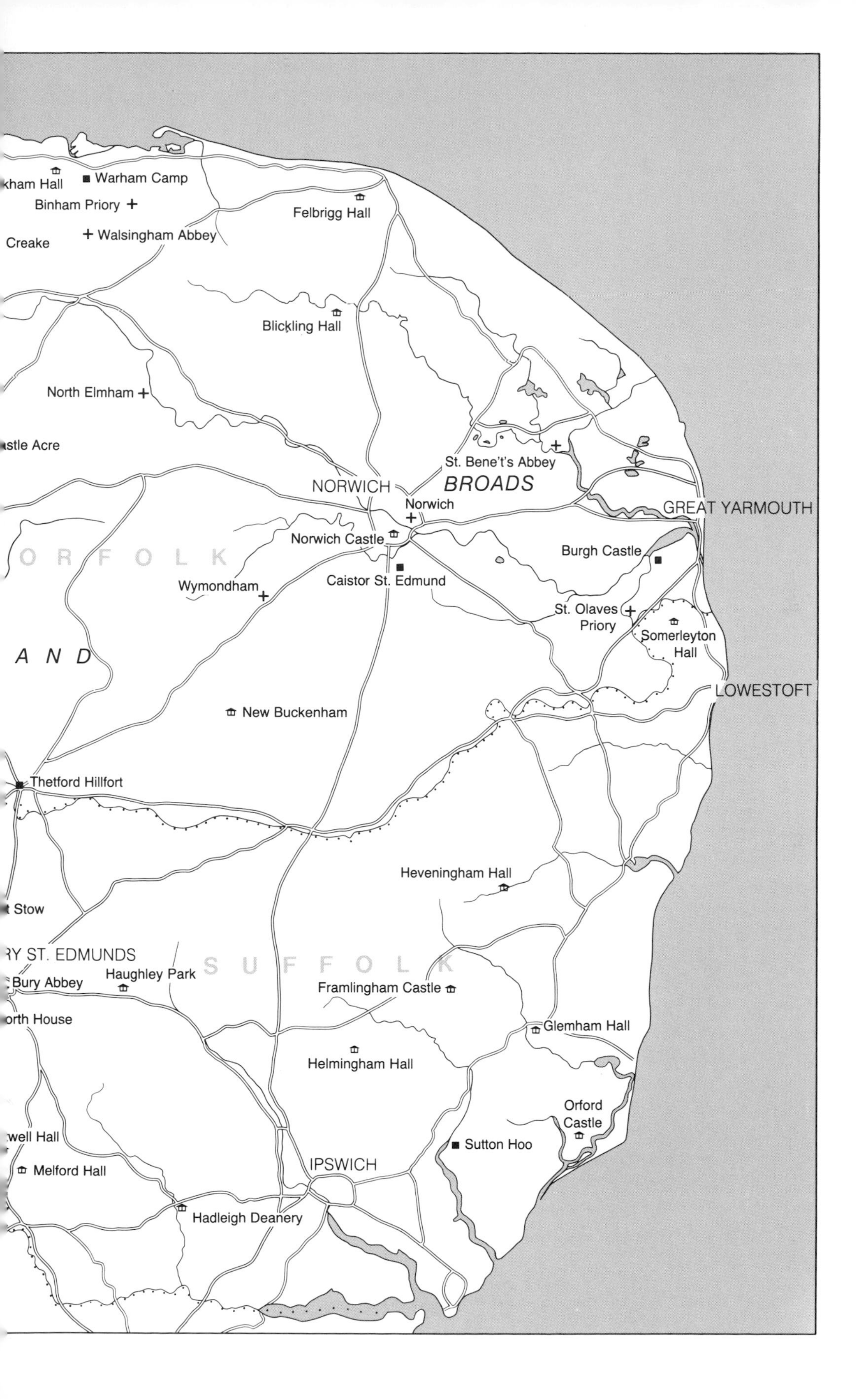

kham Hall
Warham Camp
Binham Priory
Felbrigg Hall
Creake
Walsingham Abbey
Blickling Hall
North Elmham
astle Acre
St. Bene't's Abbey
NORWICH
BROADS
Norwich
GREAT YARMOUTH
Norwich Castle
Burgh Castle
ORFOLK
Wymondham
Caistor St. Edmund
St. Olaves Priory
Somerleyton Hall
AND
LOWESTOFT
New Buckenham
Thetford Hillfort
Heveningham Hall
Stow
RY ST. EDMUNDS
SUFFOLK
Haughley Park
Bury Abbey
Framlingham Castle
orth House
Glemham Hall
Helmingham Hall
Orford Castle
well Hall
Sutton Hoo
IPSWICH
Melford Hall
Hadleigh Deanery

9
THE FENS AND FEN EDGE

Everyone has heard of the Fens. But since the region lies away from the main corridors of travel, this is an area that one does not tend to discover and enjoy on the way to anywhere else. There are no great Fenland resorts and the region is known mainly from afar, from brief written extracts and from mental images. The name conjures up visions of a watery wilderness, and so the reality of the Fens – with its well-manicured and seemingly interminable chequerboard of fields – may come as a surprise. This is one of the richest agricultural heartlands of England, with landscapes as different from the rolling, hedge-girt countrysides of deepest Shropshire, Herefordshire or Devon as one could imagine. The Fenland scene has no such scenery to entice or captivate. There are no plump villages of mellowed stone cottages nestling in its hollows – indeed, there are neither hollows nor hills of any size.

It is not easy to be indifferent to the Fenland scene. Visitors tend either to love it or to loathe it. Its admirers usually find their inspiration not in the geometrically-patterned landscape of ditch-hemmed fields, but in the juxtaposition of a low, level horizon with the soaring, restless backdrop of the Fenland sky. It is not usually the details in the landscape which draw them to the Fens, but the powerful atmospherics of the tumbling cumulus, lowering nimbus and the cirrus swirls. Others see the Fens as an unsettling and windswept plain. It is not a place for sufferers from agoraphobia, a morbid dread of open spaces. Neither is it a place for those who look for antiquity at every turn for, by English standards, the Fenland scene is mainly quite new, a Milton Keynes of a countryside.

The landscapes of a woefully large portion of East Anglia are ancient, man-made countrysides that have been battered into nonentity by the assaults of modern farming, but this is not really true in the Fens. Here, the man-made scene was to a large extent forged in the seventeenth and eighteenth centuries, and much of this Jacobean and Georgian character endures. Like it or hate it, the Fens, with its arrow-straight roads, stark brick farmsteads and gridwork of fertile fields has character a-plenty.

Bordering the Fens is a raised hem of country that is historically neither part of the Fens, nor immune to its strong influences: the Fen Edge. Here one will find countryside which at least ripples even if it seldom rolls. Here too there are prosperous villages with medieval names and churches, and with sprinklings of attractive dwellings in the timber-framing of the fifteenth and sixteenth centuries, or the warm red brick of the seventeenth and eighteenth; homes that are not stark and hard-faced like the solitary Fenland farmsteads. But this is not quite village England. Many of the Fen-Edge

settlements are not so much the timeless abodes of ploughmen as fossilised river ports which once saw their fortunes arrive and depart along the narrow waterways which threaded and wove to the sea beyond. While one might mistake the Fens for a corner of Holland, or, at least – with all the rusting tractors, wind-scattered fertiliser bags and farmyard tat on view – a rather unkempt corner of Holland, the Fen Edge dances beguilingly to a traditional English tune, even though its nooks and crannies preserve evidence of a rather unusual past.

If the Fenland landscape has its own uncompromising identity, so too do its people. For countless centuries, the rivers and marshes with their hidden fords and secret roads allowed the Fenfolk to shelter from some of the influences and controls which radiated from the interior and capital of England. Those who had learned the Fenland lore could live a little more independently, fishing, fowling and harvesting other natural resources. Rebels, patriots and traitors too could survive far longer in the Fens, emerging from uncharted pathways to strike, pillage and then dissolve again into the mist. Most schoolchildren have heard of the shadowy Saxon patriot Hereward the Wake, but Geoffrey de Mandeville, a double traitor who lived as an independent warlord, skulking in the Fens and then rushing forth to devastate vast areas of East Anglia during the anarchy of King Stephen's reign, is better known to history though not to the public at large (*see* page 157).

Succoured and insulated by their setting, the people of the Fenland were perceived as being independent, morose, volatile and suspicious of strangers. They are still known as 'Fen tigers' today. But despite its geographical autonomy, the Fens did not thrive on isolation and the region has long had strong ties with the Continent. It has accepted innovations ranging from brick building techniques, Dutch gables and improved farm waggons to the engineering of drainage systems from the Low Countries and even today it flourishes more than most places on EEC farming subsidies created to buy peasant votes for French governments.

Although the influence of the physical landscape on the affairs of man may seem more immediate in the peak and crag country of Snowdonia or the granite fastnesses of Dartmoor, the Fenland too is the product of a human response to the natural setting. The Fens were born slowly and quite recently, each formative stage representing a campaign in a long-fought battle between rivers and the sea. The region is a great basin, floored by clays that are about as old as the Cotswolds stones and fringed by rock – the chalk to the east and south, and the gilt and silver Jurassic limestones to the west.

Around 12,000 years ago, when England shed its mantle of ice at the end of the last Ice Age, the rising waters of the Wash lapped southwards to fill the Fenland basin. Here, the tides deposited thicknesses of glacial debris swept in from the North Sea bed, while the rivers too, flowing in from the south, dumped their burdens of sand and silt which they had gathered in the Midlands wastelands of glacial 'drift'. Working

---

OPPOSITE

ABOVE: *A Fenland sky, photographed during a February gale*

BELOW: *A typical Fenland landscape near Benwick*

from their different directions, the rivers and the sea gradually filled the Fenland hollow, although the slow land-building work taking place at the estuaries of the silt-laden rivers was continually threatened by marine storm surges. Gradually though, the river silts advanced over the coastal mudflats and salt marshes and the sea was nudged northwards towards the present Wash.

As the natural processes of deposition reclaimed the basin from the sea, so the wildwood which flourished in the now-balmy climates of the Middle Stone Age or Mesolithic period colonised the Fenland. The Fen of eight or nine thousand years ago was not a fen at all, but offered continuous vistas of primeval woodland with stands of oak, yew and pine while deer and wild horses, boar and cattle wandered from glade to glade. Presumably these beasts were prey to human hunting communities, although little evidence of man's presence has been found. Quite dramatic though was the discovery, datable to the next, Neolithic, period, of the well-preserved and formidably-horned skull of a wild ox or 'auroch'; it was found in Burwell Fen, along with the polished stone axe which had smashed a hole through the frontal bone of the animal.

Being so flat, the area that was destined to become the Fens developed indistinct and shifting patterns of drainage so that small changes in climate, sea level or the rates of run-off to rivers could have severe consequences. About six or seven thousand years ago, a rising sea-level had the effect of diminishing the already shallow river gradients, the lower sections of rivers were flooded and peat began to form in the poorly-drained valleys. Gradually, the forest was inundated. The stricken trees could not survive such waterlogging of their roots and when they fell, the trunks sank into the marsh plants which succeeded the forest. Unable to decay in the normal manner under such wet conditions, the successive layers of dead swamp vegetation accumulated to form an ever-thickening blanket of peat which continued to form in some places until the draining of the Fens in the seventeenth century.

The fallen trees likewise did not decay and now, as the peat shrinks, so the entombed and embalmed corpses of trees from the Mesolithic wildwood emerge just as if they were growing up from the peat. The trunks of these 'bog oaks' are hard and blackened, but the details of crevices and growth-ring structures are plainly preserved. They appear in many places, and a selection of bog oaks can be seen at the Wicken Fen nature reserve. Few people could reach out and touch one of these bog oaks, knowing that the tree might have come crashing down as many as seven thousand years ago, and doubt that Nature holds a treasure chest of wonders.

The gradual extension of waterlogging and peat formation continued for a long period and many bog oaks have been dated by the carbon-14 method to the period 4000–3000 BC. About this time, there was a major invasion or 'transgression' of the Fenland basin by the sea. In the course of this transgression, a layer of clay was deposited on top of the older peat beds. This is graphically described as 'blue buttery clay', although it turns from blue to red as its iron particles react when exposed to the atmosphere. And so, at the time when the Neolithic peasant communities in the rest of Britain were clearing farmland from the forest, building massive tombs like the West Kennet, Newgrange or Pentre Ifan monuments and beginning to contemplate massive temple projects like Stonehenge and Avebury, the Fens existed as brackish swamps, tidal mudflats and lagoons which were periodically washed over by the sea. At the maximum extent of the Fenland sea, the tides lapped close to the chalk and limestone rocks which circled the basin, and although hunters, fishers and graziers must have wandered in to exploit the resources, at most times Neolithic settlement must have been restricted to the drier margins.

Traces of a dwelling dating to about 3300 BC were excavated in the Fengate area near Peterborough which has yielded a wealth of prehistoric information on many different periods. The dwelling was quite large, around 22ft square, and the contemporary people of the area seem to have led lives not unlike those of the log-cabin pioneers during the early days of European settlement in the USA, living in dispersed farmsteads, raising garden crops nearby and grazing their livestock in temporary clearings hacked into the forest. The archaeologist Francis Pryor has described how, after 3300 BC, this pioneering lifestyle seems to have been superseded by a more structured and organised society which built great public ritual monuments.

In many places, erosion and ploughing have obliterated the traces of ancient life, but at Maxey near Stamford, relics from an ancient Fen Edge landscape were preserved beneath the headlands which divided medieval ploughlands. Around Maxey, the excavators have discovered the remains of several circular temples or henges, a 'cursus' – possibly a great ceremonial avenue – and a causewayed enclosure. Many examples of these important public monuments are known elsewhere in Britain and they were surely the settings for great gatherings which might have been concerned with ceremonial, trading or even defence. The Maxey enclosure occupied a slight rise in a loop of the River Welland and stood in an environment that was seasonally flooded

Ancient bog oaks hauled from the Fen near Wicken Fen

but variegated by stands of alder, willow and poplar. Ditched fields, paddocks and droveways patterned this landscape which was punctuated by clusters of dwellings and isolated farmsteads.

The sea lapped around the margins of the present Fens for around a thousand years. But in the course of the third millennium BC, the salt waters receded and the changes to a land and freshwater environment occurred about the time that the introduction of copper-, gold- and then bronze-working heralded the start of the Bronze Age in England. Although the land had emerged from the sea, many areas were waterlogged by the incoming rivers and a new era of peat formation began. As a result, the blue clays and silts laid down during the transgression form a sticky filling to a geological sandwich of peat, with the junction between the blue tidal clays and the upper peat layer marking both the retreat of the sea and the dawn of English metalworking. In many places, as the brackish waters receded, so the salt marsh vegetation will have been replaced by sedge fen, with alder woods and then oak colonising the landscapes of the better-drained areas. Where a very acid type of peat developed, heather, ling and pine will have grown on raised bog.

There is no doubt that these changes rendered the Fens inhabitable and attractive and the Bronze Age East Anglians exploited a range of Fenland resources. Yet sadly, as shall be explained, in most places the erosion of the upper peat layer has now reached down into the Bronze Age levels, thus removing much of the archaeological information. But as a consequence of this, the keen-eyed enthusiast may recognise familiar monuments in a most unusual guise. Bronze Age round barrow tombs are the commonest of all English antiquities and most readers will be familiar with their inverted pudding-bowl forms. In the Fens, however, the ravaged barrows can sometimes be spotted as level, circular patches of lighter soil amongst the surrounding black peat. In fact, one is seeing the levelled top of the Bronze Age tomb, emerging like the filling in a sliced Scotch egg. Numerous cemeteries of these tombs or 'barrowfields' have been discovered in the course of field-walking by the archaeologist David Hall, and they often seem to have been sited at major Fenland river junctions.

For much of the Bronze Age, the climate of Britain was warmer and drier than that of today and the Bronze Age folk will have been able to penetrate deeply into the Fens, to hunt wildfowl, fish or graze their flocks and herds. However, towards the end of the second millennium BC, cooler, wetter and more unsettled conditions became established so that grazings will have become waterlogged and old trackways rendered impassable. In some places, movement will only have been possible after the construction of artificial trackways across the swamps. A section of such a trackway, built upon long oak log piles, was discovered by a farmer and the whole track probably ran from a raised snout of land near Little Thetford and Barway across the marshes to the firmer ground of the Isle of Ely. It was dated to the closing stages of the Bronze Age, around the seventh century BC. Of course, it is very unlikely that this discovery represents the only Bronze Age trackway in the Fens and there are fragmentary records of others which were found and then perished before they could be expertly scrutinised and dated in the modern manner. There is now a well-preserved one very visible at Flag Fen near Peterborough.

The Iron Age is poorly represented by Fenland antiquities. This must in large part be due to the return of severely waterlogged conditions, but also due to the relatively recent erosion of the Iron Age peat layers containing human relics. That Iron Age life in the Fens may have been no less turbulent than elsewhere in Britain is suggested by the recent discovery of the traces of an Iron Age hillfort, dated about the time of the Roman Conquest, Stonea Camp near March (although the term 'hillfort' is rather a misnomer in terrain as flat as that of the Fens).

However, the most obvious creations which, very loosely, date from the Iron Age are works of Nature rather than of man. These are the 'roddons'. As rivers snaked and twined across the prehistoric Fen on their tortuous journeys from the bordering uplands to the Wash, so tiny particles of silt were swept upstream by the tides and deposited upon the river beds. Today, following a few centuries of shrinkage and decay which has greatly reduced the Fenland peat blanket, the silt-plastered river beds now stand above the surrounding landscape. Improved systems of drainage have eliminated most of the old, meandering rivers and streams so that the roddons are now seen as paler silty ridges which are easily discerned from ground level, while from the air they seem like bleached snakes, twisting and slithering across the black plain. Until quite recently, settlers took advantage of the firmer and slightly elevated terrain which the roddons offered and so long chains of farmsteads can be seen, from the air, to be standing on a winding roddon. And now, as the peat is eroded down to the early Bronze Age levels, so the airman can detect a less coherent but older drainage system emerging in the higgledy-piggledy patterns of branching creeks which originally traversed the salt marshes on the surface of the buttery clay.

Although parts of the Fens were affected by marine transgressions during the centuries of the Roman occupation, there is ample evidence that the region in general supported a substantial and industrious native population. The prehistoric attempts to manipulate and control the Fenland environment were small-scale and localised and seem simply to have involved the cutting of drainage ditches around the little fields. In the course of the Roman occupation, however, there were numerous attempts to improve drainage by canalising and straightening some rivers and also some important new waterways were cut across the grain of the natural rivers. The most important of these Roman canals was the Car Dyke (*see* page 55) which ran southwards for some seventy miles from its junction with the River Witham at Roman Lincoln, crossing the rivers Welland, Nene and Great Ouse, to the River Cam at Waterbeach, incorporating convenient stretches of natural rivers en route. It can still be seen as a quite impressive waterway in a few places, as near the road junction where the by-road to Landbeach leaves the Cambridge–Ely road.

The Romans, like their prehistoric predecessors, also built causeways in the Fens. One, which probably ran from near Denver to Peterborough, has been recognised in a stretch surviving between Denver and Whittlesey where it followed the south bank of a then-flowing roddon.

Fully-fledged Roman villas – the elegant country houses that were the foci of agricultural estates – are not found in the Fens, although there is copious evidence of flourishing native settlements and of Romanised dwellings. It is now widely believed that during the occupation, the Cambridgeshire Fens may have functioned as a vast imperial estate specialising in the production of sheep and cattle. Evidence to support this comes from the Roman peat cuttings which have been recognised in a number of places and which existed on quite a grand scale in the Downham Market Fen. Fenland peat was used as a fuel in the production of salt by evaporating brackish water, and so one can easily imagine that the salt was used for salting down locally-produced beef and for curing hides.

Very recently, the story of the Roman exploitation of the Fens took a curious and interesting turn as a result of a discovery by David Hall when field-walking near Stonea Camp. He noticed a slight elevation in the very smooth landscape and found that this platform was covered with stones. The name itself means 'stone island' – and stone of any kind does not occur naturally amongst the peat, silt and clay of the Fens. Here, the stones concerned were identified as having been brought from the famous shelly limestone deposits at Barnack near Stamford. Dating from about AD 117–139, it had consisted of a once lofty and very prominent rectangular tower which had underfloor heating in the form of a hypocaust served by a furnace which was attached to the south wall. A rectangular 'hall' was built against the east wall of the tower, while a semi-circular apse-like projection of a kind normally associated with Roman temples was traced by the footings of the west wall.

Various interpretations of this unique building have been offered. About $\frac{1}{3}$-mile to the south of the Roman tower lies Stonea Camp, and it has been argued that this may have been the site of a great battle in which the Romans defeated insurgent Iceni tribesmen in AD 47. Consequently, the Stonea tower could be regarded as a great monument to the victory. A second interpretation, which need not entirely exclude the other notion, regards the tower as the impressive residence of a Roman procurator who was charged with the administration of the vast Fenland imperial estate. This idea is attractive for one can envisage the old British hillfort focus being superseded by the Roman administrative centre built nearby. Elsewhere in England, after Roman power had collapsed around AD 410, many of the Roman estates survived intact and came to be administered from Saxon halls which in turn acquired churches and, sometimes, villages, while occasionally a town such as Northampton might develop. Although the Stonea tower was demolished around AD 200, some sort of influence seems to have survived beyond the Saxon settlement, for beside the tower ruins were found traces of a rectangular Saxon timber building and evidence of a pottery industry, with two kilns and pot fragments of the fifth to seventh centuries being found.

The evidence from air photography serves to underline the high density of native settlements which existed in and around the Fens in Roman times. Doubtless the folk of the many British farmsteads, hamlets and villages were able to profit from the flourishing urban and military markets for farm produce. In a few places the traces of such settlements are visible from the ground as upstanding earthworks rather than as 'crop marks', which can scarcely be discerned from ground level – as at Shell Bridge near Holbeach St John's in Lincolnshire, where droveways, field boundaries and settlement enclosures can be traced; they can be seen also at Bullock's Haste near Cottenham although recent ploughing has caused some damage while other places with interesting relics have recently been completely vandalised by ploughing.

The story of the Roman Fenland was not entirely one of prosperity and successful endeavour. There were problems with the Car Dyke as described on page 25 and severe invasions by the sea took place and a great blanket of silt was spread across the northern part of the Fens. It was thought that these inundations, which also caused waterlogging in the southern Fenlands, rendered the whole area uninhabitable in the Saxon era which followed, while the legend that the Saxons feared and shunned the marsh has often been repeated. This is disproved by the Saxon discoveries at Stonea and although many parts of the Fens were made inhospitable, in other places Dark Age communities dug cuts and ditches and they are known to have been responsible for some land reclamation schemes, as in the area to the west of Wisbech. Where islands of silt or gravel stood as higher ground, a few feet above the level of flooding, then a village was often established and many of the older Fen villages have names deriving from the Saxon *eg* and Old Norse *ey* 'island' words, like Ramsey, which may mean 'wild garlic island'. Other names, deriving from the Saxon *bece* or 'stream' and *pōl* or 'pond' are also common, as in Wisbech and Walpole.

In medieval times, the Fen was neither a wilderness nor a place where a stranger could often feel at home. That the setting held mysteries and challenges for outsiders is shown by the escapades of Hereward and Geoffrey de Mandeville, while in October of 1215, King John, who was travelling from King's Lynn to Lincoln, stood helplessly by on the side of the broad Wellstream estuary to watch his baggage train crossing the sands when 'the ground opened in the midst of the waters, and whirlpools sucked in everything, men and horses'. The quicksands consumed not only the waggons and escort, but also the Plantagenet regalia, scores of drinking vessels of gold and silver and the King's personal collection of gemstones.

The Fens held more wealth than these royal baubles, however, and in the later Saxon and Norman periods, important towns became established in and around the region, prospering on the moist richness of the Fens. Ely developed on an island of slightly higher ground in the south of the Fens (as described in Chapter 3) and the Anglo Saxon chronicle records that St Æthelthryth (Etheldreda) founded a monastery here in 673: the subsequent story is outlined on page 76.

Roman Cambridge decayed during the greater part of the Dark Ages but the town re-emerged in the later Saxon centuries and gradually the urban core drifted from the Roman, Saxon and the Norman castle nucleus on the north side of the River Cam (near the modern County Hall) to an area of ill-drained marshes across the river. There, a Norman market was developed and, for reasons that are in the initial instances still uncertain, the periodic establishment of colleges resulted in the emergence of Cambridge in the later medieval centuries as a major centre of learning.

Like Cambridge, Peterborough developed on the edge of the Fens and had a strong stake in the marketing of Fenland produce. Here, too, the market which was established in Saxon times subsequently shifted, in this case from the east to the west side of the cathedral. As at Ely, there were early monastic origins with a community being established at 'Medehamstede' in 657. Again, the Norman cathedral serves as a wonderful reminder of the monastic heritage while the town was planned and reorganised in the twelfth century. The very recent discovery of a bank which carried a later wall by archaeologists working on a site known as Peterscourt to the north of the cathedral has aroused considerable interest since it seems to demonstrate that the monastery was defended – a very unusual situation. By the start of the thirteenth century, the wall appears to have been destroyed and the most likely builder of the defencework was Abbot Cenulf (992–1005) who had charge of the community during a very unsettled period of English history. The creation of this fort or *burh* probably explains the name-change to the Borough which became Peterborough.

While Ely had taken what advantage it could of the Fenland terrain (even though the late-seventeenth-century traveller Celia Fiennes thought the town a filthy quagmire and complained of frogs, snails and slow-worms in her bedroom), the other great Fen town, King's Lynn, was developed in an atrocious setting of estuarine lagoons (as described in Chapter 3).

The character of Wisbech – or, at least, such character as still survives the ravages of modern development – is inherited from the decades around 1630 and 1800. Yet the town has a fine medieval pedigree and the great motte of the Norman castle endured to condition the layout of imposing Georgian streets which embraced it with crescents. The development of Wisbech was constrained by flooding and the periodic silting up of the River Nene. This problem was temporarily solved by drainage works in 1631 and 1638, but a permanent solution was not achieved until further canalisation works in the late eighteenth century, and so the better of the buildings in Wisbech reflect the bursts of prosperity and development which followed the different improvements.

Smaller towns too became established in the Fens and, of these, the most puzzling is March, which is given special distinction by the magnificent church of St Wendreda. The present building is mainly of the fourteenth and fifteenth centuries. The serenity of its broad open setting and the well-proportioned silvery exterior of the church are surpassed by the wonders of the Tudor double hammerbeam roof. This is so encrusted with carved angels that one cannot resist the thought that were all the outspread wings to flutter, the church might glide across the Fens like a glorious hovercraft. And yet, this gorgeous building was only a parochial chapel of Doddington, a few miles away, and was originally rather remote from the small market settlement of March. With its once isolated situation and early dedication, one must join the archaeologist Christopher Taylor in wondering whether the church commandeered an anciently sacred site?

In comparison to its church, March was a rather insignificant and humdrum place, but in 1846–7, as a result of the somewhat random processes of nineteenth-century railway development, March emerged as a major junction. Far more people are familiar with the station, therefore, than with the town – and travellers from Cambridge who leave the city in almost any direction but south know it well. In the 1930s, a set of marshalling yards which, at the time, was the largest in England was created, but the yards are now threatened by the policies and prejudices which afflict the national network.

Although in the Dark Ages and early medieval centuries, the Fens were remote and rather inaccessible, the area was by no means impoverished or lacking in potential, while the difficult environment offered the benefits of seclusion and independence – factors which clearly appealed to the monastic orders. Crowland in Lincolnshire was refounded in 946 and the Benedictines created a number of other houses in the Fens, as has been described.

OPPOSITE

ABOVE: *The market at Peterborough*

BELOW: *The river and town at Wisbech*

St Wendreda's church, March

The Fenland setting offered many challenges and opportunities for exploitation, but the environment, while doubtless stimulating a sense of communion with the Creator, must often have seemed overwhelming, for at Crowland there were 'immense marshes, now a black pool of water, now foul running streams, and also many islands, and reeds, and hillocks, and thickets, and with manifold windings wide and long it continues to the North Sea'. We can envisage the monks as pioneers, and yet the most remarkable achievements in medieval Fenland reclamation were made not by the monastic communities, but by lay freeholders. The most vigorous efforts were concentrated in the silt fen around the southern and eastern shores of the Wash. At the time of the Norman Conquest, this was one of the poorest areas in England, yet by 1334 it appears to have been regarded as the richest, with the populations in some areas having increased five or tenfold and the township assessment of that year gives the marshland villages the highest rate. This medieval prosperity has been fossilised in a number of splendid churches, including not only the building at March, but also the two Terrington churches, the three at the Wiggenhall villages and the Tilney and

OPPOSITE: *The nave roof at March*

Walpole examples, all mainly paid for from the profits derived from Fenland hides and fleeces.

Individuals, groups of farmers and small groups of village communities combined to cut ditches, raise banks and sea walls, and then colonise the newly-won lands before advancing again against the sea, or inland, into the peat fen. In this way, the salt marsh became pasture and summer grazings became ploughland. As the geographer Michael Williams has written, 'The evidence of their bustling youthfulness and energy is etched indelibly on the landscape by a series of walls or dykes, and also by many additions, each dyke marking a step in the reclamation process.'* The first attempts at land reclamation may have begun in the seventh century, but the main period of endeavour was between about 1150 and 1250. The so-called 'Roman' bank, which ran completely around the Wash and still stands six feet high in places was, in fact, almost certainly built around 1250. A glance at a map of parish boundaries in the Fens offers vivid glimpses of how village communities would forge long corridors of reclaimed land, with the snout of the parish advancing into the peat or salt marshes in the wake of the pioneers while, in other places, the particular villages controlled detached islands of summer grazing or parishes jostled to exploit a common.

But in the years following the building of the 'Roman' bank, the national economy began to ail, the climate deteriorated and the great mortality which followed the arrival of the Black Death in 1348 severely sapped the vigour for land reclamation. The monasteries which had at first been junior partners in the great reclamation bonanza extended their stakes in the Fens through various processes of bequests, purchase and coercion. Ramsey Abbey exported grain to Colchester and Ipswich, whilst Crowland, which had engaged in bitter grazing disputes with the surrounding villages, founded a swarm of new farms or 'granges' in the second half of the thirteenth century. New hamlets and villages were also established under monastic leadership, like Market Deeping in Lincolnshire which was founded by Peterborough Abbey. Despite the prominence of the monastic houses of the Fens in the later medieval centuries, fate has not treated them kindly. The most extensive remains are those of Denney Abbey; Anglesey 'Abbey' in part survives, entombed within the later, rather disharmonious house, while the beautiful gatehouse of Ramsey Abbey is also preserved by the National Trust.

In the peat Fens to the south of the main theatres of medieval activity, the changes to the landscape were less dramatic, and some were accomplished by Nature rather than by man. While some of the smaller former Fen meres may have originated, like the Norfolk Broads, as flooded peat diggings, most meres seem to have formed as a result of natural processes operating during the historical era. During the marine transgressions of Roman times, banks of clay were swept in by the tides and sea surges to bar and so pond back the Fenland rivers, so forming the shallow lakes which once splattered the landscape. Now the meres have gone, mainly as a result of drainage projects in the eighteenth and nineteenth centuries. During the centuries of their existence, however, these vast, reed-hemmed mirrors of water must have been a lovely feature of the Fenland scene.

* *The English Medieval Landscape* ed. Leonard Cantor: Croom Helm (1982)

Monastic ruins incorporated in a later house at Denney Abbey

The lost meres can still be located: many survived to appear on accurate nineteenth-century maps while names like Red Mere, Whittlesey Mere and Trundle Mere still persist. The sites and extents of the meres can also be recognised as patches of whitish soil amongst the black ploughland. The patches consist of a limey 'shell marl' which was deposited as the water plants of the meres caused chalk, which was carried in solution by the incoming rivers, to be precipitated on the lake bed where it entombed the shells of water snails and other lake floor debris.

Although originally less prosperous than the transformed silt fens around the Wash, the peat Fens offered many enticements to the peasant, farmer, landlord and monk. In addition to the cattle grazings on the vast commons, the semi-natural environment beckoned with lucrative fisheries in the rivers and meres, with the prodigious catches of eels being particularly valuable. Though timber was in short supply, the peat beds provided cheap fuel and the rights of 'turbary' or peat-digging operated in specially reserved areas. Salt pans were worked, while the Fens also yielded rush and sedge for thatching, osiers for basket work, and gliding on the waters between the reed and osier beds were wildfowl of many different types which could be stalked through the marshes or lured to special decoys. In such a setting, the peasant and small freeholder could enjoy a measure of self-sufficiency and live his life less cowed by masters and authorities than could the cousin on a Midlands manor. Not surprisingly then, the great post-medieval plans for Fenland drainage and reclamation were not universally welcomed.

The medieval achievements in Fenland reclamation tend to have been overlooked and yet, medieval society with its generally weak central government and the universal obsession with property rights, did not favour planning on the grand scale. Piecemeal drainage schemes in the Fens had various local successes, but wholesale reclamation required the forceful pursuit of a masterplan to cut through the tangled web of local interests. A few quite significant schemes were launched in the Middle Ages, notably (Bishop) Morton's Leam of the late fifteenth century, carrying the waters of the River Nene eastwards from the Peterborough area towards Wisbech. At the start of the seventeenth century, (Sir John) Popham's Eau carried surplus water out across seven miles of Fen to the River Ouse at Salters Lode in Norfolk. But most small and medium-scale schemes tended simply to divert a problem of flooding away from one man's land to that of his neighbours.

As already discussed, the 4th Earl of Bedford, who owned vast estates at Thorney, was approached by a collection of other important landowners in 1630, and in the following year an organisation of wealthy 'Adventurers' or entrepreneurs was formed. In return for staking a large amount of capital in reclamation, the Earl was promised some 95,000 acres of drained Fenland; the Adventurers became the Bedford Level Corporation and hired the Dutch drainage engineer Cornelius Vermuyden who had already won a reputation for drainage projects in England. And so it was that in the seventeenth century, as in all preceding and subsequent centuries, the wealthy and privileged masters of the countryside were able to stamp their will upon the landscape and the lesser folk who lived in it. The main initiatives in the drainage campaign have been described in Chapter 3.

The Duke's drainage of the Fens in the middle of the seventeenth century is often remembered as a major signpost on the road to modern progress and as a symbol of the break with outmoded medieval practices. Perhaps indeed it was – for the disastrous environmental consequences, which tend to have been forgotten, soon outstripped the gains. By the end of the century, serious floods were commonplace and, in 1724, the author and traveller Daniel Defoe rode down from the Gogmagog Hills and described what had become a common sight: 'We saw the Fen country on our right almost all covered with water like a sea.' Having commented on the number of rivers draining into the Fens, the incredible productivity of a duck decoy near Ely (which was reputed to despatch 3,000 brace of duck to London each week) and having also delivered the obligatory condemnation of the sloth of the county poor, Defoe then allowed himself a poetic passage which captured the ethos of the early eighteenth century Fens: 'As these Fens appear covered with water, so I observed too, that they generally at this latter part of the year appear also covered with fogs, so that when the Downs and higher grounds of the adjacent country were gilded by the beams of the sun, the Isle of Ely looked as if wrapped up in blankets, and nothing to be seen, but now and then, the lanthorn or cupola of Ely Minster.'

The Adventurers' plan for the Fens had really not worked, and the main reasons why, as sketched in Chapter 8, were fairly obvious. As the Fenland peat and silts dried out, not surprisingly, they shrank. Also, when prolonged dry spells desiccated the surface of the peat, fine particles of topsoil could be picked up by the strong and unimpeded Fen winds and blown out of the fields in choking clouds of dust. Then, as the level of the Fenland surface was lowered, so the drainage gradients were reduced, the problems of winter inundation returned with a renewed vengeance, while the estuaries of the weakly-flowing rivers became choked with silt. But there was also a more insidious dimension to the problem which had to be faced but could not be countered. When waterlogged, the peat, which is composed of organic plant debris, could not be attacked by bacteria, but once the peat was drained then 'aerobic' or air-loving bacteria could flourish in the black soils which provided them with breakfast, lunch and dinner. And so the peat was quite literally eaten away.

Meanwhile, the silt Fen to the north had no such appeal, so that the sinking peat Fen came to form a great drainage basin, exacerbating the drainage problem. At the same time, the silts which the rivers and drains deposited on the floors of their channels protected these stream beds from attack, so that soon the Fenland waters were flowing in courses which stood several feet above the sinking peat plains. Even today, when most threats of serious flooding have been countered, there are few landscapes more ominous and depressing than that of the black Fen, seen on a stormy day when the laden channels poise menacingly above the sodden, inky plain – and the oppressive ethos is heightened by the realisation that one is standing at a height that may be several feet below sea level.

Rather than solving the problems of Fenland drainage at a stroke, the Adventurers had set a whirlpool of environmental vicious circles spinning wildly. With the river gradients declining and great banks of silt building up at the coast to choke the mouths of the rivers, it was apparent that reclamation and security from flooding demanded the permanent support of a force of men and machines.

The real drainage of the Fens was achieved not by the Duke and his Dutch cohort, but by windmills and the resolute Fenmen who tended them. The mills appeared everywhere, like bizarre dragonflies hatched from the march, so that by 1748 there were 250 mills in the middle section of the Fens alone. The windmills served as pumps, with the natural energy captured by the sails being harnessed to revolve scoop wheels which raised the sluggish waters from one drain to another. Although they tapped a free source of power, they had to be directed to catch the winds and were carefully tended when storms threatened; during calm spells they were impotent no matter how pressing the threat of floods. Although ubiquitous features of the Victorian Fenland, just one wind pump survives, at the National Trust nature reserve on Wicken Fen, where a repaired and now serviceable pump from Adventurers' Fen has been re-erected.

After 1820, steam-engines began to supersede the windmills, firstly powering scoop wheels and then centrifugal pumps. About the time of the Great War, the steam-

engines in turn passed the baton of Fenland drainage to diesel-powered centrifugal pumps, while electrical pumps began to replace these after the last world war. Despite these mechanical pacemakers which pumped water through the hardened arteries of Vermuyden's drainage system, the threat of flooding was not entirely vanquished. There were floods in 1936, '37 and '39 and flooding took place more severely in 1947 and disastrously in 1953, when a North Sea tidal surge and onshore gales brought a terrifying inundation. As a consequence, in 1954, work began on a relief channel cut alongside the Lynn Ouse below Denver and regulated by a massive sluice to control the discharge of floodwater while barring the tidal surges.

Although the successive generations of pumps and the construction of the Denver sluices appear to have mastered the problems of Fenland floods and drainage for the moment, the shrinkage of the peat continues relentlessly. By the end of this century it may, like the meres, mills and marshmen, have disappeared. In one area after another, the ploughshares are biting through the last few inches of the rich peat blanket to bring up the poor soil of the buttery clay, and so the farmers that have prospered so well from the peatlands are seeing their riches blow away on the parching winds. Though more might be done to conserve the peat – for shelter belts of wind-breaking trees are still not common, and hedgerows scarcely glimpsed – the problems of bacterial attack seem insoluble. Bands of straw are set in some fields to help stabilise the footloose soils, but the microbes still munch away at the remainder of their feast, the final course in many places.

While the hanging rivers, railways and roads and the tilting Fenland farms and cottages with their distorted walls bound by trusses and tie beams all tell of the shrinking, sinking peat, the most graphic evidence was provided by the 'Holme post'. In 1848, Fens landowner and drainer W. Wells caused a cast iron pillar to be thrust down into the peat near the shores of the shrivelling Whittlesey Mere until the top of the pillar was level with the land surface. By 1892, some 10 feet of the post were visible, showing that more than 2 feet of the peat had been lost each decade. Thereafter, the rate of shrinkage continued at a slower rate, while vast areas of the Fens have lost 12 to 15 feet of peat since drainage began.

To the driver passing through, the Fens may seem to be a featureless and poorly visible landscape since the flatness of the plains and the low horizons compress the observable scene into a narrow ribbon, a slender stage that is walled and roofed by the vastness of the Fenland sky. As a result, the motorist may miss much that can be seen from the higher vantage points of a coach or railway carriage. Much of the scene may seem too modern and orderly for many tastes, although the magnificent octagon tower of Ely Cathedral is an almost universally visible reminder of more distant times, and rivals Glastonbury Tor as a gladdening beacon which once beckoned the tired pilgrim from afar. The sensual impact of the slowly approaching cathedral as it looms through the distant haze above the level green and black patterned plain

---

OPPOSITE

ABOVE LEFT: *A fragment of old Fenland at the National Trust nature reserve at Wicken Fen*

ABOVE RIGHT: *Fenland vegetation at the old brick pond, Wicken Fen*

BELOW: *A riverside view at Wicken Fen*

is one of the great passages in the English landscape saga and is perhaps most fluently delivered to the traveller on the March to Ely railway.

This chapter has tried to show that, perhaps contrary to first impressions, the Fens contain many interesting details to reward all visitors who are fascinated by the historical building blocks of the English scene. Eyes soon learn to become discerning and will recognise the sinuous ridge of an Iron Age roddon, the bleached soil marking a medieval mere or the engineering which explains the geometry of the drainage channels. But everywhere in the Fens, the impact of the broad scenic canvas dominates the fine detail. Often escaping the Atlantic cloud shrouds and the industrial hazes of the Midlands, the light in the Fens can seem purer and fresher than elsewhere, so that the brilliancy of the colours may seem to sear the senses. Then the landscape becomes a luminous psychedelic tumult of emerald, black, blue, white and silver which is seen as though through alternating golden and grey filters as the clouds glide across the face of the sun. But words are cheap and over-rated, amounting only to an invitation to readers to see things for themselves.

A broad arc of villages surrounds the margins of the Fens, like greedy children ranged around an apple-bobbing barrel. The villages of the Fen Edge were attracted by the resources of the wetland environment, some developing as river ports, some enduring the wetness of winter in order to exploit the Fenland summer grazings, with many flourishing from both trade and agriculture. As tourist attractions, none of the villages is quite in the picture-postcard class although several, like Swaffham Prior, Burwell and Swavesey have their pretty points. With villages as, perhaps, with ladies, the most overtly beautiful are often the least interesting or personable, but all the Fen Edge villages are packed with interest to beckon the thoughtful visitor. Lying quite close to urban centres of employment, the Fen Edge settlements have their fair shares of middle-class commuters who now keep the fires of village survival well-stoked. Yet written in the layouts of the village landscape and tucked away in nooks and crannies behind the titivated cottage façades can be found the evidence of an enthralling past.

Perched on the margins of the Fens, on low ridges, humps or snouts of clay, chalk or gravel, these villages needed the Fen but were sometimes lured too close for comfort so that, occasionally, floods of an unusual severity would prompt a restructuring of the village layout, the relocation of some dwellings on drier land or else launch a flurry of ditch-digging. Ditches which today may seem to be backwaters in all senses of the word could be crucial to the survival of a settlement whose toes tested the waters of the undrained Fen, while the merest swells in the watery setting could be magnets for settlement, like the almost imperceptible rise which carries Landbeach and is known by the locals as 'The Hill'. Several of the villages are linked to the Fenland rivers by artificial channels or lodes (*see* page 198). At least three, and perhaps as many as six of the lodes date back to Roman times, the others being medieval or later constructions. The lodes were maintained to carry the waterborne trade right through until the railway age and although they now serve as humble land drains, they are still held in affection by the local communities who have rallied to defend them against schemes for their destruction. The lodes provided the Fen Edge river ports with access to the major Fenland waterways and, ultimately, to the ports of the North Sea. The village port functions were gradually shed, mainly in the course of the nineteenth century but it is not easy to judge their antiquity.

There was intense native settlement on the Fen margins in Roman times and the gardens in many Fen Edge villages tend to be very productive of fragments of Roman pottery. Yet given the volatile and shifting nature of Dark Age settlement in general, it would be folly to assert that most of the Fen Edge village sites have been *continuously* occupied since Roman times. The sort of complicated changes which could take place can be glimpsed if not entirely unravelled in the case of Horningsea village, just north-east of Cambridge.

Horningsea is a place of some antiquarian note for it has given its name to a particular type of grey Roman pottery. There were, in fact, at least four Roman settlements in the vicinity of Horningsea: all were quite substantial, one covering at least three acres, two being of at least five acres, but the fourth, which lay around Eye Hall around $\frac{3}{4}$ mile to the north of the present village, was the most important, covering about 15 acres. An excavation in 1911 revealed the remains of seven cone-shaped pottery kilns from this Roman industrial centre. A medieval settlement also existed here and another lost village or hamlet lay to the SSE of Eye Hall. Clearly, then, a complex local story of village growth and decline has been enacted hereabouts.

But there is much more to Horningsea than just a rather special Roman past although the motorist passing through may be aware only of an unspectacular and elongated village with the houses, including some attractive jettied medieval dwellings, lining the roadside. The church is not very evident from the through road and the only clue to the village past is glimpsed in the name-plate 'Dock Lane' where a lane

The minster church, village and riverside at Horningsea

leads westwards from the main road. The interesting core of Horningsea also lies to the west of the modern spine, around the church and river. Horningsea church, with its thirteenth- and fourteenth-century architecture is not obviously spectacular but it has a very special pedigree, for it began as a 'minster' church with a community of secular canons who provided services for the churchless communities of the surrounding area, and its history goes back at least to the ninth century. About 970, the prosperous settlement which had developed at Horningsea became a property of the Benedictine Abbey at Ely. Just to the north of the church, two lanes, Dock Lane and St John's Lane, run down to the banks of the River Cam, and where they meet the river there are the shrunken traces of the port's former riverside wharves. And so at Horningsea, as in most other Fen Edge villages, there is far more of interest than the hasty traveller might suppose.

With its riverside setting, Horningsea was independent of the Roman lode system, but one of the most interesting of the former ports is Reach, about four miles further to the north-east. Few English villages can boast such a fascinating situation. Again there is evidence of Roman settlement in the vicinity of the village while, earlier, an Iron Age settlement had taken advantage of the little snout of chalk which juts towards the Fens. Far more important and still a very striking monument is the massive 'linear earthwork' of Devil's Dyke which runs north-westwards for 7½ miles to terminate at Reach, while the alignment of the Dyke is continued into the Fens by Reach Lode. The lode is certainly Roman and whether the great Devil's Dyke belongs to the late Roman or early Saxon period, its builders clearly decided that the existing lode could effectively continue the defences into the difficult terrain of the Fens. Much later, at some time in the twelfth century, Reach was awarded the right to hold a fair, and the Fair Green which was to be its venue was created by levelling the last 200 yards of Devil's Dyke. We have said 'Reach', but in fact we are dealing with two distinct medieval villages, East and West Reach which sat cheek by jowl on their respective sides of the Dyke and green.

The parish boundary between the buxom and prosperous villages of Burwell and Swaffham Prior ran along the crest of Devil's Dyke and, in medieval times, neither Burwell nor Swaffham Prior enjoyed direct access to the Cam river trading system. Between the two villages though, there was the Roman waterway of Reach Lode and so the two Reaches developed as medieval outports situated at the terminus of the lode, with West Reach serving Swaffham and East Reach doing the same for Burwell.

At the lode end of the shared green, a hythe or wharf with basins for the narrow Fen craft or 'lighters' was dug, and then lined with rammed chalk rubble. As well as trans-shipping the conventional medieval products like East Anglian grain and imported iron, salt and timber, Reach developed an important trade in locally dug 'clunch'. This is a white stone quarried from the harder of the chalk beds which, though easily weathered when used for external masonry, was admirably suited for the facings and fine carvings of church and college interiors. It is used at Ely Cathedral, in the lovely Lady Chapel for example, and in a number of Cambridge colleges and can be seen in the exteriors of several Cambridgeshire churches, like the one at the former clunch-quarrying village of Cherry Hinton on the outskirts of Cambridge. Although a coal trans-shipping trade developed after the Industrial Revolution, the life of Reach as a bustling little river port ended abruptly with the opening of the Cambridge–

Mildenhall railway in 1884. Packed with interest and with rambles along the Dyke or waterside close at hand, Reach is also quite pretty and preserves a wealth of fascination for all those who look for more than the glossy guidebooks offer.

Burwell gained its own improved access to the Cam river network via Reach Lode in the mid-seventeenth century when the Burwell New Lode was cut, but the townlet had already acquired a large and complicated layout and a notable history. The place-name hints that Burwell may have originated close to a spring in a place where fortifications were visible in Saxon times, but the fortress earthworks which survive today are different and of the medieval period, and the original village nucleus lay around the remarkable church of St Mary which was rebuilt in the fifteenth century, restored in the nineteenth and given a recent face-lift. From its core around the church, medieval Burwell expanded northwards and westwards until the events of the twelfth century eradicated development in the latter direction. In 1143, the rebel Earl Geoffrey de Mandeville gained control of Ely and used the town as a base for his pillaging of the surrounding countryside. As described on page 159, the castle never was finished, although an Abbot of Ramsey erected a manor house inside its earthen defences in the mid-thirteenth century. While modern visitors are restricted to the public footpath which crosses the site, the earthworks of this hastily cast-up medieval fortress are most impressive, with the immense trench of the moat surrounding a 260-ft × 160-ft raised rectangular interior.

The village core around the church, castle and the former church of St Andrew is known as High Town, and from High Town, the line of the village high street was

The ancient waterway of Reach Lode

LEFT: *The medieval church at Burwell*
BELOW: *The old port of Commercial End*

carried northwards across the village fields by a track known as the Causeway. At the northern end of this track, another settlement, known as North Street, developed in the medieval period, probably, as Christopher Taylor suggests, from the establishment of dwellings on the uncultivated headlands of the fields. Just to the south of North Street, a third settlement, which was probably planned and created towards the end of the Middle Ages and known as Newnham appeared. Newnham is linked to North Street while development along the Causeway linked Newnham to High Town, so producing the remarkable Burwell village or townlet which is almost two miles in length.

At some uncertain time, probably late in the Middle Ages, Burwell obtained its independence of Reach when a lode link to Reach Lode was cut, but this was in turn superseded by the cutting of Burwell New Lode which leaves the village near the junction of Newnham and North Street. The construction of the new lode brought great prosperity and activity to Burwell. A waterway known as 'The Weirs' runs behind the houses in this section of the village, terminating at its Newnham end in what was a public wharf or hythe, while around twenty-five basins and canals ran from The Weirs to give barges access to the landings behind the private houses lining the west side of North Street. The former prosperity of the merchants and traders living here is still evidenced by a collection of good houses dating from the decades around 1600 and surviving after the infilling of most but not all of the house-backing canals and basins which sustained the prosperity.

Relics of the old Fen Edge river trade abound, but space allows only one more village example. Villages with names like Shakespearean actors or Tory MPs are common here and elsewhere in England, but 'Commercial End' is hardly of the Boothby Pagnell or Hemingford Abbots genre. Just to the south of Commercial End is Swaffham Bulbeck which, were it not a quite attractive village, might not sound out of place on the stage of *Hamlet* or the right-wing benches. Unlike some of its neighbours, Swaffham Bulbeck has a fairly simple layout in the form of a parallel line of medieval and later dwellings set out along a road running northwards down a gentle chalk scarp towards the edge of the Fens. At the northern end of the village, this road forks around a farm and paddock and its north-eastern branch takes a couple of sharp bends and finds itself in Commercial End.

In the medieval period, there were both a Benedictine priory and a nunnery near Commercial End, and although the undercroft of the nunnery is plainly visible as the bottom storey of a nearby house, neither foundation is prominent today. Commercial End may have begun its life under a different name as a hamlet associated with the monastic houses, and until the nineteenth century it was known by the common name of Newnham – but its real fascination derives from the quite recent past. There are no medieval dwellings standing here, the closest approach to antiquity being a peripheral thatched cottage of the seventeenth century. This appendage of Swaffham Bulbeck is really very much a product of the early nineteenth century so far as the surviving dwellings are concerned. It seems likely that at some uncertain stage in the post-medieval period, the building of a mill on the village lode obstructed navigation into the heart of Swaffham Bulbeck, causing trade to drift a little downstream. In any event, Commercial End began to prosper as a river port during the eighteenth century. In 1805, a merchant called Thomas Bowyer constructed warehouses and some ter-

The two churches at Swaffham Prior

raced dockside dwellings here and the port is known to have handled imported wine, timber, salt and coal and despatched export cargoes of East Anglian grain, flour and malt. In 1821, a New Cut improved the link to the River Cam via the village lode and the cut ran towards the Fens from a large wharf of the seventeenth century (still partly intact but on private land), which lay beside the late seventeenth-century Merchant's House which Bowyer purchased and enlarged after 1805.

Although the briefly dynamic Cambridgeshire coprolite industry boosted the port trade at Commercial End in the latter part of the nineteenth century, the business died away. (The coprolite diggings exploited beds of phosphate-rich nodules which were reputed at the time to be dinosaur droppings.) Now this offshoot of Swaffham Bulbeck, with its neat brick terraces, fine Merchant's House, warehouse, maltings and waterways has been colonised, revived and prettified by the commuters and professional classes. The setting seems quite rustic and so it is strange to think that one is visiting industrial archaeology, and stranger still to realise that the trade perished scarcely a century ago and that the communal horizon once extended outwards, embracing both Cambridge and the North Sea.

A mere handful of Fen Edge villages have been mentioned, and yet there are twenty or thirty more with tales scarcely less fascinating. Do visit those mentioned, and include nearby Swaffham Prior with its most unusual complement of two churches sharing the same churchyard, a legacy of some old manorial rivalry. Then there are attractive Fen Edge villages like Swavesey, described by Jack Ravensdale in his book and television series *History on your Doorstep* (BBC, 1982); the former county of Huntingdonshire has some delightful villages, not the least being Houghton with its fine broach-towered church and watermill. To the north-east, the fascination extends into Lincolnshire with the Deeping villages, and the cornucopia of prehistoric and Dark Age archaeology associated with Maxey just south of the county boundary, while to the north-west it continues into Norfolk, where Denver and the Wiggenhall churches all charm the eye. More detailed biographies of a series of Cambridgeshire Fen Edge villages are provided in the Royal Commission on Historical Monuments volume for the region, while Jack Ravensdale describes the history of Cottenham, Landbeach and Waterbeach in detail in *Liable to Floods*.*

Very few people would consider spending a holiday just pottering in and around the Fens – and this is just one good reason for considering the possibility. Another good reason is that the summer climate is one of the very driest and sunniest in Britain, and the roads are freer of traffic than most and plied by tractors rather than the frenetic Cortinas or thunderous juggernauts so common elsewhere. For many people, the region could not hold a candle to the fish and chips of Benidorm and all who find the world and ideas of the Sloane Ranger even remotely interesting will be far better off elsewhere. But for all the many, many people who love and respond to the varied English landscapes, the Fens and Fen Edge have much to offer. Though pancake flat, the Fens have a bold and gutsy character, while the colleges of Cambridge, the antiquities of King's Lynn and the cathedrals of Peterborough and Ely all lie close and beckoning.

**Liable to Floods* J.R. Ravensdale, CUP (1974)

10
THE BRECKLAND

Imagine a virtual desert: a place of poor, sandy soils that has been largely abandoned by its farmers and carved up between the military and the conifer growers. One will surely picture a sad scenic disaster zone. Yet the Breckland has a very special allure, and in between the army's no-go zones and the tedious forest plantations, there are patches of wild and soulful heathland scenery which are as distinctive and as full of character as any English countryside. But the Breckland landscape is far removed from most perceptions of an idyllic English scene. It has a fleeting likeness to the Suffolk Sandlings and is vaguely reminiscent of some of the wilder and flatter corners of Central Europe although really this tiny region, its true core only about the size of Anglesey, has a personality that is all its own. It is a personality distilled from heather, bracken and sand, from meres which rise and fall in the strangest ways and from the tattered friezes of Scots pine, whose silhouettes are the hallmark of the landscape. The name itself seems only to have been coined by the local naturalist W.G. Clarke in 1894, who based it on the local word 'brecks', which describes impermanent fields periodically broken into the waste.

The previous chapter described how an appreciation of the geological basis of scenery is fundamental to an understanding of the Fens, and this is also true of the Breckland. The region is floored with chalk, even though the Breckland heaths seem a million ecological miles removed from a typical chalk landscape (such as the racing industry has helped to conserve on the downs near Newmarket, just a few miles from the Breckland frontier). Before the Ice Ages, the area existed as a chalk basin, but in the course of the glaciations, a thin, pancake-like smear of glacial debris or 'drift' was plastered across the basin by the ice, while rivers of meltwater also dumped their burdens of sand and chalk particles here. This glacial coating contained sand, clay and chalk particles and is known technically as a 'chalky boulder clay'. As the centuries rolled by, however, percolating rain water flushed down the fine chalk particles, leaving behind the surface blanket of unstable sands. And so it is that in the Breckland one finds the strange anomaly of an area that is floored in alkaline chalk but in most places supports acid-land ecology of heather, pine and bracken which flourishes on the surface skim of sour sands.

This is also one of the very driest corners of England, with a low rainfall and soils which allow the swift downward drainage of moisture. The footloose sands, which brought many disastrous sandstorms (page 211) and are still inclined to blow in some places, the old dunes which have been stabilised by vegetation, and the scars of recent sand-blows combine to produce a feeling of semi-desert – and yet the Breckland is generously sprinkled with small lakes or meres. In such a sandy setting, the meres seem quite incongruous and the strangeness does not end here, for they often appear to be quite heedless of the laws of Nature and can sometimes be seen to be well-filled with water during a relative drought, yet be shrunken and partly overgrown after a deluge. The level of water in the meres is now known to be governed by the degree of saturation in the underground chalk. If the chalk is quite dry, then a torrent of rainfall can be absorbed and the level of the meres will seem unaffected by a cloudburst. Only when the chalk is fully saturated will renewed rainfall cause the level of a mere to rise; therefore the state of the meres at any particular time is not so much a reflection of yesterday's rainfall or drought, but of the wetness of preceding weeks or months.

The origin of the meres is even more tantalising and is still partly mysterious. When faced with odd landforms or puzzling prehistoric relics, our distant forbears often grasped at the straws which religion or the supernatural offered, so that while the great East Anglian frontier earthwork is known as Devil's Dyke, one of the most attractive Breckland meres is The Devil's Punchbowl. Even in the modern era, the unsupportable notion that the meres might be flooded shell craters has been given an airing. As to the possible origins of the meres, the 'geomorphologists', who study such problems, offer a number of plausible explanations.

Unlike the Norfolk Broads, the meres are natural rather than man-made landforms, although some have been re-shaped by the digging of marl pits. A minority interpretation of the meres sees them as 'solution hollows' similar to those which have formed in limestone districts like the Pennines as a result of the underlying lime-rich rocks being dissolved by rainwater. The majority of experts believe that the meres were formed by processes that were active in the immediate aftermath of glaciation. They just might be 'dead ice hollows', marking the places where great blocks of ice which had become severed from a retreating ice sheet stood stranded as islands in a landscape awash with silt-laden meltwaters. More probably, the meres are 'ground ice depressions' which were formed where great masses of underground ice lay entombed until thawing, when the ground above collapsed into the sludgy chasm. The ground ice features closely, but not exactly, resemble the ice-filled blisters or 'pingos' often shown in films of Arctic exploration.

Although it is not obviously apparent, the meres are aligned along two gentle troughs. Several lie inaccessible amongst the military zones, but there are others, like The Devil's Punchbowl, Fowl Mere and Ringmere which have roadside locations, while Langmere lies in the East Wretham Heath nature reserve: *see* page 218. (Currently, the environs of Ringmere are afflicted by an adder epidemic and all explorers of the Breckland should be aware of the snake hazard.) In the Saxon and medieval periods, the meres existed like oases in the parched heath, and so it is not surprising that the surrounding communities were anxious to control a section of the waterfront as a watering-place for their cattle. No less than ten parishes converged upon the now desiccated Rymer Mere to the south of Thetford, and six focussed on Ringmere to the north of the town. (One or other of these meres was probably the site of the terrible battle of 'Hringmara Heath' of 1010, one of the terminal rounds in the long contest between Saxon and Danish leaders.)

While the meres and the surface skim of glacial drift are the most obvious legacies

Sunset at Ringmere

of the Ice Ages, there are other relics which are as fascinating though harder to recognise. Glaciation did not end suddenly in a golden sunburst, and for many centuries winters remained bitter, while the summer thaws turned the countryside into a morass of meltwater and mud which stood upon the rigidly frozen subsoil. When such 'periglacial' conditions held sway – as they did for most of the final Ice Age when the ice only formed a frigid fringe around the Norfolk coast – the succession of freeze and thaw created contortions in the ground and produced some quite peculiar features.

Patterned ground is visible from the air and is evident from the ground in newly-ploughed fields and in the vegetational patterns of the undisturbed areas. Periglacial processes that are not entirely understood have sorted the surface soils and stones so that chalky soils form polygons that are around 30 ft across, these polygons being edged and defined by bands of sandy soil. But as soon as the ground begins to slope, the polygon patterns are transformed into alternating stripes of chalky and sandy soils. As a result, the discerning visitor will recognise a detailed ecological patterning of the vegetation, with lime-loving grasses alternating with the heathers which thrive on acid soils. Since the onslaughts of myxomatosis drastically reduced the rabbit population after 1954, the patterns traced by the sand sedge, which used to be held in check by the rabbits, have become quite striking. The plant thrives on sand but soon dies on chalky soils and it spreads by creeping underground stems or 'rhizomes' at such a rate that a single plant can obtain a diameter of over 200 yds, pursuing the sands and failing on the chalky soils; the older, weaker growth at the centre of the plant contrasts with the vigorous young shoots at its edges.

Vegetation patterns also help to reveal the underlying soils in the areas of the meres. The raised chalky rims of the meres support grasses and lime-lovers like the thistle, horseshoe vetch, cowslip and scabious; fen sedge, black bog rush and cotton grass grow in the peats which have accumulated in the meres themselves, while the heathland around may be patterned by heather, bracken and sand sedge and dotted by trees like birch and ash, and shrubs like gorse, hawthorn and blackthorn which have gained a foothold since the decline in grazing by sheep and rabbits. As a result of its peculiar glacial and periglacial history, the contrasting environments of the Breckland offer a great deal of interest to all serious nature lovers.

It is not difficult to contrast the scenic and botanical richness of the patches of preserved heathland with the modern coniferous wasteland all around, and so compare good old unspoilt countryside with the sterile modern product. At the same time, one must remember that all our countrysides are man-made – although some are better made than others. The Breckland heaths can seem wild and untamed and yet they are just as much the product of human endeavours as the sombre Forestry Commission plantations. In fact, the saga of man's transformation of the natural environment is nowhere better demonstrated than in the Breckland. The fragmentary heaths do not represent a threatened vestige of the natural environment but result from several millennia of use as livestock grazings. The damp peat layers beneath the meres have preserved ancient pollen grains which allow us to reconstruct the story of the colonisation of the Breckland, first by a natural woodland vegetation, and then by plants which could withstand the pressures of grazing.

The first trees and shrubs to colonise the post-glacial landscape were rugged pioneers like the arctic willow and birch. Gradually, they were largely succeeded by the pine, while as the warmth and the amount of humus present in the soil increased, so the pioneers were supplanted by the more demanding deciduous trees like the alder, elm, hazel, lime and oak. Had man not intervened to change the Breckland ecology, then the region would still be blanketed by an expanse of mixed deciduous forest.

In the closing stages of the last glaciation, bands of migratory hunters began to wander into the Breckland. They were not the first men and women to do so, for evidence of previous Old Stone Age intrusions exists in the form of the very ancient pear-shaped flint 'hand axes' which have been found quite frequently in the area and which can still be found on the shores of the River Lark which must often have served as a corridor for movement into the Breckland.

It has often been said that after the introduction of farming to Britain, around 5000 BC, the devotees of the new agricultural lifestyle sought out areas with light, sandy or dry, chalky soils. It is argued that on such land, the primeval forest would have grown less thickly, while the simple prehistoric farming implements could have coped more easily with the lighter, drier soils. The Breckland has therefore often been considered as an important heartland of Neolithic farming. This may or may not be true, for in recent years it has been demonstrated that Stone Age agriculture exploited a wide range of different environments and farming expanded quite rapidly from the pioneering farmsteads established in clearings in areas with chalk, limestone and alluvial soils. In the Breckland, the prehistoric farmers must have appreciated the limited fertility of the dry, sandier soils and so they will have developed a form of farming which emphasised livestock production rather than grain. In the pioneering phases, cereals may have been grown in clearings which were abandoned after a couple of years of cropping, with sheep and cattle being put to graze on the crop of weeds and seedlings which followed. Such grazing prevented the re-establishment of the deciduous woodlands so that the clearings will have merged to form an open heathland of heather, grasses, gorse and bracken. Some areas of surviving heathland may never have been ploughed since the first crops were planted by the Neolithic pioneers.

Throughout England, the eruption of activity which accompanied the First Agricultural Revolution created an enormous demand for axes which were needed to fell the forest, to cut useful timber for poles, tool handles, fuel or fencing, while they also served as weapons and, perhaps, as ploughshares. The most suitable and amenable stone for axe-making was flint which was tough, could take a very sharp edge but which, by virtue of the way in which the flint lumps or 'nodules' fractured when struck, could be easily worked by expert 'knappers'. But the bands of flint nodules only occur in chalk rocks, while most English regions have a different geological base and not all the chalk districts yielded top-quality flint. As a result, a trade in flint axes developed and certain localities were systematically exploited to produce flint for export, while the flint-mines of the south and east of England had their counterparts in the axe-factories of the Lake District, Cornwall, Wales and Northern Ireland where other types of hard rock were worked. The greatest complex of flint-mines, however, was at Grimes Graves in the Breckland, already discussed on page 20. Some of the flint-mines which were developed on the Sussex Downs are older than Grimes Graves, but this is the best collection of ancient workings to visit. Many of its axe 'rough outs' were exported to Wessex via the ancient Icknield Way and Ridgeway tracks, the former passing close to the Grimes Graves mines.

There are many other places in the Breckland where the observant visitor can pick-up waste flakes or even discarded tools, and a substantial flint-working industry existed at the Breckland town of Brandon in living memory, surviving until quite recently at a small workshop which produced gunflints for antique firearms enthusiasts and, reputedly, for Arab warriors who still favoured the flintlock gun. As well as littering many a modern field, Breckland flints can be seen displayed in most of the region's medieval churches and in the neat cottages of the late eighteenth and nineteenth centuries which predate the extinction of the vernacular building tradition by imported bricks.

Bronze Age round barrows are very common in the Breckland and are often seen as domed mounds crowned by the Scots pines planted on them during the last couple of centuries. Here, the barrows seem generally to have been built on the poorer marginal lands or on ground abandoned by agriculture. The large number of Breckland barrows implies that the area had a substantial Bronze Age population, although so too did many other English regions where most barrows have been destroyed by ploughing. The region does not seem to have produced any magnificent Bronze Age ritual monuments to compare with the final stages of Stonehenge, and stone circles appear to be completely absent in eastern England. Like their Neolithic forbears and Iron Age descendants, the Bronze Age population of the Breckland will have worked mainly as stockmen and graziers, with temporarily cultivated fields being periodically hacked into the heathland.

ABOVE, LEFT: *Boating at Burnham Overy Staithe*
ABOVE, RIGHT: *The Roman brick and flint masonry of Burgh Castle Saxon Shore fort*
BELOW: *The landscape of the Broads seen from Burgh Castle*

OPPOSITE: *The last surviving Fenland windpump, restored at Wicken Fen nature reserve by the National Trust*

RIGHT: *An agricultural landscape near Overy Staithe*
BELOW: *A typical Fenland landscape near Benwick*

A Breckland landscape at Langmere

There are no spectacular Iron Age remains in the Breckland apart from the hillfort at Thetford (page 24) and one site, very recently excavated and developed, which offers all sorts of important and interesting challenges. When the Romans invaded in AD 43, they created two puppet kingdoms, one in Sussex which was ruled by Cogidubnus, and one in East Anglia amongst the Iceni, a complex of smaller tribes over which Prasutagus was installed as ruler. Prasutagus died without a male heir in AD 60 and the Romans decided that this was an opportune time to absorb the Iceni kingdom into the Empire. This, and other diplomatic blunders, caused the bloody, destructive but ultimately ill-fated uprising. Had Cogidubnus rallied his subject tribesmen to support the revolt, then the outcome and the whole shape of English history could have been different. But he stayed loyal to his Roman masters, and the opulent Romanised palace which has been excavated at Fishbourne in Sussex may later have been provided for him as a recognition of the political services he rendered to the Romans.

This very challenging site belonging to the decades around the Roman Conquest and Boudicca revolt was recently discovered at Gallows Hill on the outskirts of Thetford. It was excavated by a team led by Tony Gregory who has very kindly provided us with a summary of the evidence as it currently exists. Adventurous spirits have suggested that this Thetford site was the palace of Prasutagus and Boudicca, although archaeology, being bound by the limitations of physical evidence, can often neither confirm nor deny such claims about the functions and occupants of buildings. If there had been such a palace here, one might have expected that prestigious trade goods would have been revealed, although the Iceni were a conservative people in comparison with the tribal federations to the south who engaged in much more continental trading.

Around 200–100 BC a small settlement existed here. In the AD 30s an imposing double-ditched enclosure was constructed, surrounding three large timber roundhouses. This house and ditch complex could easily be interpreted as the base of an aristocratic family, the focus of a large estate or perhaps of a tribal territory. In the years around and following the Claudian landing and invasion, the buildings were demolished, the innermost ditch levelled, a new outer ditch dug and the intervening space was filled with rows of timber fences to create a most unusual and puzzling monument. In the centre of the enclosed area, no signs of dwellings or occupation were found, and this has led the excavators to suspect that the site had been converted into a monumental ceremonial or ritual centre. After the Iceni uprising in AD 60, the whole complex was systematically but not violently dismantled, presumably by the victorious legions. They might have been reducing a centre of hostile religious ideology, removing what could have easily been converted into a dangerous native stronghold or, more prosaically, simply have desired the masses of timber posts for their own fort-building operations.

In the centuries following the uprising of AD 60, the Breckland must have enjoyed a good measure of prosperity and have had a quite rapidly growing population, for Romano-British settlement sites tend to be found at close intervals of about half a mile. Even so, the Breckland does not contain imposing Roman remains, although the Roman impact on the life of the area should not be underrated. The historian David Dymond reminds us that the peculiar rectilinear parish patterns in the Wangford area in the eastern Breckland might well be a legacy of some sort of Roman reorganisation of the landscape. A more obvious legacy of the Roman period is the route known as Peddars Way, which traverses the whole of Norfolk from the Little Ouse near Brettenham to reach the coast at Hunstanton. It does not seem to be an entirely Roman creation, but rather a Roman remodelling of an ancient branch of the Icknield Way. Like most Roman roads, it has been partly absorbed into the living countryside so that it hops and skips across the landscape, in places destroyed and invisible, then re-emerging as a hollowed lane, the boundary of a forest or a military track, although in some stretches it is still possible to recognise the embanked 'agger' of the Roman route. An accessible section of the old highway is signposted from the A 1075 at Stonebridge.

It was during the last century of Roman rule that Saxon settlers became established in various parts of East Anglia. Some must have arrived as mercenaries and have chosen to settle in Britain after their service expired; others may have come as peaceful settlers – and there is certainly nothing military about the pagan Saxon settlement established at West Stow on the Suffolk margins of the Breckland, and here the Saxon villagers seem to have traded peacefully with their British neighbours. West Stow, overlooking the ancient thoroughfare of the Lark valley, and described in more detail on page 108, is one of the most important of the excavated early-Saxon settlements, and by far the most interesting to visit.

In the Dark Ages, the prehistoric tradition of using the Breckland as a vast area of grazings interspersed with ploughlands on the less sandy soils persisted. At the start of the medieval period, the records show that some of the great estates were supporting flocks of 1000 or more sheep. In many ways, the Breckland favoured the rearing of sheep: they could feed on the coarser vegetation which had little appeal to cattle, the freely-draining sandy soils eliminated the problem of foot-rot, while the emergence of an important East Anglian wool export and textile industry provided a ready access to the main wool markets. In the earlier medieval centuries, the region was far more usefully productive and more densely populated than today, although some severe threats were beginning to emerge.

We might lose many friends amongst our readers were we to suggest that the Breckland is full of villages that are picture-book-pretty and packed with handsome medieval dwellings. There are hamlets of modern forestry workers' houses, several re-organised estate villages of the nineteenth century, but most Breckland villages are the merest shadows of their former selves, tattered remnants of villages which have shrunk and decayed, while many others have vanished completely. Gone too are most of the farmsteads and small hamlets which seem to have been numerous here in medieval times.

The emptying of a packed medieval countryside is a common theme throughout Norfolk and Suffolk, where the landscape was often closely partitioned between a multitude of tiny parishes and studded by scores of churches and villages. Even at the time of Domesday in 1086, Suffolk had 410 churches standing and some parishes covered less than 500 acres. While we can discover why a number of specific villages perished, the enormous scale of the losses is much harder to explain. In the Breckland, the depopulation seems to have been even more severe than in the surrounding areas and at least thirty lost village sites have been discovered; more still await discovery, along with the sites of scores of vanished farmsteads and hamlets. Here as elsewhere, village communities multiplied in the earlier medieval centuries, with the mounting

A round tower and cottage in Breckland flint: Croxton

pressure of population on the resources of existing villages causing a budding-off of new settlements to exploit settings which were ever more marginal and uninviting.

The Breckland environment was always a fragile one and there were limits to the numbers of families and livestock that the thin, sandy soils could support. Over-grazing and over-cropping must have exposed the weakened soils to the terrible sand-blows which were encountered at the end of the thirteenth century. The grazings will have deteriorated through over-stocking, while hunger will have encouraged peasants to plough areas of 'outfield' land which had had insufficient respite under fallow from ploughing and cropping. Sand-blows occurred at frequent intervals during the Middle Ages and they continued to be a despairing feature of Breckland life for centuries to follow. In 1668, a particularly notorious sandstorm almost buried the village of Santon Downham and the footloose sands obstructed the Little Ouse; nine years later, John Evelyn described the migrant sands as 'rouling from place to place and like the Sands in the Desert of Lybia, quite overwhelming some gentlemen's whole estates'. Even today, one can see impoverished fields which seem to be on the verge of blowing away, and several biographies of the region repeat the apocryphal tale of the Breckland farmer who, when asked whether his lands lay in Norfolk or Suffolk, replied that it depended upon which way the winds were blowing.

It was probably in response to the destructive sand-blows of the thirteenth century that the great landowners introduced a new form of livestock. Today, the rabbit is regarded either as a cuddly animal or as a minor pest, and younger readers will not be able to remember the bobbing brown masses of rabbits so often seen in the countryside before the introduction of the horrible myxomatosis disease in the mid-1950s. In previous centuries, however, the rabbit (which is thought to have been introduced to England by Normans in the twelfth century) was often reared on a grand scale as a valuable source of meat. By 1300, the Prior of Ely is known to have had a rabbit warren at Lakenheath and it seems that at least seven other warrens had been created. The territories of these warrens could cover thousands of acres and they had to be licensed by a Charter of Free Warren – the sale of such privileges being a useful source of crown revenue. Several warrens continued to be systematically exploited right through into the nineteenth century and could yield up to ten rabbits per acre, with the larger examples producing tens of thousands of rabbits each year.

The names of many warrens still survive, Thetford, Santon, Blackrabbit, Sturston and several others being marked on the modern map. There are also some interesting medieval relics in the form of fortified Warren lodges, built to accommodate the warrener and his helpers. In a countryside which contained many hungry peasants, the lay and ecclesiastical landlords needed such gamekeepers to guard their coneys. Armed bands of poachers were clearly a serious threat so the warreners would sleep on the upper floor of their robust stone lodges, protected by stoutly-barred doors and thick walls pierced by tiny window openings. Most of the lodges, like the three which guarded Lakenheath warren, have disappeared. The remains of the Mildenhall lodge survive, as do fragments of those at Eriswell and Methwold, but the best-preserved and most accessible is the Prior of Thetford's Warren Lodge, previously mentioned on page 139, which is to the north-west of the town and signposted from the B 1107. It is a gaunt cube of flint edged in Barnack stone and one could never regard it as a pretty or romantic medieval fortlet, yet one can still imagine how isolated and insecure the drowsy warrener may have felt, even though the lights of Thetford were burning just a couple of miles down the track. But it is easier to sympathise with the peasants who could be whipped or transported for poaching a single rabbit until well into the nineteenth century.

While the medieval Breckland landscape was being forged, the local capital was moribund. Thetford is distinguished by the fact that after the passage of a thousand years, the town is probably no larger than it was in Saxon times. Thetford lies where a branch of the Icknield Way crosses the Little Ouse near its junction with the River Thet. The existence of a Roman and even older capital here is hinted at by the hillfort and the 'palace' discoveries described above, while in the Saxon period, Thetford emerged as a major regional centre. The Saxon town was embraced by defensive earthworks, although its remains have been obliterated by recent expansion. This town lay on the southern side of the river junction, and the shifting of Thetford's centre of gravity to the northern side of the river occurred in medieval times. New fortifications, in the form of the massive motte at Castle Hill were added by the Normans and the mound was crowned by a keep that was demolished by Henry II in 1174 after one of the periodic Plantagenet family revolts. (*See also* page 31.)

In 1075, the reorganisation of English diocese in accordance with Archbishop Lanfranc's decree that episcopal sites should be based in large towns brought the East Anglian see from the Saxon focus at Elmham to Thetford, and the cathedral of St Mary stood in the heart of the Norman town. It was in keeping with Thetford's developing tradition for fluctuating fortunes that the see was moved again, to Norwich, in 1095. Better luck returned in 1103–4 when the Norman warrior, Roger Bigod, established a community of Cluniac monks in the town, and they used the abandoned cathedral until work on new priory buildings was begun in 1107.

A healthy pilgrim traffic sustained many a medieval religious foundation, and the necessary stimulus for pilgrimage came to light in the form of 'holy relics' with sensational curative powers that were most fortuitously discovered to be lodged in an image of the Virgin at the old cathedral. In the years that followed, Thetford acquired an impressive array of monastic houses for, as well as the important Cluniac priory, the town gained a Benedictine nunnery, a Dominican friary and houses of the Canons of the Holy Sepulchre and Austin Friars – all these foundations now having either vanished or become very ruinous. At the close of the Middle Ages, Thetford is said to have had some twenty parish churches in addition to its generous monastic endowment, but it was almost inevitable that the town would decline following the dissolution of the monasteries. The decline was advanced by the seventeenth century, and Celia Fiennes found the town 'now much decay'd and the ruines only shews its dimensions'.

In the eighteenth century, the exploitation of local chalybeate springs gave Thetford a brief lease of life as a minor fashionable spa, but the Norfolk town was to make a more lasting contribution to civilised life. Were the outlooks of modern East Anglians accurately represented by the opinions one finds expressed in the correspondence sections of local newspapers, radio and television, then one could expect the region to be a dauntingly reactionary preserve, a last bastion of the belief that unemployed people are scroungers and that sufficient hangings and floggings will solve all the nation's ills. As the unpredictable capital of an enigmatical little province, Thetford gave the world Thomas Paine who was born in the town in 1737. It was here that he wrote *The Rights of Man*, a most influential work, packed with ideas for radical reform: it is a book which is still revered in the USA even if its sentiments may not cut much ice in East Anglia.

During the first half of the twentieth century, Thetford remained wedded to its involuntary no-growth policy, but then began to grow quite rapidly as a reception centre for London overspill. Relatively little of its important Saxon and medieval heritage has endured into the modern era, but Thetford is not without character. With its brash new shops, bright modern factories and suburbs that press right up to the forest, Thetford can seem more like a dynamic little German boom-town than an elder statesman of the English urban ranks.

Of the other Breckland settlements, Mildenhall is the most attractive. Its name will be well known to many aficionados of the British Museum who have never visited the townlet, for it was nearby, in 1942, that a farmer – or rather, his plough – discovered the celebrated Mildenhall treasure, a magnificent collection of Roman silverware, perhaps hidden during the traumas of the collapse of the Empire in Britain. In the medieval period, Mildenhall was a royal manor of Bury St Edmunds Abbey and supported a renowned fish market. Today it is still distinguished by the majestic Church of St Mary. Though built mainly in the Perpendicular manner, the church has a fine and unusual window of the early fourteenth century surviving in the east end. Like some other noted East Anglian churches, such as those at March and Swaffham, the roof is embellished with carved angels, although those on the hammerbeams of the north aisle had their wings clipped by Puritans in the seventeenth century.

Brandon is neither a particularly ugly nor a notably picturesque townlet, but it can claim to be very much a native of the Breckland, for its former glories, such as they were, were based on flint knapping and the manufacture of top hats from the pelts of Breckland rabbits.

The margins of the old Breckland have responded to agricultural improvements so that the real Breckland ethos only survives in a broad arc of country which lies mainly to the north of Thetford. Within this area, the charms of the settlements are rather modest, although a series of fascinating places punctuate the Breckland fringe. They include Methwold with its outlandish tower, corona and spire attached to the Church of St George; Oxborough Hall, one of the loveliest buildings in England (page 139); Great Cressingham priory, a fine but partly decayed mansion of the sixteenth century, and Attleborough where the Church of St Mary contains a painted rood screen of the late fifteenth century. Across the county boundary in Suffolk, there are interesting churches at Euston, Redgrave and Bardwell as well as the medieval splendours and excellent museum at Bury St Edmunds. But in this lightning tour of the Breckland fringes, mention must be made of the ribbon development along the A 11 near Barton Mills. Its ugliness can scarcely be surpassed outside the USA, but doubtless it brings memories of home to the US servicemen stationed nearby.

Returning to the landscape – for the Breckland is distinguished by its countryside rather than its settlements – the themes of sheep, rabbits and sand-blows persisted into the post-medieval centuries. In the eighteenth century, however, the Agricultural Revolution swept fashions for farming improvements across the face of Britain and some of the less impoverished estates on the Breckland fringes were able to respond. On others, the improvements amounted to little more than the planting of game cover, and in the Victorian and Edwardian eras, the Breckland became the setting for some of the grandest shooting orgies. The fashionable parties who ventured forth from the mansions here would often kill more than 1000 birds in a single shoot, a curious achievement. Pheasants are still reared in large numbers in the Breckland. Stupid and unairworthy, they clatter through the thickets waiting for the day when they are blasted into oblivion by creatures scarcely more sensitive than themselves.

Until a couple of centuries ago, the Breckland had still not acquired the full visual character which can be enjoyed in its unspoilt corners today. The Scots pine was an early colonist of the deglaciated Breckland scene, but it was elbowed aside by the advance of deciduous trees and eventually displaced to Scotland and relegated to a few suitable ecological niches in the Lake District. In the Scottish Highlands, the tree is said to have been admired by the Duke of Cumberland, so that one of the few good things to result from the carnage of Culloden and the butchery of the clansmen which followed seems to have been the reintroduction of this most distinctive and personable tree to the estates of England, where it was used for landscaping, shelter and game cover. In 1849, H. Raynbird published his advocacy of the use of shelter belts, but by this time the tree was already being adopted in the Breckland where the need to protect the fragile soils against sand-blows was profound.

ABOVE: *An ageing shelter belt of Scots pine*

BELOW: *A beautiful Scots pine shelter belt near Ringmere*

The Scots pine may lack the stately grace of the lime, the solid grandeur of the oak or the delicate charms of its northern cousins, the birch and the rowan, but no tree creates a more haunting silhouette than this one, with its mops of blue-black foliage draped on a twisting frame of tortured branches. No two Scots pines have quite the same outline; seen singly, they are starkly impressive and when planted in rows, each member of the troop remains a personality. A succession of rows can be a wonderful sight as they step towards the horizon, the nearest row seeming black, the next slate, the next blue-grey, with perhaps a pale violet row being just visible in the distant haze. Without its windbreaks of old Scots pines, the Breckland would often seem like a stage without a backdrop.

By the end of the nineteenth century, large areas of the Breckland margins had been reclaimed as improved pasture or ploughland, but the improvements had made less headway in the sandy core. Sheep were still very numerous, sharing the heathland grazings with rabbits which were sometimes welcome and sometimes not, and with the scuttling pheasants. Early in the twentieth century, the age-old sheep economy began to decline. The heaths and warrens had supported several flocks of between one and two thousand sheep, but competition from New World wool and mutton, a difficulty in meeting the high costs of folding sheep and the shortage of men willing to endure the harsh life and low wages of the shepherd all conspired against the flocks. (More recently, the astronomical subsidies available to arable farming have further undermined the rearing of sheep whose grazing is essential to the maintenance of a heathland landscape.) During the agricultural depression of the inter-war years, thousands of Breckland acres came onto the market at rock-bottom prices. The cheapness of land never denotes that nobody wishes to own it, however, and the recent history of the Breckland has involved an intense competition to control the heathland estates, resulting in the loss of many scenic and biological treasures.

In the 1920s, the new Forestry Commission began to purchase an empire of bankrupt holdings. In the area around Thetford, estate owners encountered great difficulty in finding tenants for their farms while the existing tenants, who were usually unable to afford or contemplate improvements, eked out a living by selling rabbit pelts to the fur factories at Brandon. In 1922, the Forestry Commission began to purchase land here, and today the Thetford Forest alone covers some 80 square miles. Initially, the new holdings were planted with Scots pine, but then the emphasis shifted to the cultivation of interminable rows of drab alien species like the Corsican pine and Douglas fir. Whether anyone really needs it or not, a Breckland output of about 140,000 cu/m of timber per annum is targeted to be reached by 1985. In the post-war era, stung by the deluge of complaints from naturalists and country lovers, the Commission has become conscious of public relations. Where the hideous plantations meet a thoroughfare, a face-saving belt of more personable deciduous trees may be planted; picnic areas have been provided, while access to some forests is allowed along designated 'nature' trails. In the face of such earnest PR work, it may seem churlish to suggest that the disciplined lines of graceless trees are visually repugnant and biologically rather uninteresting, a poor substitute for the ecological richness of the lost

OPPOSITE: *A drab Breckland conifer plantation near The Devil's Punchbowl*

heaths. Also, the invitations to explore a forest trail must have limited appeal so long as any old heathland remains – for who would desert the rose garden to inspect the cabbage patch?

The story of the forests is not entirely one-sided. The destruction of the English countryside is often masked by lies and coloured by arrogance and one cannot fail to admire the candour of the statement in the Commission's own guide to the East Anglian forests that 'With the afforestation of Thetford Chase, the rarer species characteristic of Breckland have diminished and are now to be found mainly in Nature Reserves.' It should not be assumed that had the Commission not intervened, then vast expanses of the heath would survive, for the incredible levels of subsidies now available to arable farmers would perhaps make it 'profitable' to plough up the Gobi Desert, let alone the Breckland. The forestry has also brought much-needed employment into the Breckland, producing some new hamlets and revitalising other settlements like Santon Downham.

The identity of other inheritors of the Breckland will be clear to all visitors who have been deafened by the military aircraft screeching skywards from the British and American bases at Mildenhall and Lakenheath, and who have found large areas to be permanently inaccessible as NATO training grounds and others temporarily but unpredictably closed by the army. In 1940, when the need for army training areas was indisputable, some 118,000 acres in the Breckland were commandeered and in 1942, a further 16,000 acres became a 'battle area' where live ammunition was used. During the war, the populations of a number of villages were evicted from the designated battle area and have never been allowed to return. Their houses were blown to pieces long ago, but the village churches are still intact in the protective embrace of wire mesh cages. (A more detailed account of this story has been provided in Richard Muir's *The Lost Villages of Britain.*) Whatever the rights or wrongs of the modern military presence in the Breckland may be, one of its prime effects is to close a large area of attractive heathland to the visitor. On the other hand, the military uses have proved less fatal to Nature than the commercial afforestation, and a number of valuable bird and plant species continue to survive amongst the rehearsals for war.

For all these onslaughts, agriculture, forestry and the military have not extinguished all the old heathland. Sufficient still endures to entice the naturalist and lover of the landscape, surviving to remind the nation of the qualities of loveliness that have been lost. The best of what is left lies in areas of East Wretham Heath which is managed by the Norfolk Naturalists' Trust and sandwiched between Forestry Commission land and the Stanford battle-training area, north of Thetford. The reserve of 362 acres was bequeathed to the Trust by the late Mrs Claire Rich in 1938 and it includes several meres, the three largest being Langmere, Ringmere and Fen Mere. Part of a fourteen-mile-long drove road which runs through the reserve and passes close to Langmere is believed to have originated as a Neolithic track, while just to the north and west of the mere is a fine Scots pine plantation which still harbours the red squirrel and contains some of the earliest of the introduced pines, with some trees dating back to the Napoleonic wars.

Anyone who glances at the East Wretham Heath booklet will begin to appreciate the extent of the destruction of habitats and species in the areas lying outside the confines of the reserve, for it lists almost 100 species of birds which can be commonly

The mere and Scots pines at Langmere

seen within the reserve and almost forty less frequent visitors. It harbours a number of rare and threatened species including the stone curlew, hawfinch, two types of shrike and two of harriers. In addition to the red squirrels, there are two family groups of roe deer as well as most common wild animals, while the absence of pesticides allows at least twenty-four different species of butterfly to survive here. The reserve is also a haven for scores of rare heathland plants as well as others which flourish along the fluctuating shorelines of the meres. The nature trail which runs around the Langmere area offers interest at every step, but the ramble which provides perhaps the most haunting vision of the old Breckland can be enjoyed by those who leave their transport at the lay-by beside Ringmere and proceed away from the mere in a south-easterly direction, taking the path which follows an exceptionally fine shelter belt of Scots pines. This narrow zone is also conserved and access to the Trust's reserves is by a permit which can be obtained at the house of the warden, clearly visible near the roadside from the East Wretham Heath lay-by: at the time of writing, the fee is 50p.

The recent past of the Breckland has, in most respects, been tragic and the future for the surviving fragments of heathland must be uncertain. Planning in Britain tends

The stone curlew still survives in a few unspoilt parts of the Breckland

to have a poor reputation, perhaps because many people associate it with bureaucratic interference of a petty, domestic nature. But if ever there was a case for land-use planning guided by the national interest, it is to be found in the Breckland where a glorious landscape packed with threatened species of plants and animals and full of conservational and recreational potential has been systematically dismantled by sectional interests. What the nation has been given is surely not what the nation would have wanted – but then the people are not asked about such things. They pay the piper, but he seldom plays their tune.

11
THE NORFOLK BROADS

Many of the pleasures of East Anglian life derive from the fact that the region embraces a series of quite distinctive environments, each one having its own particular history and qualities of landscape – the Fens, the Breckland, the rolling farming countrysides of Suffolk and, of course, the Norfolk Broads. Scores of readers from outside East Anglia will have made their first acquaintance with East Anglia – just as this writer did – by way of a holiday spent boating on the Broads. Memories of windmills and waterside pubs; moorings hit and moorings missed; of irate yachtsmen looking comical in naval outfits and London girls looking better in very little; of chugging along to the races at Yarmouth, and of watching the invader coypu slip silently into the reed-edged waters – all spin in the kaleidoscope of recollections, a clutch of images surely shared with countless holiday-makers. The Norfolk Broads has provided a small playground for the nation for several decades and so it is strange to think that the actual forces which created the landscape have only been understood since the late 1950s, and stranger still to realise that this recreational and conservational wonderland faces the threat of dismemberment by the greedy local farming interests.

The name itself is misleading for the Broads are not simply natural widenings of local rivers like the Bure and the Ant; their actual life story is far more interesting than this. The Norfolk Broads is a man-made landscape, and when the nation's greatest biographer of the scenic heritage, Professor W. G. Hoskins, tells us that the Broads 'represent perhaps the most extraordinary manipulation of the natural landscape by our medieval forbears', then we should be sure that the time has come to sit up and take an interest. Vague suspicions that certain of the Broads might be artificial have existed since at least the 1830s, but the scholarly elucidation of Broadland origins represented a major triumph of the interdisciplinary approach to environmental challenges and was a combined exercise in historical geography, botany and geomorphology (the study of landforms). The story was fascinatingly and unequivocally revealed in 1960, with the publication of *The Making of the Broads* as a research monograph by Drs J. M. Lambert, N. Jennings and C. T. Smith. As all good landscape detectives should, these specialists garnered their clues from every possible source: they listened to the testimony of ancient pollen grains and other materials recovered from the peat; studied the detailed topographical evidence as seen from the ground, the air and the water margins and as it was revealed in venerable maps and medieval documents. When the strands of evidence were combined, they not only provided an answer to the mystery of the Broadlands, but also told a detailed landscape story.

As so often happens when highly-skilled and diligent work unravels a challenging problem, one is left to wonder how such a lucid and rational answer could have remained elusive for so long. For despite the trappings of water, reeds and wildfowl, the Broadland scene does not seem natural. The broadenings of the rivers can occur quite suddenly; water and shore often meet at a vertical bank junction rather than merging at a gentle shelf, while one cannot conceive the natural processes which could create the raised peaty causeways, like the one which strides across Barton Broad in a most deliberate manner.

The Norfolk Broads are flooded medieval peat diggings and they reveal the exploitation of this fuel on a truly gigantic scale. Man has exploited such peat deposits since time immemorial and the evidence from the Fens has revealed an organised industry there in Roman times. The Romans were also present in the area that is now the Broads. Their most remarkable memorial is the vast fortress of the Saxon Shore, Burgh Castle, now inland overlooking Breydon Water at the mouths of the rivers Yare and Waveney while, across the water, a Roman town lies buried near the outskirts of modern Caister-on-Sea. In the second century, it was an important *entrepot*, handling cargoes arriving from the Rhineland, and was enclosed by a prestigious stone wall measuring 1,300 by 900 feet. In addition to these massive developments, there were many lesser Roman settlements in the area: Roman bases are thought to have existed at Reedham and Horning while Potter Heigham may have had a Roman pottery, and a millstone of this period was incorporated in the walls of St Olave's Priory. However, the extraction of peat on the phenomenal scale necessary to gouge out the Norfolk Broads was only achieved in the twelfth, thirteenth and fourteenth centuries when a total area of about 2,600 acres was quarried by peat diggings.

At first, these diggings formed dry workings which must have resembled the neat, steep-faced brown fuel quarries that are still worked in Ireland and the Scottish Highlands and islands. The word 'broad', describing a flooded area, does not seem to have been used until the fifteenth century. Peasants living in this timberless locality must have been obtaining fuel from peat diggings for countless centuries before their activities attracted the attentions of the communities established in the nearby monastic houses. Now, if there was anyone who could be relied upon to recognise the chance to make a relatively honest buck, it was the medieval monk, and the organisation of peat digging on a vast commercial scale was achieved by these monastic communities. It is amusing to picture a flock of monks at work, slicing away at the peat beds with habits hoisted, sandals splashing and tonsures flashing. But if the medieval monk had a second talent, it was for getting someone else to do the dirty work, and so the peasants dug the peat, the monks warmed their feet and the profits rolled in. The monks gained control of the fabulous fuel resources around the River Bure and its tributaries by buying up the rights of digging and drying or 'turbary', and in this way, the priory of St Benedict (St Bene't's) created an empire of turbary which embraced a dozen parishes.

OPPOSITE: *The ruins of St Bene't's Abbey are dominated by those of a much later tower mill*

The undercroft at St Olave's Priory

This wealth and prosperity came to St Bene't's in late middle age, for the house was an old one, founded by a small Benedictine community in the ninth century on lands near Ranworth donated by the Saxon lord Horn (whose name could be preserved in the village of Horning: 'the place of Horn's people'). In 870, the original buildings were razed by Danish raiders, and the monks put to the sword. Another Dane, King Cnut, was responsible for refounding the community. Legend tells that, later, the monks of St Bene't's resisted the Norman invaders but were betrayed by the monk Ethelwald, who coveted the leadership of the community. When the Normans took over, they enthroned Ethelwald, but then hung him from the bell tower – suggesting that the invaders were as Teutonic in their humour as they were in other ways. Following several centuries of unspectacular survival, St Bene't's grew in wealth and influence from the profits of the peat industry. But after the Dissolution, peasants from the villages whose sweat and toil had created this prosperity greedily pillaged the monastic site for building stone. As a result, the surviving remains are modest in scale and the most prominent feature amongst the ruins is the conical base of a massive eighteenth-century windmill which was built into the fabric of the ruined gatehouse. A second Broadland monastery, the Augustinian priory of St Olave and St Mary at St Olaves near Great Yarmouth and dating from 1236, has been excavated and partly restored by the Department of the Environment.

Conveniently close to the monastic peat workings and easily accessible by water was the great medieval city of Norwich. Then ranking amongst the largest towns in England, Norwich had an enormous appetite for fuel, and the cathedral priory alone is known to have burned 200,000 blocks or 'turves' of peat in a single year. Bog oaks were a useful by-product of the peat diggings, and these were also sold for fuel. The turves which did not end smouldering in the hearths and ovens of Norwich were consumed by the monastic fires, or else exported as fuel to the settlements along the Norfolk coast where salt was produced by evaporating brine. Over a period that was probably no longer than two centuries, around 9 million cubic feet of peat was quarried from Broadland.

These great operations were made possible by the fact that during the High Middle Ages, the relative sea level was about 13-ft lower than today, so that simple methods of baling will have been sufficient to keep the peat cuttings dry and workable. But a rising sea level and a climate which was beginning to deteriorate in the thirteenth century conspired to end the bonanza. The story is most easily learned in the South Walsham diggings and at St Bene't's Priory itself, for although the monastic buildings are now tumbled, the records survive to be read as freshly as when they were written. In prophecy of the doom to follow, an exceptional storm surge swept brackish water across the monastic site in 1287, so that the floods rose above the altar of the priory church. Early in the fourteenth century, the diggings at South Walsham were still yielding a fifth of a million turves a year, while those at another of the priory's cuttings at Holme were even a little more productive. In 1315, however, the records show that a lake of some kind had developed in part of the South Walsham cuttings. Gradually, it must have expanded, causing the large-scale extraction of peat to end around the close of the century, although in other places that were similarly afflicted by rising water levels, peat is known to have been scoured from submerged beds. This was done by means of a device called a 'dydle', consisting of a rake and drag net. But by the fifteenth century, the rush for the brown gold was over and the Norfolk Broads now existed to provide its lovely epitaph.

Some evidence still survives to show that the peat was extracted in a planned and purposeful manner. Adjacent diggings were separated by uncut ribbons of peat which sometimes still stand above the surface of the water as narrow balks. As well as marking the divisions, these balks served as useful causeways, while some preserved the courses of parish boundaries traversing the region. In medieval times, the old boundaries were always revered and could not be consigned to a watery uncertainty.

After the inundation of the medieval peat workings, the landscape of the area will have displayed steep-edged, geometrical broads set in periodically flooded surroundings which will have resembled the countryside of the undrained Fens. The neatly-edged broads can still be recognised in places, but in others the pattern has become blurred and, in many more, the old landscape has been wrecked. During the post-medieval centuries, many acres of the surrounding marshland were reclaimed by embanking the Broadland rivers, although these drainage schemes had only limited success until, as in the Fens, windmill-powered pumps were introduced in large numbers in the late eighteenth and nineteenth centuries. The windmills were superseded by steam engines, and these by diesel and then electrical pumps. The classical Broadland scenery, which was widespread at the time of our grandfathers and which still exists in pockets today, is one of broads surrounded by partially-drained meadowland grazed by cattle whose wanderings amongst the marshes are restrained by water-filled dykes.

Clear descriptions of the countrysides as they existed in the nineteenth century are preserved in the detailed maps of the period. The tithe maps of the 1830s and 40s show that the geometrical indentations of flooded medieval peat diggings were then still evident in many areas. Those of Hoveton Broad in 1840 and Malthouse Broad in 1839 show that a reduction of at least 60 per cent has affected the broads at Hoveton and Ranworth; that Malthouse Broad, near Ranworth Broad, has been reduced even more, while other broads, like Sutton and Strumpshaw have vanished since the maps were drawn.

The constriction and the destruction of broads is due partly to natural processes, partly to the side effects of human activities, and partly to the unadulterated greed of members of the influential local farming community. The natural processes result from the deposition of river silts in the peat cuttings and the advance of the marginal reeds and reed-grass which encroach upon the broads and cause the accretion of new land. In recent times, however, several factors have tended to retard the natural reclamation of such broads. In 1937, coypu – which resemble buck-toothed, spaniel-sized water rats – escaped from neighbouring fur farms (we can hardly blame them for that), and their grazing habits kept the advancing reedbeds in check. Now, as a result of their depredations in the surrounding farmlands, the coypu are also kept in check by extermination programmes. Other factors which have caused a retreat of reedbeds in many places result from a more complex interplay of ecological forces, involving the effects of the discharge of nitrates and phosphates deriving from agricultural fertilisers, the slurry from intensive livestock units and effluent from sewage works, with the foul mixture being churned up by the propellers of the tourist craft.

This problem has many unhappy dimensions. The 'over-enrichment' by nitrates and phosphates leads to the proliferation of algae which cloud the water. The fall-out of dying algae increase the rate of sedimentation on the beds of the broads where a bacterium, *Clostridium botulinum*, flourishes in the accumulating muds. It produces a toxin causing avian botulism which has caused countless thousands of deaths in the Broadland wildfowl population, while one of the algae, *Prymnesium parvum*, releases another toxin responsible for the fish mortalities which have afflicted the area during the last two decades. The over-enrichment problem is also thought to be the

A coypu

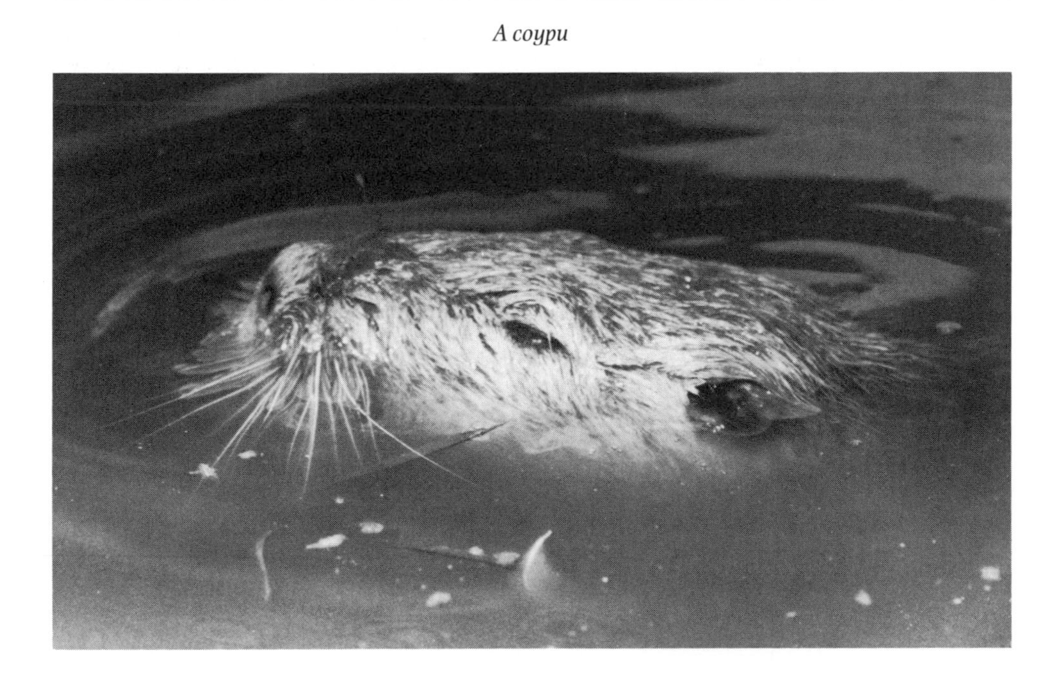

main agent causing reedswamp 'dieback'. The killing of the waterside reedbeds exposes the riverbanks to accelerated erosion caused by the wash from passing tourist craft, while the churning propeller blades often destroy those waterweeds which have escaped death from pollution. Although successive maps show the steady encroachment of reclaimed land and reedbeds on Hoveton Broad, post-war research work has shown a reverse in the trend with the broad having grown since 1949 through the destruction of its marginal reedswamp.

This catalogue of environmental ills should not discourage the tourist from visiting the Norfolk Broads and the pressure of public opinion from the countless thousands of visitors who love the Broadland landscape could yet be instrumental in saving this threatened fragment of the national heritage. An even greater threat to the still-lovely countryside comes from the farmers who would impose the barren wheatfield landscapes of Iowa or Kansas upon this fragile but beautiful corner of England – a threat discussed below.

As with all man-made landscapes, the Norfolk Broads has been very sensitive to changes in human activities and lifestyles. The traditional patterns of management, which evolved in the centuries following the creation of the Broads, helped to check the natural processes which would have seen the encroaching reedbeds eventually yielding to a 'carr' vegetation of tangled alderwoods. The reed and sedge beds were regularly cut to provide litter, hay and thatch, while the alder thickets were coppiced to yield useful poles. Meanwhile, dykes or ditches were cut and maintained to allow boats to ply between the marshes and to control the movements of cattle. The wetland environments which these activities helped to preserve attracted a scintillating diversity of wildlife, and in those fragments of the area which are preserved and unspoilt, the fascinating plants and creatures still have a toehold on survival.

From the naturalist's point of view, the Norfolk Broads is an invaluable area of wetland because it contains such a wealth of different damp environments. Tidal influences extend far upstream to affect the middle courses of the main Broadland rivers, and so in different sections one can find plant communities which vary in their tolerance of the tidal ebb and flow and demand different degrees of brackishness in their water supply. A variety of different environments are protected as nature reserves. In 1945, the Norfolk Naturalists' Trust, which performed so much good work in salvaging fragments of the Breckland, purchased a part of Hickling Broad which later formed the core of a larger national nature reserve of 1,361 acres, where a large observation hut and a water trail have been provided for visitors. Though only around 3-ft in depth, this is the largest surviving broad and the proximity between the surface and the food resources of the gravel-strewn lake-bed make this broad particularly attractive to swans and diving ducks. Migrant ospreys – the rare fish-catching bird of prey – periodically visit Hickling, but the most celebrated of its threatened inhabitants is the magical swallow-tail butterfly. This is perhaps the most colourful of the British butterflies, but also the most vulnerable, since its caterpillars depend on the milk parsley plant which still grows around the edges of the broad.

The lovely Martham Broad is also shallow, and here the Trust manages 140 acres of the area as a nature reserve. In addition to the commoner wetland bird species, Martham, like Hickling, harbours the bizarre bittern whose booming call may often be heard, although the visitor must be very observant to see the brown, slightly heron-

Alder Carr vegetation at Ranworth Broad

like birds as they stand frozen like tawny statues amongst the waterside stems. Although the bittern is still declining in numbers, a second rare but characteristic broadland bird, the marsh harrier, seems to be increasing. The last member of the trio of distinctive Broadland birds is the bearded tit; the male sports a smart black mustachio, although this bird, like the bittern, is more often heard than seen, having whirring wings and a metallic 'pink pink' call. The Norfolk Naturalists have a reserve on Barton Broad, where bitterns, bearded tits and swallow-tails may sometimes be glimpsed and where a heronry is established in a patch of wet alder wood.

In all, the Norfolk Naturalists' Trust manages a total of thirty-five reserves in the Broads, covering a total of 5,500 acres and it has the distinction of being the first county conservational organisation, originating in 1926. In 1928 it began to acquire its network of reserves by purchasing the Starch Grass reserve in the Martham area and controls other important wildlife refuges in Alderfen, Ranworth, Cockshoot and Surlingham Broads. The Nature Conservancy Council manages the national nature reserves at Hickling Broad and at Bure Marshes, where a programme of scrub clearance and dyke scouring is in progress. While these conservational organisations have done so much to protect the threatened plants and creatures of Broadland, the strength of the conservational stake in the battle for the future of the area is put in perspective when one realises that while there are 8,031 acres of unreclaimed fen in Broadland, some 52,262 acres have been drained, and of this area about 12,355 acres is now devoted to growing arable crops, and is lost both to wildlife and tourists.

Although in an area such as this, the wholly man-made landscape of villages and churches must take a second place to the Broadland countryside, the region contains a number of settlements of genuine charm, as well as some others that have been submerged by the brash buildings, bustle and commercialised tat produced by the tourist industry. At Woodbastwick there is a fine church in the traditional Norfolk flint and thatch, with good painted glass windows and an unusual dedication to SS Fabian and Sebastian. Horning was once a dynamic little commercial river port but has now been rather overwhelmed by tourism. Its church stands a little detached from the dwellings on a knoll, and along with the neighbouring church of St Helen's at Ranworth it combines in a distinctive pairing of landmarks. Though mainly built in the Perpendicular style of the later medieval centuries, the Ranworth church stands on the site of its Saxon predecessor and it contains a remarkable rood screen that has recently been restored to its original splendour. Stokesby is a pretty village and Honing is another; Stalham and St Olaves boast fine flint churches and Ludham has a very large one, a Perpendicular building with a hammerbeam roof, a superb screen of 1493 and a mural of the Crucifixion painted on the chancel arch.

The Broadland church towers and spires provide valuable reference points and foci in the flat countryside of water, reedbeds and pasture, but they are not the only graceful intrusions on the Broadland skyline. Moving sails of quite different kinds add their own distinction to the setting.

During the medieval period and for countless centuries before, movement in the area was mainly accomplished by water transport. The position of Norwich as a leading city was facilitated and sustained by a lively water traffic, and it seems that two types of vessel were important: the square-rigged 'keels' which were used for moving cargoes from river ports to the sea ports, and 'wherries' rowed by a quartet of oarsmen which provided passenger transport. At the close of the medieval period, the forerunners of a type of boat which was especially adapted to the local conditions of navigation began to ply the Broads. These craft were also known as wherries, but they differed considerably from the old row-boats and resulted from the marriage between them and Dutch trading vessels which carried a fore-and-aft rig. In its fully-developed form, the Norfolk wherry had a single mast that was set unusually close to the bows; it had a capacious hold running aft from the mast, leaving only a minimal accommodation for the crew, and a 'slipping' or false keel which could be removed from its housing beneath the main keel. This allowed the wherries to operate in very shallow waters, while the unstayed mast could be rapidly dropped to permit the boats to pass beneath bridges. The fore-and-aft rig allowed these boats to sail very close to the wind, assisting navigation amongst the tortuous Broadland channels. Although new wherries were being built in the years leading up to the Great War, the last commercially trading vessel was withdrawn from the Broads in 1950. There is just one Norfolk wherry which may still be seen sailing these waters: the *Albion*, which has been preserved and restored by the Norfolk Wherry Trust.

While the wherries have sailed away into history, sails are still a characteristic of

OPPOSITE:
The thatched church at Woodbastwick

RIGHT: *The painting on the chancel arch and rood screen at Ludham church*
BELOW: *The beautifully restored rood screen at Ranworth church*

the Broadland scene. Long before the water comes into view from behind its screening reedbeds, the visitor will often be made aware of its presence by the sight of a moving triangle of canvas which seems to be slicing through the lush vegetation like the fin of a great white shark that glides through a green ocean. Broadland still contains about 125 miles of navigable waterway and it supports around 7,500 privately-owned boats and 2,000 hire craft, most of which are motor cruisers. Each holiday season the cruisers cater for some 250,000 holidaymakers.

Just like the Fens, the Broadland landscape was once sprinkled with windmills which were mainly used as pumps to assist drainage, although some served as grain mills. They were mainly simple timber structures and most have perished, although a number of the later and sturdier brick-built tower mills have survived to be restored by modern enthusiasts, with the Norfolk Windmills' Trust being formed in 1963. One of the finest mills, Horsey Mill near Horsey Mere Staithe is a National Trust property and was a working mill until forty years ago. Other fine survivors include the Stacey Arms drainage mill on the River Bure south-east of Acle; the waterside Hunsett mill near Stalham, which is a privately-owned and restored tower mill; the large Berney Arms mill, near the junction of the rivers Yare and Waveney, which is still in working order and preserved by the Department of the Environment, and Palmers Hollow post mill at Upton Dyke, a renovated wind-pump. Several other wind-pumps are earmarked for restoration by the Norfolk Windmills' Trust.

The mention of nature reserves, the *Albion* wherry and the rehabilitation of many windmills might seem to suggest that the corner in Broadland conservation has been turned. Sadly this is far from being the case, and there is a distinct threat that sectional agricultural interests will continue to drain the damp pastures until very little of Broadland remains for the tourist and naturalist to enjoy.

In the past, the problem of conserving the Broads was undermined by a lack of scientific understanding of the workings of the complicated Broadland ecosystems, and also by the lack of an authority which could both regulate the conflicting recreational and environmental interests and oppose the voracious farming and drainage lobby. There were countless dimensions to the problem, just one facet being the clash of interest between the boating and fishing fraternities. The two activities are not easily compatible; the regular passage of boats disturbs the angler and upsetting slanging matches often result when boatsmen try to dislodge anglers from moorings. Detailed work by Peter Owens has shown that the undeclared hostilities are being won by the boatmen as anglers gradually desert the Broads. However, recent research, much of it accomplished at the University of East Anglia in Norwich, has provided the understanding of Broadland ecosystems which allows the necessary strategies for conservation to be devised. Also, the Broads Authority was founded in 1978 to form and integrate policies to 'arrest the environmental deterioration of the area'. Some critics saw the creation of the authority as a half-hearted response to the problem which fell short of the formation of a Broads National Park, and this more forceful solution is thought to have been opposed by the county council and the drainage authority. Even so, the Broads Authority has carried out invaluable research and enjoyed some successes in resisting the relentless farming pressures.

Yet the destruction of Broadland by drainage and then the conversion of damp pastures into prairie wheat fields continues at a terrifying rate. It is estimated that

ABOVE: *Masts and windmill silhouetted against a Broadland sunset at Thurne*

RIGHT: *The windmill at Stalham*

BELOW: *The Stacey Arms mill is now open to the public*

LEFT: *The Broads at Thurne*

RIGHT: *Angling on the Broads at Thurne*

in the postwar period about a quarter of the grazing marshes, amounting to the 12,355 acres already mentioned, have been converted to arable farming, while in the period 1980–83 alone, some 1,200 to 1,500 acres of grazing marsh have been destroyed. Two major threats are particularly worrying at present. A scheme to drain the Halvergate Marshes south of Acle has caused a barrage of protests from naturalists and conservationists, and although the minister responsible has turned down the larger component of the scheme, the possibility of piecemeal attempts to 'reclaim' the marshes for grain farming continues to threaten the wildlife and landscape of the area.

The second great threat comes from the proposed Yare barrier across the estuary which would remove the threat of occasional flooding of Broadland areas by the sea. In this way, it would provide an extra incentive to the 'reclamation' schemes. Initially, the barrier was advanced as a drainage and flood control project to facilitate the ploughing up of vast areas around the Yare but while the proposal was being debated, the local farmers moved in – and many of the threatened pastures surrendered immediately to the plough. Currently a cost/benefit analysis is reassessing the barrier, not any longer as a means of permitting drainage, but as a means of safeguarding the destruction already accomplished.

Whether the Norfolk Broads will be allowed to survive as a national recreational and conservational wonderland, or whether it will be relegated to the role of an anonymous prairie growing subsidised grain by virtue of subsidised drainage schemes, remains to be seen. Most conservational interests agree that it would be prohibitively costly to enlarge the Broads by removing expanses of encroaching alder wood and flooding 'reclaimed' areas in such a way as to create the landscapes and environments of, say, 1900 or 1850. But it *is* possible to preserve the Broads in the present form. Were this issue to be decided by a national referendum, the outcome would not be in doubt, but the powerful interests at the Department of the Environment and Ministry of Agriculture tend to regard the nation's heritage in a different light.

12
THE EAST ANGLIAN COAST

THE EAST ANGLIAN SHORES

As well as offering great fascination to all those who have an interest in the plants and wildlife of coastal environments, the East Anglian seaboard is a source for many dramatic and plaintive stories concerning the rise and fall of towns and villages: places that were both sustained and threatened by the grey, uncaring sea. At the same time, this coastline would not win many prizes in a beauty contest were its charms to be pitted against the rugged grandeur of those of Cornwall, Gower or old Aberdeenshire. Even so, the sand spits, salt marshes and sandlings have their own appeal, and provide inviting counter-attractions for visitors who are tired of treading the shingle of the crowded holiday beaches. The coast of Norfolk has exerted a powerful attraction to artists, and the bright, silvery light, which narrows the eyes and mutes the colours in its glare, is best portrayed in the thin, limpid tints of watercolour rather than the solid strokes of oil painting. Painters often see the landscape with eyes that are more aware and penetrating than those of writers, and some have said that the Norfolk coast is landscape in a minor key – a point more easily appreciated by readers who have seen it for themselves. Groping for a word that will not upset the tourist interests, let us say that the climate of the East Anglian coast is – bracing. When the wind blows from the north-east, it is very bracing.

This brief sketch of the coastline begins in the north-west of the region and tacks along the shores to the Essex borders.

Around the Wash, the former Fenlands approach the sea in a series of stages, each one marked by an old sea bank which commemorates a small victory in the relentless campaign to wrest a little more dry land from the sea and salt marsh. Moving northwards from the medieval 'Roman' bank, these frontier defences of the reclaimed zone become progressively younger, with those which lie close to the mudflats of the Wash dating from the late eighteenth, nineteenth and twentieth centuries. Beyond and to the east of the great medieval port of King's Lynn (page 81), the hem of Wash salt marsh tapers away at the holiday resort of Hunstanton on the north-west Norfolk coast and cliffs appear. Although they might lack the grandeur and celebrity of other chalk cliffs like those at Dover or the Needles, these are amongst the most colourful in the country, with white chalk, red chalk and the chocolate-olive greensand being exposed where the sea has bitten into the geological layer cake, while huge slabs of tumbled rock litter the cliff base. None of the East Anglian cliffs was built to last.

This stretch of cliff coastline is brief, and as the coast trends eastwards, the salt marshes of Brancaster Bay begin. Along much of the north Norfolk coast, a series of parallel man-made and semi-natural zones can clearly be recognised, with each zone existing as a quite distinctive environment. To landward, one can often see a line of fossilised sea cliffs, hewn by the sea but long since abandoned. The narrow ribbon of old arable farmland at the foot of such cliffs has long been valued and tends to carry the main coast road and many of the villages, townlets and little sea ports established in Saxon and medieval times. Seaward of these villages lies a band of reclaimed salt marsh, an emerald zone of grazings which is criss-crossed by geometrical networks of drainage channels. Then one generally encounters a strip of unreclaimed semi-natural salt marsh with pungent branching creeks and violet patches of sea lavender: an ecological wonderland which can only develop when protected from the buffeting waves by the dunes and spits which mark the junction with the maritime world.

Norfolk still boasts the finest expanses of salt marsh to be seen in Britain and, fortunately, substantial areas are managed by various conservational organisations. From some vantage points on the ancient cliff-line, the complete panoramic sequence of zones unfolds. The view from the heath-carpeted cliff above Salthouse is particularly engrossing, displaying the fruits of human endeavour and the natural marvels of the seaward zones.

Between the dunes and salt marshes of the Scolt Head Island nature reserve and Cley next the Sea, the pattern is rather different. While the woods which guard the sea frontage of the Holkham lands (where the Queen has a private beach) are of the mid-nineteenth century, the landscape hereabouts was transformed by eighteenth- and early nineteenth-century improvements. The Coke family of Holkham, the Earls of Leicester, owned around 45,000 acres in Norfolk. Between 1734 and 1761, the wealth and energy of the dynasty were directed into the creation of the magnificent family seat. As previously described William Kent designed the house and Capability Brown landscaped the lake and gardens, while the vast parkland setting was won from barren sands and salt marsh. In the process, the old village of Holkham was destroyed and its successor still stands metaphorically tugging its forelock at the park gates. There were several Cokes at Holkham, but one of them is known to history as Coke of Holkham because of his remarkable achievements in the area of enlightened land improvement.

Born in 1752, Thomas William Coke inherited the estate in 1776 and lived until 1842. While he enlarged the park at Holkham, his vitality and talents were channelled into highly efficient land improvement. The Earl imposed a regime of reclamation upon his sandy inheritance so that the value of the estate quadrupled within the space of fifteen years, and continued to rise. The barren wastes were improved by digging through the blanket of sands into a layer of marl, which was then spread on the land to give body to the topsoil. Excellent crops of wheat and barley were produced, and they were grown in rotations, with improved strains of sheep being grazed on the fallowing acres. Coke's 'sheep shearings' were amongst the first agricultural shows and did much to disperse the doctrines of livestock improvement.

During the Napoleonic wars, grain prices rocketed and gave an extra incentive to land reclamation. Miles of sea bank in the coastal strip between Holkham and Cley were built at this time, while shelter belts protected the light soils from the North Sea gales. In the farmland near Holkham Park, one can see geometrical patterns of magnifi-

The neat estate village at the park gates of Holkham Hall in Norfolk

cent, well-tended and sturdy hedgerows which put the squalid, battered hedges which have managed to survive the attentions of modern farmers in counties like Cambridgeshire to shame – along with their owners. For many eighteenth-century aristocrats, life was an aimless sequence of idleness and debauchery, but there were others, like Coke of Holkham and the Townshend dynasty (page 106) also of Norfolk, who contributed profoundly to the achievements of an age when 'agricultural improvements' really did *improve*.

To the west of Cley, the coastal landscape does not bear the stamp of reclamation by an aristocratic proprietor, but rather is the product of peasant endeavour. They advanced into the medieval salt marshes, digging dykes and embanking rivers to drain the land and building sea banks to exclude the tides, leaving the winter rains to flush out the sea salt from the reclaimed grazings. Though each settlement had its complement of peasants and several part-time farmers, most had other important occupations. Salthouse – a place with an honest name – was an eleventh-century warehouse centre for the collection of salt produced from the brine at several places along the north Norfolk coast. Most of the shoreline villages doubled as little seaports, although their fortunes were ever at the mercy of the tides and currents. Wells-next-the-Sea is the only village on this coast which can still claim even a minor role as a seaport today and is still visited by small coasters, even though now some two miles from the sea at low tide.

Environmental forces and competition from larger ports have undermined the ambitions of the other little harbours which used to jostle for shares in the coastal and North Sea trade. Often too, the peasants' reclamation activities posed problems to those more interested in the sea. Cley is one of several little ports which responded to changes in the coastline by relocating its harbour, only to lose the race with the retreating sea. Until the seventeenth century, its harbour seems to have been a little to the west of the present settlement, where the River Glaven enters the salt marsh. The embanking of the Glaven to reduce the flooding of reclaimed land probably stemmed the tidal rises, rendering the old harbour inaccessible. A new one was built and Cley drifted closer to the sea, leaving behind the prestigious church which tells of medieval prosperity and marks the setting of the old dwellings and green. But this harbour in turn became silted and inaccessible to ships, while the great spit of Blakeney Point now claws over the approaches to Cley, shaped just like a dead man's hand and forearm.

The sequence of events at the Burnham villages to the west was not too different. Burnham Thorpe, renowned as the birthplace of Horatio, Lord Nelson, could once be reached by barge at high tide, but the main traffic gravitated seawards from Burnham Overy to the outport developed at Burnham Overy Staithe. Schooners and brigs called at this bustling little port in the nineteenth century, and although competition from the railways reduced the commerce of Overy Staithe, the harbour was still visited by the colliers, until the Great War. A few warehouses remain, but now the old outport is a vibrant little centre for amateur yachtsmen. Sheltered by the withered forearm of Blakeney Point, Blakeney is another former port that is now used only by pleasure craft. At Salthouse, as at Cley, the reclamation of farmland was achieved at the cost of navigation. Although Salthouse's channel to the shipping lanes became silted in the seventeenth century, the North Sea could not be entirely forgotten and in the great floods of 1953, the church, with its old sailing ship grafitti, became a village refuge.

The most easterly settlement on the north Norfolk coast is Cromer, also an old fishing port, but now a sizable resort with hints of gentility lingering in the buildings inherited from the town's eighteenth- and nineteenth-century development as a health resort.

At Cromer, the coastline begins to bend to the south-east and runs very straight, right down to Winterton-on-Sea. Between Weybourne and Happisburgh are cliffs composed of glacial drift which seem to have been cut from dirty tallow with a hot, blunt blade. At places they are low, although at Trimingham, they tower to over 200 ft. Particularly where they consist of poorly-compacted silts, sands and gravels, these cliffs are very unstable and vulnerable to erosion, so that while the coastal settlements on the north Norfolk coast have had to come to terms with a retreating sea, those on this coast often have their footholds gnawed away by the surges. Overstrand lies in an area known as Poppy land – or at least it did until the farmers discovered chemical herbicides. Where it will lie in a few decades' time is open to question, for here the destructive tides have an ally in underground springs which help to sap the cliffs. Several houses have already found themselves not over the strand, but on it. Here, as almost everywhere else in Norfolk, the grand old churches bear witness to the

Pleasure yachts lining the roadside at Over Staithe

region's medieval prosperity, with those at Trimingham and Happisburgh being amongst the most splendid of the coastal beacons.

After Happisburgh, the tacky cliffs disappear and a long ribbon of coastal dunes carries the shoreline down to the Broads and Great Yarmouth. The coast between Happisburgh and Winterton suffered badly in the terrible storms of 1953. The coastal defences were breached at Sea Palling, but the effects of the storm were felt along the whole of the vulnerable East Anglian sea frontier and also well inland, in the Fens, where the Great Ouse burst its banks and Wisbech was rendered awash by the overflowing River Nene. Fishing boats working off the Scottish coast warned of the approaching tragedy as north-westerly gales piled up the high spring tides in a rushing surge which rolled down the exposed east coast of England, devastating Spurn Head, parts of Lincolnshire and Norfolk and Canvey Island. In all, 307 lives were lost and 32,000 people made homeless: in Great Yarmouth, ten people died and 10,000 were evacuated; at Felixstowe in Suffolk, the death toll was forty and an entire estate of prefabs was carried away, while at the other extremity of East Anglia, at Hunstanton, a USAF corporal carried twenty-seven people to safety. Even on the less exposed west coast of Britain, the losses were terrible, for the ferry *Princess Victoria* sank on the crossing from Stranraer to Larne. After the floods, there was a grievously overdue

ABOVE: *Salt marsh vegetation beside a creek at Salthouse with the sand dune barrier beyond*

BELOW: *The church at Salthouse seen from the old cliff line*

LEFT: *The church at Happisburgh was an important landmark for navigators and many shipwreck victims are buried in the churchyard*

BELOW: *The old core of Great Yarmouth as seen from the air (© Cambridge University Collection)*

strengthening of coastal defences, but there are still many people in Norfolk who believe that the defences are still some way from perfect.

The erosion of beaches north of Winterton produces material which the sea, in its relentless and insatiable manipulation of the East Anglian outline, can use to build new land further south. Great Yarmouth is notable in several ways, not least for the structural awfulness of its site, for the town is built on a spit of shingle and sand accreted in post-Roman times. By ignoring the supposed dictates of geography, however, Yarmouth became 'Great' in 1272, when Henry III conferred a charter. At some stage in the medieval period, this bustling trading port acquired a layout (*see* page 66) which is both unique and partly unexplained.

Just across the county boundary, in Suffolk, is Lowestoft, which has also experienced the ills resulting from the over-exploitation of fisheries since the times, earlier this century, when the quays would bustle with Scottish fisherwomen who followed the herring boats southwards. Today, it is hard to imagine the prosperity which the 'silver darlings' brought to these towns and, even in 1772, Daniel Defoe reported that the merchants of Yarmouth and 'Leostof' told him 'that they have cured, that is to say, hanged and dried in the smoke, 40,000 barrels of merchantable redherrings in one season . . . this is besides all the herrings consumed in the county towns of those populous counties, for thirty miles from the sea, whither very great quantities are carried every tide during the whole season'.

An important fishing port since the fourteenth century, Lowestoft captured the trade of several smaller centres when the railway was established in 1847 to export the catch arriving at the new harbour. The town suffered more than most from bombing and then from planned destruction and hideous redevelopment, with the conservational controls of the early 1970s arriving too late to redeem much of the Victorian, Georgian and older heritage.

Though lacking cliff bastions against which the surf might crash to remind one of the savage might of the sea, this is a deceptively cruel and wilful coast. Defoe recalled how, in 1692, a fleet of 200 colliers left Yarmouth for the Newcastle coalfields and was struck by an onshore storm off Winterton. Some raced for the shelter of Yarmouth or made a longer dash for Lynn, but 140 vessels were smashed to pieces on the shore. Meanwhile, a laden southbound fleet of colliers as well as coasting grain ships and merchantmen bound for Holland were also driven aground on Winterton Ness, so that, in all, 200 ships and 1,000 seamen perished on this single night.

In its way, the sea could be as cruel to the merchants, chandlers and dock workers of the Suffolk seaboard as it was to mariners. Between Southwold and Dunwich, the landscape resounds to tales of fortunes gained and lost. The tale of Dunwich has been retold so many times that its impact on the eighteenth-century mind of Defoe might now seem insular and exaggerated: 'The ruins of Carthage, or the great city of Jerusalem, or of ancient Rome, are not at all wonderful to me . . . But for a private town, a sea-port, and a town of commerce to decay . . .' It was, in short, almost incredible. At this time, Dunwich was still shipping out local butter, cheese and corn, but Defoe found it hard to credit that the sea alone could wreak such havoc. Although long dead as a town, Dunwich has had a longer life than most places now flourishing as described on page 67.

In the fourteenth century, when the River Blyth cut a new outlet to the sea and

Dunwich harbour began to choke, some of the borough's trade drifted northwards to Walberswick, on the new mouth of the Blyth, where a lively fishing port developed. Gradually, Walberswick in turn declined, and if the modern village errs towards the twee, the ruins of the fifteenth-century church of St Andrew is a splendid epitaph to a prosperous and gutsy past. In the mid-seventeenth century, after the Commonwealth's iconoclast, William Dowsing, had caused the windows and monuments to be smashed, the people had all but the tower and the south aisle closed. The port was decaying, and the community could no longer support its majestic building.

At Blythburgh, the currents had an unusual ally in the reduction of the former estuarine port, for a series of severe fires in the seventeenth century hastened the decline. As at Walberswick, a magnificent fifteenth-century church tells of the former glories (*see* page 41). A little further north is Southwold which was a modest hamlet for most of the medieval period, but grew to become a borough in 1505 and became very prosperous in the sixteenth century, although in 1590 a cut had to be made through the shingle banks which had begun to choke the harbour. Defoe found a lively sprat-curing trade here, although he was not impressed by the 'lousy creek' at Swoul (Southwold), 'which our late famous atlas-maker calls a good harbour for ships, and rendezvous of the royal navy'. Things must have changed since the maps were drawn. Later in the eighteenth century, attempts were made to develop a revitalised fishing industry here, but the sea remained the master and so Southwold progressed, attractively, as a Victorian resort and its harbour is now used only by holiday craft.

The coastal land strip between Covehithe, with its spectacular ruined church, and Aldeburgh offers natural as well as historical interest. The coastal marshes like Easton Broad, Dingle Marshes and Minsmere have both Fenland and brackish water ecosystems, for seawater from beyond the coastal sandbanks manages to percolate into the marshes. Part of Minsmere was drained at the time of the Napoleonic wars, although in the face of the next great invasion threat, 1,600 acres of reclaimed grazing land were deliberately flooded in 1940. A reedbed environment soon became established and, in 1950, Minsmere became a nature reserve of the RSPB.

Inland lie the beautiful but greatly reduced heathlands of the Suffolk sandlings. From the lovely heaths near East Bridge, visions of the surreal modern architecture of the Sizewell nuclear power station bring one starkly to the realities of the modern world. At the time of writing, an inquiry on the building of Three Mile Island-type reactors is going through its motions. There will be no prizes for guessing the result, but one cannot resist the personal thought that perhaps East Anglia should not push its luck in such matters: on 27 July 1955 an American bomber crashed onto a hangar at Lakenheath airbase which contained a store of nuclear bombs; later the commander expressed relief and mild surprise that East Anglia had not 'become a desert'.

Just to the south of Aldeburgh is the astonishing spit of Orford Ness. All along this coast, the sea currents sweep sand and shingle southwards to create sand spits which bar the mouths of sea-bound rivers and divert their courses to the south. Without the deflection of the Yare, there would be no spit-perched Yarmouth, while Orford Ness now forces the Alde to parallel the coast for some eleven miles before its waters can mingle with the North Sea. The steady growth of this spit literally turned the town of Orford into a backwater, and it decayed to become a pocket borough of Sud-

The partly-ruined church at Walberswick

bourne Hall that was disenfranchised in 1832. The old quay has been built over, the market place is vacant, while old town streets remain only as paths through vegetable gardens. The castle here (*see also* page 135) was built in 1165–71 by Henry II against insurgency in a region until then devoid of royal castles. At this time, the spit extended only about a mile south of Orford, to Stonyditch Point, where The Gull and The Narrows join. Here it stabilised for several centuries, providing the medieval port with useful protection against the north-east storms, but subsequently it has lengthened by some five miles. Orford was still a going concern in Elizabethan times, for the town gained free borough status in 1579 and a map of this reign shows moorings lined by fishermen's dwellings running up to the church. In Defoe's time, the spit was still used by mariners seeking shelter from the storms, but they had lost all interest in the decayed port at the head of the coastal river Ore.

And now, via the attractive Victorian resort and modern port of Felixstowe and the great old and modern harbour of Ipswich, Orford Ness points our way out of East Anglia and into Essex. One cannot leave our region without pausing at Sutton Hoo, high up the Debden estuary and across the water from Woodbridge and described in Chapter 1.

The East Anglian coast has seen many tragedies, but it has also witnessed the arrival of many useful innovations. Its cosmopolitan awareness has contrasted with the rural conservatism of inland Norfolk and Suffolk, where even visitors from 'The Shires' to

LEFT: *A recent collapse of the unstable cliffs at Covehithe*

BELOW: *The ruins of the once magnificent church at Covehithe*

the west are deeply suspect. Some Celts, Saxons, Danes and saints landed here, bringing new ideas and cultural stimuli, while the eastern seaports saw the arrival of diverse and useful continental creations ranging from bricks, textile techniques, and architectural forms ranging from Dutch gables to improved farm wagons. One may doubt whether the flooding of Minsmere caused the Führer to cancel his invasion plans, but this has long been a potential invasion coast as we said at the beginning and, as the Romans knew well when they sited Saxon Shore forts at Brancaster on the north Norfolk coast, at Burgh Castle, and Walton Castle which lies awash below Old Felixstowe. A century and more ago, romantics were encouraged to contemplate ancient ruins and so discover the fickleness of fortune and the frailty of human achievement. Some went to Athens, others to Carthage or Egypt. But if a salutary lesson in human weakness in the face of Nature's forces was what was needed, they might as well have saved their fares, for the beguilingly placid East Anglian coast offers lessons a-plenty.

INDEX

Italic folios indicate black-and-white illustrations in the text